GOD'S LABORATORY

Elizabeth F. S.
Roberts · GOD'S LABORATORY

Assisted Reproduction in the Andes

University of California Press

Berkeley   Los Angeles   London

University of California Press, one of the most distinguished university presses in the United States, enriches lives around the world by advancing scholarship in the humanities, social sciences, and natural sciences. Its activities are supported by the UC Press Foundation and by philanthropic contributions from individuals and institutions. For more information, visit www.ucpress.edu.

University of California Press
Berkeley and Los Angeles, California

University of California Press, Ltd.
London, England

Library of Congress Cataloging-in-Publication Data

Roberts, Elizabeth F.S., 1970–
    God's laboratory : assisted reproduction in the Andes / Elizabeth F.S. Roberts.
        p.   cm.
    Includes bibliographical references and index.
    ISBN 978-0-520-27082-4 (hardback) —
    ISBN 978-0-520-27083-1 (pbk.)
    1. Human reproductive technology—Ecuador.   2. Human reproductive technology—Andes Region.   3. Fertilization in vitro, Human—Religious aspects—Catholic Church.   4. Medical anthropology—Ecuador.   5. Medical anthropology—Andes Region.   I. Title.
    RG133.5.R615   2012
    616.6'920609866—dc23   2011048549

21   20   19   18   17   16   15   14   13   12
10   9   8   7   6   5   4   3   2   1

For Sophie and Thea Spindel—
daughters of substance and sustenance

In memory of Gay Becker, 1943–2007

CONTENTS

ILLUSTRATIONS

FIGURES

MAPS

ACKNOWLEDGMENTS

By rights these acknowledgments should be longer than this book. Countless colleagues, teachers, friends, and family members have made indispensable contributions to the project, as well as to my perpetual life of learning.

This research would not have been possible without the patience and openness of the patients, gamete donors, and clinicians who allowed me to scrutinize their involvement with assisted reproduction in Ecuador. The time I have spent with clinicians and laboratory biologists has changed my understanding of the work lives of doctors and medical technicians. I came to feel solidarity with the lab biologists whose fascination with and dedication to their work I admired and whose generosity with their time and expertise seemed boundless.

IVF patients and their families, as well as gamete donors, allowed me into their recovery rooms and homes to relate what were usually painful experiences. I hope they received some benefit from sharing their stories with a stranger. I also hope that I've adequately portrayed their encounters with reproductive medicine. Their accounts form the backbone of this work. The thoughtful comments of Ecuadorian priests, lawyers, and bioethicists who spoke with me enhanced my understanding of these people-making technologies.

In Ecuador a welcoming group of scholars and friends helped to make my fieldwork and subsequent writing more informed, rich and varied. These include Diego Quiroga, Victor Hugo Espin, Brian Selmeski, Kim Clark, Marc Becker, Chris Garces, Fernando Ortega, Ellen Mitchell, Chad Black, Lisa Madera Swanson,

Diana Defaz, Chris Krupa, Liz Lilliot, Raul Midiros, Eduardo Larrea, Maria Larrea, Eileen Willingham, Patrick Wilson, Jean Colvin, Maria Guzman, Carlos de la Torre, Nancy Castro, William Cevallos, Jim Trostle, Carmen Martinez, and Rudi Collorado Mansfield. Kate Swanson and Esben Leifsen became especially dear friends and colleagues. Conversations with them led me to a deeper understanding of child welfare and the state in Ecuador.

The always-hospitable Espinel family allowed me to stay in their lively family compound for long periods. Martiza Cordova was an efficient transcriber and more: her insightful comments on my interviews with doctors and patients prodded me to understand the material through another lens. The Chaluisa family in Zumbagua—Heloisa, Nanci, Alfonso, Olga, Blanca, Adriana, Jenny, Elsy, Guadalupe, and Wilmer—were my guides to the beauty and harshness of rural highland life. Carmen Vibanco cleaned our house and cooked for us in Quito, making our lives easier in many ways. She and her children, Maythe and Mauricio, provided invaluable commentary on daily life in urban Quito.

Before, during, and after my time in Ecuador I was sustained by a life shared with Joe Eisenberg. His kindness, care, and meticulous intellect nurtured this project through many of its phases. Joe had his own project in northern, coastal Ecuador—a site very different from mine, in urban, high-tech clinics—but with people increasingly connected (and made more marginal) to the global order of things. The juxtaposition of our projects greatly strengthened my own.

Scholars and comrades in the study of the technical and social formations of biotechnology have given me new horizons to contemplate in the last decade. The insights of Lynn Morgan, Megan Matoka, Stefan Beck, Janelle Taylor, Marcia Inhorn, Elly Temen, Marcia Ochoa, Seline Quiroga Supinski, Kelly Raspberry, Charis Thompson, Susan Kahn, Linda Layne, Melissa Pashigan, Sharon Kaufman, Carolyn Sargent, Ian Whitmarsh, Carlos Novas, Michal Nahman, Margaret Lock, Carole Browner, and Sahra Gibbon have thoroughly illuminated my work. Aditya Bharadwaj and Susan Erickson are fellow travelers who have shaped the very ground of how I think.

The anthropology department at the University of California, Berkeley, provided a site of intellectual ferment and vigor for me to begin my research trajectory as an anthropologist. My dissertation committee, which supervised the formative stages of this book, was made up of five scholars whose generosity with their knowledge and support I someday hope to reciprocate. Nancy Scheper-Hughes continues to be good to confer with, good to think with, and most of all good to argue with. The occasions of Lawrence Cohen's stream-of-consciousness erudition were among my most cherished experiences of learning at Berkeley. Tom Laqueur's attention to and enthusiasm for my ethnographic research were unanticipated and appreciated, given that I inevitably botched the history. Mary Weismantel opened a door to the study of kinship and the intimate exchanges of daily life in the Andes. Her scholarship and honest criticism of my work have become models for my own efforts in writing about the Andes. She is an exemplar of the best kind of mentor and friend. More than anyone, Gay Becker at the University of California, San Francisco, guided me through fieldwork with her generous e-mails, full of practical and wise advice for navigating ethnographic work. Her research on IVF in the United States provided a masterful example of a humanistic and sensitive study of assisted conception. Her untimely death was a huge loss for medical anthropology and the anthropology of reproduction.

Friendships begun in graduate school seeded the intellectual project of this book. Kira Foster, Lisa Stevenson, Natasha Schull, Eduardo Kohn, Lucinda Ramberg, Kate Zaloom, Naomi Leite, Chris Roebuck, Andy Lakoff, Sue Wilson, Cristiana Gordiano, Duana Fulwilley, Adrienne Pine, Misha Klein, Zeynep Gursel, Eric Kleinenberg, and Fouzieyha Towghi were all models for what I wanted to be, scholars and engaged social critics of the world. Each one of them has contributed to my sense of anthropology's captivations.

I worried that I would never find another place like Berkeley, with its combination of intellectual energy and the good life, but I have found it at the University of Michigan. The department of anthropology is a wonder of collegiality and conversation, and the university as a whole makes it very easy to do one's work. Elisha Renne, Webb Keane, Gillian Feely Harnik, Tom Fricke, John Mitani, Holly Peters Golden, Janet Hart, Amal Fadlallah, Gayle Rubin, Zeynep Gursel, Charlie Bright, Jennifer Meyers, Bruce Manheim, Aliana Lemon, Michael Lempert, Jennifer Roberston, Mark Padilla, John Speth, Krisztina Fehérváry, Judy Irvine, Andrew Shryock, Julia Paley, Damani Patridge, Stuart Kirsch, Carol Boyd, Anna Kirkland, Erik Mueggler, Ayn Reineke, Linda Bardeleben, Julie Winningham, Sarah Hallum, Laurie Marx, Melinda Nelson, and Darlinda Flanigan-Dascola all contribute to making the U of M campus a place where I want to think, teach, and learn every day.

It's been a privilege to share my in–progress chapters of this book with scholars at Brown, Johns Hopkins, MIT, the University of North Carolina at Chapel Hill, Northwestern, McGill, Yale, Humboldt University—Berlin, the University of Oslo, the University of Edinburgh, the University of Amsterdam, and the London School of Economics. I hope all of the challenges raised by the erudite audiences have been adequately addressed within these pages.

One of my greatest forms of wealth is writing groups and writing partners. At the University of Michigan, the Science, Technology and Medicine Group, including Gabrielle Hecht, Paul Edwards, John Carson, Joel Howell, and Alex Stern, generously read and commented on the first half of my manuscript. During my first years in residence at Michigan, the Writers Group, composed of Rebecca Hardin, Julia Paley, Nadine Naber, Gayle Rubin, Miriam Ticktin and Damani Partridge, took me in and helped me refine my manuscript as well as providing a nourishing social life. Over the last few years, the members of the Oxidate Working Group—S. Lochlan Jain, Jake Koseck, Miriam Ticktin, Diane Nelson, Joe Masco, Jonathan Metzel, Joe Dumit, Michelle Murphy, Jackie Orr, and Cori Hayden—have pushed and prodded me toward a more macro and materialist view, which is just what this ardent observer of the micro needed. Kate Zaloom, Janelle Taylor, Naomi Leite, Stefania Pandolofo, Kira Foster, Lucinda Ramberg, Natasha Schull, Chris Roebuck, Sharon Kaufman, Adi Bharadwaj, Kim Clark, Megan Matoka, Genevra Murray, Mark Padilla, Pamela Waxman, and the Adoption and Infertility Reading Group organized by Marcia Inhorn all patiently waded through earlier drafts.

Another great debt I owe for assistance in shaping this manuscript is to my trusted writer comrade Matthew Hull, who has read every word over the last years, many of them multiple times. He has helped me clarify my arguments and saved me from my worst impulses. Another debt goes to Ara Wilson for her intensive interventions as the manuscript neared completion. This is a vastly better book because of the way she called me to attend to the project's framework, compelling me to rethink so much of what I'd thought was nearly done. She offers a similarly bracing engagement in nearly all realms of life, for which I will always remain grateful.

Gary Smith and Sandra Mojica of the Reproductive Sciences Program at the University of Michigan generously read portions of the manuscript to check for technical accuracy. Editorial guidance from Brad Erikson, Polly Rosenwaike and the incredible Erika Büky was invaluable for shortening and tightening the manuscript. Ken Wissokur and Dorothy Duff Brown were two other crucial writing guardians. At the University of California Press, Reed Malcolm has been a wonder of calm and enthusiastic guidance. Hannah Love and Kate Warne made the process easy. The insights from three anonymous reviewers were invaluable.

Funding for this project came from many sources. The bulk of my initial research was funded by the National Science Foundation and the Wenner Gren Foundation for Anthropological Research, with smaller grants from Berkeley's

Center for Latin American Studies, the Lowie Olson Fund in the Department of Anthropology, and Sigma Xi Grants in Aid of Research. Other funds and writing support came from the UC Berkeley Chancellor's Dissertation Research Award and the Doreen B. Townsend Center for the Humanities. Since arriving at the University of Michigan, I've received abundant time, space, and resources from the Institute for Research on Women and Gender, research and mentoring money from the Department of Anthropology and the Residential College, and time off made possible with a NIH-funded BIRCWH fellowship.

Parts of this manuscript were previously published in *American Ethnologist*, *Medical Anthropology Quarterly*, and *Culture, Medicine and Psychiatry*, as well as in the edited volumes *Assisting Reproduction Testing Genes: Global Encounters with New Biotechnologies* (Birenbaum-Carmeli and Inhorn 2009), *The Problem of Ritual Efficacy* (Sax and Weinhold 2010), and *Bio-socialites, Genetics and the Social Sciences: Making Biologies and Identities* (Gibbon and Novas 2008).

I have been blessed with supportive friends and family who mostly (and wonderfully) live outside academia. My natal family—Alison, Byron, Annemarie, Candace, and William Roberts—helped set me on a path toward anthropology. They assisted me in developing a thick skin, a tendency toward nosiness, and a belief that dignity is overrated. These traits have served me better than any formal training for fieldwork in medical anthropology, the social science of bodies and the strange things they do. My relations—the Roberts, Raymonds, Luca and Francesca Lorenzini, and the Duncans, Sedehis, and Garouttes—are the loudest, most entertaining, and most grounded bunch from whom to claim origin and connection. The Eisenbergs, Mullowneys, and Ryles also offered me great support throughout this project.

Writing can happen because of life's fantastic abundance in other realms—commensality shared with friends and relations near and far. Lori Freedman, Ori Tzveli, Hannah and Ruby Tzveli-Freedman; Lynne Wander, Pamela Waxman, Adrienne and Laney Waxman-Wander; Natasha Schull and Kate Zaloom; Cindy Haag and Elia Lara; Sue Wilson and Darla and Dan Lawson; Gila Wildfire; Karen Blanpied; Julie Emden and Micheal and Eliana Tertes; Naomi Leite and Jason Head; the Y Swimmers and Knackered Tyres of Berkeley; the Masters Swimmers of Ann Arbor; Michael McGowan, Dave Whitesman, and Alison Badger; my dearest *comadres* Marie Mohapp, Shauna McCosh, Tanya Stemple, and Katie Shaffer; Damani Partridge, Sunita Bose, and Jasmine Partridge; Rebecca Hardin, Arun and Nena Agarwal; Mark Padilla; Erik and Max Mueggler; Jean Henry, Ada Banks, and Esra Lee; Ara Wilson, Stephanie Grant and Augusta and Josephine

Grant Wilson—all of them are the kinds of people you keep near you forever because of their lives lived with integrity and collective welcome.

Finally, my daughters Sophie and Thea Spindel, the mostly enthusiastic travelers, have accompanied me wherever they have been made to go. In Ecuador, especially, their incessant questioning provided ample opportunities for reflection on Latin America's inequalities and saturated beauty. Their existence gifted me with limits on my time that has made researching and writing this book a rich and workable endeavor. My participation in their "civilizing process" is the sort of daily gift that never allows me to forget that persons are even more difficult to mold than words. And they both make me laugh all the time.

CAST OF CHARACTERS

The practitioners and clinical personnel listed below worked at the clinics where I made the bulk of my ethnographic observations in 2002 and 2003. They are organized under the names of the clinic directors, an ordering that speaks to the hierarchical nature of the IVF enterprise in Ecuador. I refer to some practitioners by their first names, indicating the informality of my relationship to them. Although I observed and interviewed more than one hundred patients, this list includes only those patients mentioned frequently in the book or whose encounters with IVF I describe at length. I have changed the names of all of the patients and practitioners described throughout the book.

PRACTITIONERS AND CLINIC PERSONNEL

DR. MOLINA'S CLINIC

The largest IVF clinic in Ecuador, in terms of both patient volume and staff

Dr. Molina   Clinic director

Diego   A physician and laboratory biologist who underwent training in Brazil and returned to work in his father's clinic

Wilson   The oldest son of the clinic director, and a physician who worked mostly in a clinical capacity. He underwent advanced training in reproductive medicine in Spain and returned to work in his father's clinic.

Dr. Lucero   A gynecologist who also had his own obstetric-imaging and genetic-test counseling practice

Milena   A physician who managed patients' IVF cycles and aided in egg aspirations

Silvia   A laboratory biologist

DR. HIDALGO'S CLINIC

A small IVF clinic, located in a large private Catholic hospital in Quito

Dr. Hidalgo   Clinic director

Antonia   A laboratory biologist who underwent advanced laboratory training in the United States

Dr. Castro   A gynecologist who also managed patient IVF cycles

DR. PADILLA'S CLINIC

A small, private gynecological hospital in Quito where IVF is one of the services available

Dr. Padilla   Clinic director

Linda   The laboratory biologist who managed the IVF program

DR. CABEZA'S CLINIC

A small IVF clinic in Quito, located within a private Catholic hospital

Dr. Cabeza   Clinic director

Dr. Escobar   A laboratory biologist

DR. LEON'S CLINIC

A small IVF clinic in a private consultation office in Quito

Dr. Leon   Clinic director. She carried out her laboratory work at Dr. Cruz's clinic nearby.

DR. CRUZ'S CLINIC

A obstetric and gynecological clinic that also offered infertility and other assisted reproduction services

Dr. Cruz   Clinic director

Dr. Cruz-Espinel   Codirector of the clinic; daughter of Dr. Cruz

Ecuador's second largest IVF clinic, located in Guayaquil

Dr. Vroit   Clinic director

Dr. Vroit Jr.   Codirector of the clinic; son of Dr. Vroit

Dr. Castillo   A physician and laboratory biologist, and a distant cousin of Dr. Vroit

Nancí   A laboratory biologist

Sandra   The administrative coordinator

Dr. Vega   A psychologist who consulted with patients at the clinic

DR. JARAMILLO'S CLINIC

A small IVF clinic in Guayaquil, located within a private hospital, with IVF cycles performed in groups by visiting specialists

Dr. Jaramillo   Clinic director

Eugenia   The laboratory biologist

PATIENTS AND DONORS

Anabela   The wife of Javier, who donated her eggs to Javier's aunt Frida

Consuelo   A patient at Dr. Jaramillo's clinic in Guayaquil

Eliana   A patient at Dr. Vroit's clinic in Guayaquil who had triplets

Frida   A patient at Dr. Molina's clinic

Sandra   A working-class patient at Dr. Molina's clinic in Quito

Tatiana   A patient at Dr. Hidalgo's clinic in Quito

Teresa   A patient with very few economic resources who underwent IVF at Dr. Hidalgo's clinic in Quito with an egg from an anonymous donor

Vanessa   A patient at Dr. Molina's clinic in Quito, who underwent IVF three times, giving birth to quadruplets after the third transfer

Ximena   An upper-class IVF patient at Dr. Vroit's clinic in Guayaquil who underwent four IVF cycles

PREFACE

On November 3, 2002, the volcano Reventador erupted, dumping tons of ash over northern Ecuador, including the capital city of Quito. The world shut down for days. The streets were empty except for the piles of ash. Eventually, the cleanup crews emerged—manual laborers with push brooms. Still, ash covered everything for weeks: trees, cars, the corn patches in empty lots, the forever-barking dogs, the stoic llamas, the crevices of our necks, and the slits of our eyes. The airport was closed for nearly two weeks. No matter how carefully we swept the entryways or arranged towels on window sills, the ash left a fine grit on every surface and every pore.

Ash also seeped in through the air vents of the in vitro fertilization (IVF) clinics in Quito where I was observing and working. The morning after the eruption, I went into Dr. Molina's clinic, the biggest in Ecuador, to watch an embryo transfer. Even though I changed into scrubs, surgical mask, hat, gloves, and booties, and no matter how many times I washed my hands and wiped my shoes, I couldn't get the ash off of me. Though it was hard to see, the ash crept into the laboratories— into the incubators and the petri dishes used to maintain harvested eggs and sperm. Most devastating, the ash contaminated several cycles' worth of embryos that had been readied for transplant back into the wombs of patients. None of those procedures resulted in pregnancy.

For the next few weeks, laboratory biologists at IVF clinics throughout Quito mulled over the damage most likely caused by the ash. How different would it have been if they had had air-filtration systems like those in North American and European labs? Such systems were incredibly expensive in Ecuador, but they probably would have kept the embryos safe and the labs free of the invisible but pernicious ash. Purity is a trait associated with laboratories—it is how they are supposed to be kept, free of contaminants from the outside. At professional meetings and workshops for laboratory biologists and IVF practitioners around the world, one of the pressing topics of discussion is how to keep labs pure in order to improve fertilization rates. In Ecuador, maintaining lab purity was already a challenge. Everyone in the Quiteño clinics agreed that the ash posed yet another challenge for the practice of assisted reproduction in Ecuador, where it was already so difficult to assemble the equipment to combat impurities. The practitioners required a good deal of help, not only from purified water and sterile test tubes but also from God.

Like the majority of practitioners, laboratory biologists, physicians, and IVF patients I encountered in Ecuador, Dr. Molina relied on God and the Virgin Mary for assistance with IVF. Soon after I met him, he told me, "God is in the laboratory." Although the Catholic Church claims that IVF takes reproduction out of God's hands, threatens the sanctity of the heterosexual and dyadic marital bond, and murders innocent human life through the destruction of embryos (Ratzinger 1987), Ecuadorian IVF practitioners, the vast majority of whom are Catholics, invoked God's assistance and attributed their successes to his intervention. In a nation that most people, including IVF practitioners and patients, experienced as being in a state of perpetual failure, God's patronage was considered essential to IVF success.

In vitro fertilization—the process of mixing eggs and sperm in a petri dish and transferring the fertilized eggs into a woman's uterus—was first performed in 1978 and came to Ecuador in 1992. Although IVF fails most of the time there—with or without volcanic eruptions—as it does in IVF clinics throughout the world, the babies born through Dr. Molina's clinic are just a few of the more than three million IVF babies that have been made in petri dishes around the world.[1] The number grows each year, along with the number of children born through other techniques of assisted reproduction, such as gamete donation and after-embryo cryopreservation.

In many nations, especially the United States, Western Europe, and Australia, these new technosocial practices have troubled boundaries between nature and culture, matter and spirit, love and money, life and death, and individual and collective. Consider a baby conceived through the mixture of anonymously donated eggs and sperm and frozen as an embryo for a few years before being implanted with the goal of providing a child for a heterosexual couple. Or a baby born from a surrogate mother in India for married heterosexual parents-to-be living in the United States. Or a baby born to a lesbian couple, with one partner impregnated with the other partner's eggs mixed with sperm from a known donor. These contemporary ways of making children have forced a reconsideration of our understanding of nature, life, family, and inherited traits. Who are these babies related to? How do genes mold a child? Does a woman's uterine environment shape a child to whom she is not genetically related? If a family member or friend donates sperm or eggs, how does that complicate parenthood? Could a child have more or less than one mother and one father?

Assisted reproduction has also forced a reckoning about the divide between the natural and the artificial, the natural and the spiritual, the family and commerce, and the status of human life and dignity, within what I call "life debates"—contestations over the status of recently made and visualized technobiological entities, such as fetuses, embryos, and the brain-dead (Roberts 2007, 2011). If children are made outside a human body, does that make them artificial? Are the doctors who made these children "playing God" or making "designer babies"? If a fetus is carried by a paid surrogate, is the surrogate exploited? If parents pay for gametes or a surrogate mother, do they love their children less or treat their children like consumer goods? Do embryos count as human life? How old is a child if she was cryopreserved as an embryo for a long period before birth? If that embryo had instead been used for stem-cell research or discarded, would that have been murder?

The work of ethnographers—researchers who find out about how people experience the world through long-term observation and interviews—has demonstrated the diverse answers that ordinary people in the United States, Europe, and Australia have figured out in response to such questions. These ethnographers (mostly medical, cultural, and feminist anthropologists, who in recent decades have invigorated kinship studies with research on topics such as assisted reproduction and queer family formation) have found that people involved in assisted reproduction sometimes produce new and startling configurations of nature, kinship, and love. At other times they reinforce long-standing normative practices of descent through a deterministic view of nature.[2] In other words, these new practices can either reinforce or destabilize the status quo, and sometimes both at once.

Yet medical anthropologists have also shown that for many people around the world who use assisted reproduction, many of the questions above are simply not relevant.[3] These questions are not universal but come from a specific history of European and North American thought and practice. Some of the key elements that form the practice of assisted reproduction in the Europe and the United States—assumptions about biogenetic reproduction and related anxieties about mixtures of commerce with kinship and the beginnings and ends of life—do not necessarily inform its use elsewhere. Ethnographic studies of assisted reproductive technologies outside the global North show us how this Euro-American sense of nature and kinship is constructed. These studies also help us look harder at North America and Europe, allowing us to see that the use of assisted reproduction in these sites isn't uniform either.

This book explores assisted reproduction in one of those "other" places. In Ecuador, where I conducted ethnographic fieldwork in IVF clinics from 2000 through 2007, many of the questions and anxieties that I had encountered in my research on assisted reproduction in the United States were not as pervasive (Roberts 1998a, 1998b). In the infertility clinics in Ecuador's major cities, Quito and Guayaquil, I found that assisted reproduction was more readily accepted than in the United States. It did not force the same kinds of reconsiderations of nature, life, and kinship because such ideas were differently configured to begin with. To put it broadly and abstractly, nature, life, and relatedness in Ecuador are not predicated on individual autonomy. Nature is not seen as a fixed object, waiting to be discovered by people, to the same extent as in the United States or Western Europe. Instead it is experienced as malleable, shaped through interactions with people who exist in relation to the material biological world, as well as with other people and divinities. Existence emphasizes not individual autonomy but interdependence. The more assistance someone or something receives from these sources, the more it exists. Throughout this book I trace this emphasis on interdependence by focusing on the ways in which IVF and gamete donation are used and reshaped in the context of care and the value placed on assistance, rather than on autonomy. In Ecuador, assisted reproduction is an extension of earlier reproductive practices. Making new people was already perceived as an assisted process. These new technological practices are seen as supplementing God's intervention.

This emphasis on assistance, whether from technology, other people, or spiritual entities, was enmeshed in long-standing forms of stratification and domination, extending from the colonial era to the neoliberal era. The women and men involved in assisted reproduction are largely engaged in normative projects of forming heterosexual families in a racist and hierarchal terrain. Naming their specific attachments to God, money, biology, kin, and doctors to help themselves and their families make children, and to get by in a difficult world, often meant that these individuals avoided attachments to other kinds of collectivities, such as "the nation" or "civil society." It also meant marking difference, excluding and denigrating some of the people they were most attached to, like domestic servants, who occupied lower places in Ecuador's racialized and racist hierarchy. Most of the people I encountered in and out of the clinics were both subject to and promulgators of racism. This racism is a significant part of assisted reproduction, because, as the social-science literature on the Andes and my observations of IVF makes clear, in Ecuador the kind of assistance and attachments people lay claim to, and receive, determines their race.

The necessity of assistance for existence that I found in Ecuador has affinities with arguments made by philosophers, historians, sociologists, and anthropologists of science, technology, and medicine in the field of science technology studies (STS).[4] Throughout the book I reflect on their arguments about the intersections between culture and nature in addition to the literature on kinship, reproduction, and race in the Andes.[5] Considering this scholarship in conjunction with my own research in Ecuador, I analyze how these approaches to nature and relatedness, with their greater emphasis on attachment and assistance, can contribute to ways of thinking about assisted reproduction in the United States as well as, more generally, how people come to exist.

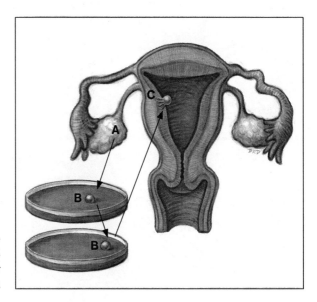

Introduction

Reproductive Assistance

A PICTURE OF ASSISTED REPRODUCTION

Figure 1 is an abstracted image of the in vitro fertilization process, similar to those found in informational brochures distributed by infertility clinics in Ecuador and throughout the world. The purpose of the image is to explain the process of IVF for the uninformed, but it takes some previous knowledge to understand it. The viewer needs to be able to recognize what she or he is looking at and what has been omitted. A cutaway view of female reproductive organs shows the fallopian tubes, the uterus, and the top of the cervix. Next to these free-floating organs are two free-floating petri dishes. A line runs from the egg follicles in the fallopian tubes (A) to the petri dishes (B) to indicate that eggs are removed from (A) and placed in (B). Another line runs from the petri dishes into the uterus to indicate that the fertilized eggs (which, in a step not shown, were fertilized with sperm) are transferred into the uterus (C). The image concentrates on the relationship between female reproductive organs and petri dishes: the movement of eggs between fallopian tubes, petri dishes, and a uterus. These are represented as separate from the rest of the woman's body and the equipment, medical specialists, and other resources required to make eggs and embryos exist outside the body.

Science and technology studies (STS) scholars acknowledge that crystallizing complicated processes in images like this one has been a powerful strategy that allows scientists, doctors, and engineers to isolate and concentrate on smaller and smaller pieces of the world (Bowker and Star 2000; Cole 2000; Gordon 1988). Such representations, in turn, give these pieces autonomy to engage in relationships with other autonomous pieces. Though highly relational, they are depicted as separate. Small, autonomous units can be abstracted and compared to each other on a vast statistical scale, which is a very robust way of making claims about reality. However, STS scholars also caution against the danger of such abstractions. They would argue for the importance of representing the network of attachments that make up the relations between an IVF egg or embryo and an IVF patient. Not only is it essential to illustrate the context of the material reality of fallopian tools and petri dishes; it's also important to understand how those relations actually mold and make these objects.

Scholars have devised various terms that trace this reciprocal process. The medical anthropologist Margaret Lock coined the term *local biologies* to describe how biological processes are produced within fields of thick historical and economic relations. For example, she observed that while women in mid-twentieth-century Canada and women in mid-twentieth century Japan both cease to menstruate in midlife, the endocrinological changes associated with menopause in North America are by no means universal. At the time of her study, women in Japan did not experience hot flashes (Lock 1993; Lock and Nguyen 2010). Women from these different nations literally possessed different biologies, brought about through different local material and cultural conditions. The anthropologist Sarah Franklin draws our attention to how embryos produced in laboratories, as well as heart valves and skin, are not only "born and bred, or born and made, but made and born" through rigorous quality control that takes away impurities, making these lab-made entities as "good as nature" (Franklin 2006a, 171–72; Franklin and Roberts 2006). The philosopher and historian of science Donna Haraway talks about the natures and cultures that make humans and other organisms into cyborgs, and how humans and dogs have co-made each other's evolutionary trajectories (Haraway 1999, 1991). The anthropologist Paul Rabinow described emergent "bio-socialites" like activist patient collectives, which coalesce around disease status, and genetically engineered tomatoes, both of which might over overcome "the nature/culture split" (Rabinow 1996, 99). The STS scholar Bruno Latour and a host of others describe the process of "construction," whereby people and things are all actors constituted in networks constantly making one another. Proponents of actor-network theory argue that a scientist like Louis Pasteur did not employ his individual and solitary genius to discover microbes but instead enrolled, and was enrolled, in the agendas of a vast array of actors, including the public hygiene movement, the military, milkmaids, microscopes, and the microbes themselves (Callon 1989; Latour 2005, 2010). Shifting the emphasis from the completion that the term *construction* implies, the philosopher of medicine Annemarie Mol uses the term *enactment* to indicate the ongoing processes by which things must be continually "made" in order to exist. Mol argues that diseases, for example artherosclerosis, have multiple realities depending on their enactment within various contexts: in a lab with a microscope and slides, in a clinic with an exam table and patient, in a journal with statistical measures, or in an informational brochure with images of abstracted body parts (Mol 2002). All of these scholars are making claims about the interrelated processes through which the world of people, things and ideas is made.

For many of the Ecuadorians I encountered in my research, an argument that there is an enactment of local biologies in Ecuador would make sense. They already experience the world in ways similar to the ones these scholars advocate in their understandings of existence. I was able to notice this in Ecuadorian IVF clinics, guided by the scholars who have studied the historical and contemporary configurations of race, nature, and kinship in Latin America, particularly in the Andes. These scholars have shown that bodies, including attributes like race, are cultivated and transformed through material circumstances of dress, language, education, diet, and occupation. Historical, economic, and political processes built into these attributes mark and make people's bodies and their racial realities (Cadena 2000; Clark 1998; Pitt-Rivers 1973; Swanson 2010; Wade 1993; Weismantel 2001). Adding to these attributes, I trace how the care relations—inputs of time, money, and bodily attention—involved in medical treatment (specifically within IVF clinics) enact racial and other realities.

The phrase *nuestra realidad* (our reality), commonly used throughout urban Ecuador, also speaks to the similarity between Ecuadorian and STS scholars' understanding of the world. The term is used to describe the specific sets of relational contingencies, connections, and constraints that shape a particular reality in Ecuador. *Nuestra realidad* denotes nonuniversality. Sometimes it refers to the lack of infrastructure in Ecuador, as in "That project won't work in *nuestra realidad*." Sometimes it refers to a social norm or law, as in "No one will follow that regulation in *nuestra realidad*." It's also used more positively to denote the warmth, attachment, and flexibility of people in *nuestra realidad* (in contrast to the harsh individuality of people from the United States), as in "Gringos don't understand how to be in *nuestra realidad*." *Nuestra realidad* involves materially contingent relations that often shape biological organisms.

The people I encountered in urban Ecuador, both inside and outside IVF clinics, experienced biology and bodies, as well as race, as contingent. IVF doctors tailored their drug regimens specifically for the bodies of Ecuadorian women and in relation to economic and bureaucratic circumstances, such as the high cost of fertility drugs and the difficulty of bringing them through customs. Hormones actually work differently in *nuestra realidad*. Female IVF patients had heard that fertility hormones caused mood swings in women in other countries, but they attributed their own feelings of emotional tumult to the complexity and messiness of managing their lives during a difficult reproductive project. Physicians' deviations from standard international protocols, as well as patients' sense of their own bodies as different from other women's bodies, were the result of specific, intertwined biological, economic, and institutional configurations in *nuestra realidad*.

This take on reality resonates with the insights of STS theorists who show that technologies that are envisioned to work everywhere sometimes do not, because of different material circumstances. For example, pharmaceuticals that require refrigeration do not work well in places with intermittent or no electricity (Crandon-Malamud 1993). Additionally, objects made in laboratories are not everywhere the same. A frozen embryo in Delhi is not the same as a frozen embryo in London or Quito. They are constituted in material relations that make them differently. The term *nuestra realidad* also helps me describe IVF in Ecuador without having to make claims about the relationship between the global and the local (Latour 2005). This is not a book about IVF in Ecuador as a local version of a global practice but rather about the ways in which IVF in *nuestra realidad* is shaped by relational and material processes both immediate and far away.

Nuestra realidad has shaped the way I analyze my ethnographic observations in Ecuador. I came to this project with a comparative approach based on my prior research on assisted reproduction in the United States. I was concerned that this approach might make it difficult to show how assisted reproduction in Ecuador matters without defaulting to a comparison with a reality that North Americans and Europeans know best—a reality that tends to be understood as singular and universal, even though it does not always hold in North America and Europe, either. I learned that comparisons to the global North dominated the thinking of my research subjects as much as, or more than, it did my own. The urban Ecuadorians I encountered possessed a "decentered" understanding of themselves and their world (Rofel 1999): that is, they considered their sense of self and their material and relational surroundings to be particular. They never had the luxury of universalizing their own experience. Whereas many North Americans are privileged enough to see themselves and their material reality as universal, *nuestra realidad* was already comparative.

.   .   .

Picture, if you will, another, hypothetical image of the IVF process. This representation considers the context of *nuestra realidad*, along with the insights of feminist and medical anthropologists and STS scholars with regard to the crucial attachments between people and things that produce particular IVF patients, eggs, embryos, pregnancies, and babies. The abstracted reproductive organs from the first image are situated in the body of a woman, acknowledging that IVF is dependent on her body. Her body and her biology are particular, shaped by her specific life history and material circumstances. The petri dish appears on a table in a laboratory that also contains a microscope, an incubator, and bottles of hormones. Flying overhead, an airplane filled with expensive jet fuel reminds us to consider the political and economic aspects of transporting IVF equipment and resources.

The picture is also crowded with people, starting with doctors and lab personnel, mostly trained in faraway countries. The woman's male partner stands next to her, usually providing support and sperm, in a step that is missing in the first picture.[1] Nearly equal in importance are the female relatives who help her through the process. They might lend her money to pay for the treatment or donate eggs if she needs them. Both forms of care are part of a long history of reciprocal female economic exchange. Maybe, off to the side, there is someone the patient has never met, who sold her eggs to the clinic for this woman to use. Probably there is a female domestic servant nearby, an *empleada*, who takes care of the patient and her family while she recovers from her IVF cycle. Dollar signs (Ecuador uses U.S. currency) fill some of the space between these relations, as well as the relations between doctors and patients, and doctors and equipment. Money makes it all possible. Floating alongside the money, God and the Virgin Mary offer their assistance every step of the way.

Far off to the side, we see a crucifix and an Ecuadorian flag. Neither the Catholic Church nor the state offers much explicit assistance with the potential IVF baby in whom this woman and her family have invested so much. The church condemns assisted reproduction, and the Ecuadorian state ignores it, so as not to interfere with private medicine or be forced to take a stand on the status of human embryos. Despite this overt distance, though, institutions of church and state shape the way that IVF babies are born, and especially how a woman is assisted and cared for when she enters a private IVF clinic.

To understand this cluttered picture, it's useful to take up the question of existence, or ontology. *Ontology* refers to beingness, how things are. To use words of the STS scholar Charis Thompson, Ecuadorian IVF participants are involved in an "ontological choreography," assembling people and things to bring into existence new kinds of people and things (Thompson 2005). This hypothetical second image, nearly impossible to draw, illustrates how the ontological choreography of IVF in Ecuador is different from that in the first-world clinics where Thompson and so many other scholars have made ethnographic observations. In Europe, North America, and Australia, IVF participants often work to minimize these relations among people and things. They situate IVF within the framework of the accepted "facts" of life, where reproduction is seen as primarily a biological process, disconnected from money or kin relations except for the sperm-meeting-egg scenario of a dyadic couple (Franklin 1997; Martin 1992; Modell 1986; Strathern 2005). In these contexts, IVF is often choreographed to seem less assisted. The de-emphasis on assistance and assertion of autonomy is encapsulated in the first picture, which divorces the female reproductive system from all of the relational factors in IVF.

In my observations, many of the choreographies common to North American clinics didn't come into play in Ecuador, because it was assumed by Ecuadorians that relations between larger family groups, as well as relations with God and money, always assisted in producing children. It was not that these relationships were considered easy—quite the opposite. In the words of one young woman undergoing IVF amid the ministrations and stifling care of her relations, "Como sangre duele" (How blood hurts). Painless relations these were not. But reproduction in general and IVF conception in particular were presumed to take place within them, instead of through a modern and transcendent "agency freed of the press of other people" (Keane 2006, 310). Coming into existence as an IVF baby meant coming into being within a relational network. Like all reproductive endeavors, IVF entailed not only making children but also making and reinforcing relations among adults, and between adults and God.

Choreography between people and things—such as pipettes, drugs, and money—was more difficult in Ecuador than in the United States. It was hard to count on them or to determine how they would interact with the nonuniversal, economically produced, and malleable bodies of patients in *nuestra realidad*. Harnessing these material resources through the care relations of clinicians, egg and sperm donors, relatives, and God and the Virgin Mary took enormous effort. Although the relations were collective—reaching beyond the dyadic couple or the nuclear family—they weren't public. They were personal, modeled on the hierarchical, paternalistic relationship between God and his human children, instantiated within highly unequal race, class, and sex relations. For urban Catholic patients and practitioners alike, God's involvement in private IVF was like his participation in all other areas of their lives. It was considered vital for getting by in a hostile world with a nearly nonexistent social welfare system, unstable state institutions, and constant economic insecurity.

IN VITRO FERTILIZATION IN ECUADOR

A cycle of IVF involves many phases, some more dramatic than others. In Ecuador, some of these steps were similar to the IVF process elsewhere, and others were more specific. After a consultation and diagnosis, an IVF cycle was initiated in a female patient through hormone injections designed to stimulate the egg follicles so that mature eggs could be produced and retrieved. Clinicians measured the patient's follicles with a sonogram every other day. When the follicles were large enough (usually around day 12 to 15), the patient was put under anesthesia, and oocytes (eggs) were vaginally retrieved in an operating room. (In U.S. clinics at the time, women were typically given only local anesthesia.) A physician, usually a man, then suctioned the follicular fluid containing the eggs out of the patient and deposited it into test tubes. These were delivered to the waiting biologist, usually a woman, in a darkened laboratory next door. She emptied the contents of the tubes into petri dishes, which she then placed under a microscope to look for eggs. As she searched, she called out the running egg tally from the laboratory to the participants in the operating room next door. If she failed to keep them informed, the nurses and doctors would shout queries into the lab. When the biologist was satisfied that she had isolated all the eggs, she placed them in biological growth media to await further preparation a few hours later.

The next stage involved the biologist alone in the laboratory, the inner sanctum of the clinic, preparing the eggs for insemination. After placing the sperm in a petri dish, she would check them for fertilization eighteen to twenty hours later. She would assess the symmetry of the gametes and pray to God or the Virgin Mary. In Dr. Padilla's clinic in Quito, Linda, the laboratory biologist, would kiss and caress the incubator as she asked God to fertilize the eggs. She would often say a short prayer, addressing God familiarly: "Que Diosito quiera que los ovulitos fertilicen" (May God want the little eggs to fertilize). In another Quiteño lab, the biologist Dr. Escobar would make the sign of the cross before he placed the petri dish with

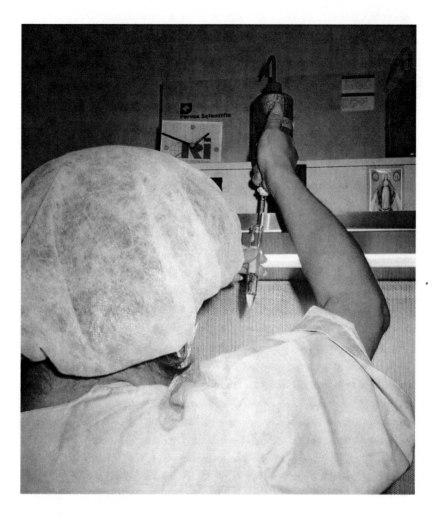

FIGURE 2.
The Virgin on the microscope. Photo by author.

the ovum and sperm in the incubator. With the gametes safely inside, he would pat it, saying, "Vayan con Dios" (Go with God).

Across town, when Dr. Leon finished combining ovum and sperm, she would touch the image of the Virgin Mary hanging over the microscope and make the sign of the cross (figure 2). As she closed the door to the incubator after placing the petri dish inside, she would touch a crucifix that hung from the incubator in a sterile plastic bag and again make the sign of the cross (figure 3).

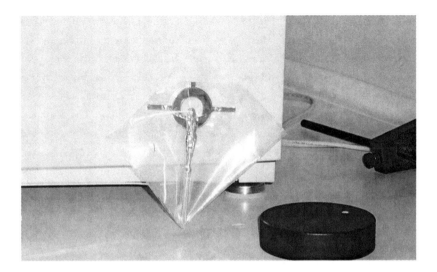

FIGURE 3.
The crucifix on the incubator. Photo by author.

In Dr. Vroit's clinic in Guayaquil, there were fewer visual images of God or the Virgin, because Catholicism takes a less slightly less materialistic form there, but the practitioners did pray. At every aspiration, Nancí, a laboratory biologist, would appeal to God "to allow us get the number of eggs we need and that we get good results." She would pray before each aspiration. "I have Christ in the laboratory," she told me. "Whenever I go to do a procedure, I ask that he enlighten me to do things well."

The morning after the retrieval, the biologist would check the eggs for fertilization. If the gametes were *bonito* (beautiful), that is, symmetrical, rather than *feo* (ugly), or asymmetrical, fragmented, or not fertilized at all, the biologist would give thanks to God and make the sign of the cross. After this crucial check, the new embryos were monitored daily for cell division and cell regularity until the transfer of selected embryos into the woman's uterus. Finally, before the transfer, another prayer was offered: "God, allow me to select good embryos." The transfer of embryos to the patient was a moment of great consequence. During the transfer (which was performed between forty-eight and seventy-two hours after the aspiration of the follicular fluid), clinicians would tell the IVF patient to relax to allow the embryos a better chance of implanting.[2] But relaxing could be difficult. Clinicians often gave the patient this directive with an abrupt tap to her inner thighs as she lay with her feet spread in stirrups. She was usually nervous and uncomfortable, especially because she was required to have a full bladder for the procedure. Doctors placed a catheter inside the patient's cervix for one timed minute before injecting the embryos into her uterus. During this minute, everyone held their breath, staring at the catheter or at the clock positioned over the doctor's head, which was positioned between the patient's thighs. The lab biologist then took the catheter back into the lab to inspect it under a microscope and ensure that no embryos remained inside the tube. With the shout of "¡Está bien!" (It's fine!) from the lab, the tension would dissipate, and the regular bustle of the OR would begin again.

Dr. Molina's son Diego was both a physician who managed patient cases and a laboratory biologist. One afternoon while Diego held the catheter in the supine patient's cervix, he turned to a visiting biologist and remarked, "Wouldn't it be great if everyone got pregnant?" He mentioned a recent North American study about the hormone selectin, which in the future might allow them to understand and control implantation better. Nodding, the biologist replied, "But for now only God can help us." Diego agreed. When he removed the catheter, he said to the patient, "Felicitaciones. Que Dios nos ayude. No podemos hacer mas hasta la prueba." (Congratulations. May God help us. We can't do anything more until the test.)

Similarly, in Dr. Padilla's clinic, when Linda brought the prepared embryos in the catheter into the OR, Dr. Padilla intoned, "God help us, may these implant," as he inserted the catheter into the patient's cervix. Meanwhile, the nurse guided the patient's hand in the sign of the cross. After Linda checked that the embryos had transferred from the catheter, she would announce, "This all depends on God. It's in the hands of God if they will stick." She would say to the patient, "There is a high chance you'll get pregnant, but we don't know. If God helps us, all will go well." As the practitioners left the room, they would kiss the patient on the cheek, saying, "God willing, you will be pregnant," or "We need to have faith."

God's help was invoked most frequently and fervently at fertilization and at the transfer, the moment when the clinicians, after preparing as best they could, ceded control of the gametes to the unknown. At fertilization, the biologists put the eggs and sperm in a sealed incubator, where they remained unexamined for a day.[3] After the transfer, a two-week waiting period ensued, punctuated by frequent hormone injections and testing. This period was marked by greater uncertainty than other stages of IVF, such as stimulation, when follicles were monitored each day through ultrasound imaging of the patient's body.

God was invoked at these moments of heightened lack of control. When biologists checked the quality of embryos, they frequently offered thanks to God. The embryos themselves, though, did not necessarily elicit reverence. After a transfer, "extra" embryos were often dumped unceremoniously in the trash (see chapter 5).

God's intervention was also considered a factor in clinical outcomes. After a spate of negative pregnancy results, Linda reflected on why things were going so badly. She recalled an embryo transfer that I had observed a few weeks before. When Dr. Padilla pulled the catheter out from the patient's uterus, it had been covered with blood. (Clinicians maneuver carefully to avoid this kind of bleeding, but sometimes they cannot.) My stomach sank when I saw Dr. Padilla and Linda exchange a look. Linda later explained: "Blood is invasive and damaging for embryos. In that case, it's the only explanation we have [for why the patient didn't get pregnant], because we did nothing different. Nothing! God is not giving me a hand. Lately he has forgotten me. When we transfer the embryos, and I see that [they] are good quality and could achieve pregnancy, and nevertheless they do not, it is because, unexpectedly, God did not want it."

Linda's lament illustrates one of the most pressing questions posed by IVF practitioners, especially the laboratory biologists. When everything has gone perfectly, when embryos are beautiful, why doesn't the patient get pregnant? In this particular case, the answer wasn't genetics, or the biological particularity of the patient, or volcanic ash, or a faulty incubator: it was the will of God.

As the anthropologist Bronislaw Malinowski documented more than seventy-five years ago, calling for spiritual assistance was a common means of managing uncertain outcomes for Trobriand Islanders (Malinowski 1922, 1984). Not long afterward, E. E. Evans-Pritchard examined related questions of causality and attribution for misfortune among the Azande. He demonstrated that "Why now?" and "Why me?" were questions that could be answered satisfactorily through witchcraft (Evans-Pritchard 1937). Both of these discussions furthered anthropological debates about rationality, magic, science and religion (see Leenhardt 1979; Lévy-Bruhl 1935; Tambiah 1990). The debates suggested that it's not only Trobriand Islanders or the Azande who seek assistance and explanation from deities and spirits, but modern people as well (Favret-Saada 1980; Taussig 1986).

Malinowski, Evans-Pritchard, and others who took part in these "rationality debates" tended to assume that scientists, working in the purely material world of inert objects, didn't provide explanations based on spirituality or call for assistance from unseen forces. In recent decades, STS scholars have pointed out that scientists and biomedical practitioners engage with unseen forces like "neurons," "black holes," and "society" all the time in making their attributions and seeking assistance for their endeavors. They do this while presuming the separate autonomous reality of the objects of their study, as well as a separate autonomous reality of their own (Latour 1987; Mol 2002). The majority of Ecuadorian embryologists did rely on an unseen force for assistance and for explanation, and they did not presume that these forces, God, or technology were separate from themselves.

TECHNOLOGY AND GOD

The different valences of the word *assisted* in the United States and in Ecuador underpin a central argument of this book.[4] Assisting reproduction in Ecuador through technological means isn't as problematic as it has been in the United States and Europe, where IVF has frequently been regarded as interfering with the "natural" biogenetic processes of reproduction. Especially in the early years of IVF, technologies like catheters, hormones, and microscopes; third parties, such as egg and sperm donors; and the efforts of physicians were often seen as artificial additions to the heterosexual act of intercourse that produces children. These anxieties did not stop people from using these technologies, of course, but the concerns had to be taken into account. A number of twentieth-century social scientists in Europe and North America worked to historicize and critique this sense of the artificiality of technology and its separation from humans in Euro-American nations. Countering René Descartes's Enlightenment assertion that the world can be divided into matter and spirit, into inert objects and animated, reasoning souls, Georges Canguilhem, the mid-twentieth-century French philosopher of science and medicine, argued that "machines should be considered as an organ of the human species" (Canguilhem 1992, 55). Canguilhem's proposition that tools and technologies are biological, and thus part of our humanity, is reflected in the work of STS scholars today. These social scientists, feminist theorists, and philosophers insist that all sorts of things—humans, scallops, water pumps, computers, legislatures, tomatoes, microorganisms, divinities—co-make each other.[5] Microbes and quarks can be made real only through a long series of attachments between people and things. We need microscopes, telescopes, and university infrastructures to establish their reality. Ethnographers who study how people practice assisted reproduction, and social scientists who study science, technology, and medicine, note that although the use of technology to produce relationships and people can have a dehumanizing effect, this isn't an inherent property of technological interventions (Mol, Moser, and Pols 2010). Humans live with and through the assistance of many technologies.

The people I met who were involved with IVF in Ecuador already perceived reproduction as an assisted experience. Their comfort with the technological interventions of IVF was related to their comfort with the idea of God's intervention in reproduction. This comfort was shared by IVF practitioners, who were trying to make things, namely embryos, with God's assistance, through biological principles formulated within laws of nature that excluded the presence of God. The Protestant Reformation postulated a God who no longer intervened in the natural world. In combination with ensuing Enlightenment thought, this view posited physical matter as devoid of animation or intelligence. This was arguably a more drastic shift in the Western worldview than any in the preceding millennia (V. Nelson 2001). As part of this disenchanted world, biological reproduction became a natural phenomenon that could be observed and understood separate from the newly separated "social" and "spiritual" domains. Within these principles of scientific materialism, laboratories came to house objects that were understood to be inert.

Descartes described a God who put the world on autopilot: "God has so established nature . . . and concluded His work by merely lending His concurrence to nature in the usual way, leaving her to act in accordance with the laws which he had established" (Descartes 1996). By that reasoning, the animation of inanimate matter in a laboratory might be seen as miraculous: however, as the Scottish philosopher David Hume declared in the eighteenth century, "A miracle is a violation of the laws of nature" (Hume 1964). With God's interventions written out of everyday life, many (but not all) Europeans became "reluctant to believe that physical objects could change their nature by a ritual or exorcism and consecration" (V. Nelson 2001, 57). Failure to believe in miracles came to distinguish the modern from the primitive, the civilized from the barbarous, and the reasonable from the ignorant (Favret-Saada 1980).[6] God and spirits cannot be proved to have an independent existence devoid of relations to things and people. It follows that an unreal God cannot affect the world of nature, considered real precisely because it is seen to exist autonomously from humans.

As STS scholars have argued for the co-construction of people and things in order to counter the emphasis on autonomy established in the Enlightenment period and continuing into modernity, they have also noted that the valorization of autonomy crossed God out of existence. If humans exist autonomously from nature, and nature exists autonomously from humans, God cannot exist, because

God cannot be established autonomously. Bruno Latour is perhaps the STS theorist most concerned with the question of the reality of deities in relation to the reality of nature. Latour argues that science and religion are not opposite modes of thought and do not involve different mental competencies, that is, knowledge versus belief. Instead, both ways of thinking make real things through mediators, despite the fact that within Enlightenment cosmologies, real things are supposed to exist autonomously. In his view, science builds "long, complicated, mediated, indirect and sophisticated paths so as to reach the worlds . . . that are invisible because they are too small, too far, too powerful, too big, too odd, too surprising, and too counterintuitive through concatenations of layered instruments, calculations and, models" (Latour 2010, 111). Scientific mediators, such as microscopes, air pumps and graphs, are "indirect" and "artificial" means of transforming the faraway and the counterintuitive into an objectively seeable, knowable reality (Latour 2010, 114). Similarly, religious images or mediators have the ability to bring things close through transformation. A Russian icon, a West African fetish, or a Peruvian crucifix renews the presence of deities, bringing them near, confirming interdependence and existence (Latour 2010). When the Enlightenment God became a being with an independent reality "out there," religious mediators like icons and fetishes became false symbols. But, Latour argues, these mediators call attention not to the spiritlike Cartesian God far away, but to the presence of an up-close God.

This scholarship resonates with the work of postcolonial theorists who argue that God and spirits are not *social* facts but rather are "existentially coeval with the human." When the postcolonial theorist Dipesh Chakrabarty argues that being human means "the possibility of calling upon God [or spirits] without being under the obligation to first establish his reality" (Chakrabarty 2000, 16), his claim is strikingly similar to STS arguments about the fabrication of facts in science. Just as quarks and embryos are fabricated, so is God. Latour argues that it's only Enlightenment moderns who predicate reality on the denial of the fabrication of both God and nature through mediators.

Both postcolonial and STS theorists have discussed how the Enlightenment reshaped people's relationships with God. Latour's argument that a distant God reduced the transformational ability of religious icons to invoke God's presence is similar to Talal Asad's genealogy of belief and ritual in Enlightenment thought. Asad argues that "belief" became predicated on the assumption of ritual as a signifying behavior for something else far away, "to be classified separately from practical, that is, technically effective, behavior" (Asad 1993, 58). In early Christian monasteries, the liturgy, the routine ritual of mass, was not seen as a separate, symbolic enactment of faith in a distant God, but, like copying manuscripts, was a practical and technical means for monks to develop virtue (Asad 1993, 64). Calling on God in a patterned way was a form of rote behavior intended to invoke God's presence and transform the speaker. It had little to do with the idea of interior belief in a faraway, noninterventionist God.

Ecuadorian IVF participants were vocal about the assistance they received from both technology and God in their pursuit of children. In fact, they linked the two. An IVF baby was unabashedly technological as well as miraculous. As Hilda, a patient in Quito, explained to me: "God helps us in this. . . . All of science is thanks to him. If [patients] don't have children, it's not because they don't deserve it, or they are bad. It's because they had the destiny that God wanted. Without the will of God, there is nothing." Another patient told me that "doctors are instruments of God." A woman who had received donated eggs from her sister explained, "God and science are the same." As if to illustrate this point, the donor vividly recounted the dream she had had the night before the donation: she visualized the embryos swimming inside her sister's womb, with God guiding them toward implantation. For the majority of Ecuadorian IVF practitioners and nearly all of the patients I met, God manipulated the material world on behalf of family continuity. His actions did not unsettle the laws of nature, as "all of science is thanks to him." God's direct interventions in biological processes were real, not unnatural or supernatural, and were consistent with the way people and things could come together to mold the material world of assisted reproduction.

By invoking God in word, deed, and object, by caressing placards of the Virgin Mary on the microscope or touching the crucifix on the incubator, IVF practitioners and patients repeatedly reminded themselves and others of their need for assistance. In Ecuador God is the patron of IVF, the director of the lab. He dispels uncertainty about the process and contradicts Church arguments about human trespass on his terrain. And for all of these interventions, these everyday miracles, IVF practitioners and patients give back to God by paying attention to him. Patients made promises to God to hold church weddings, to make pilgrimages, and to engage in charitable acts to honor him for his assistance in their IVF cycles. They also insisted that others acknowledge this assistance. Once, when I asked a patient how many embryos the doctor had implanted, she corrected me, saying: "No, you mean transfer. Only God decides if they implant." These negotiated exchanges of attention, practice, and material goods were essential to the success of assisted reproduction.

While exchanges with God were essential, an interior state of belief in God was not. When I began giving presentations about God's role in Ecuadorian IVF, North American audiences tended to be amused and skeptical. To them, invoking God in the lab sounded like rote behavior, rather than a deeply felt interior state of belief. But instead of questioning the inner convictions of Ecuadorian IVF practitioners and patients, we can understand them as engaging in an integral practice. Prayers to the Virgin and exchanges with God constituted existence through this disciplinary and external ritual of self-oblation, making clear to all present— patients, practitioners, and God—that the power of life rests in his hands, in a world where individual autonomy is not possible or even desirable. The repetitive invocations I witnessed involved a renewal of the awareness of God through practice (see Kirsch 2004; Roberts 2010, 2006). During the most fraught moments of an IVF cycle, when the potential for the creation of a new family member hung in the balance, clinicians and patients performed a kind of divine service by reminding themselves and others that they were not responsible for the creation of life. Both the repetitive checking of the temperature gauge on the incubator where the gametes were stored and the repetitive calling on God while caressing a crucifix attached to that incubator were calls for assistance from unseen forces that directly assisted the growth of embryos.

In Ecuadorian IVF clinics, attachments and the fundamental need for assistance from both technology and God were regarded matter-of-factly. By no means were the IVF patients happy about the fact that they needed expensive biomedical assistance to have children. Their infertility was devastating in a multitude of ways, and more so for women than men. But IVF itself did not elicit criticisms about artificiality or the intrusion of third parties. Technological intervention was not necessarily something to hide or overcome; nor was that of God. Third parties were not always painful additions to the process. Couples did not feel that their reproduction had to be nucleated from the rest of the world to legitimize their connection to a child. A multitude of objects, processes, and beings had to be harnessed, cajoled, and invoked to produce children in a reality where it's very hard to imagine that any two people could have and raise children alone. These Ecuadorians might agree with Annemarie Mol when she claims that "to be is to be related," whether to microscopes or the Virgin Mary (Mol 2002, 54).

MALLEABLE REALITY

In vitro fertilization is the umbrella term for an array of techniques, processes, and relations between objects and actors. It can include pipettes, petri dishes, paperwork, reimbursement systems, test tubes, incubators, sperm spinners, medical education, state regulations, civil codes, electricity, microscopes, garbage disposal, jet fuel, taxis, clinic buildings, gamete donors, hormone meters, and much more. These various elements often come together quite smoothly in North America. In *nuestra realidad* coordinating them can be more difficult, making it harder for IVF participants to assume a singular and universal reality. When Ecuadorians who have the ability to travel abroad return, they sometimes need to be reminded that they have reentered *nuestra realidad*. IVF doctors arriving home from overseas training often had a difficult time adjusting to the slower pace and the looser schedules for procedures at the clinics, characteristics of practice in resource-poor settings. Nurses who bore the brunt of a doctor's ire would whisper to each other that the doctor had not adjusted to *nuestra realidad*. These same doctors would have to be reminded how difficult and expensive it was to get clinical supplies. They would register supply orders with clinic administrators, who would chide them, "Do you think it's Christmas and you can order anything you like here?"

When Dr. Molina's son Wilson returned from a year and a half of training in Spain, his father told me that the Spanish clinic had thirty-three incubators, whereas Dr. Molina's Quito clinic had only one. Differences like this affected Wilson's homecoming. For the first month or two after his return, a frustrated Wilson seemed to be suffering from reverse culture shock. The genetics counselor told me laconically that Wilson was coming back to *nuestra realidad*, where he couldn't order as many genetic tests as he was able to in Spain.

Maintaining clinic infrastructure was difficult in Ecuadorian IVF clinics. Selecting and purchasing new microscopes and incubators was an enormous undertaking because they are so expensive and hard to maintain. Customs delays made it difficult to obtain properly handled growth media for culturing embryos or infertility drugs that weren't about to expire. I was often recruited to transport hormones, small devices, instructional videotapes, books, and specialized micropipettes from the United States. Personal deliveries eliminated the cost of shipping and handling fees, thus substantially lowering the costs for patients.[7] It was difficult to service some of the equipment in Ecuador. Once I spent an entire day with Linda, the biologist at Dr. Padilla's clinic in Quito, as we both tried to figure out a problem with her U.S.-supplied micromanipulator microscope. We couldn't call any one to come look at it, and we couldn't call the company's toll-free technical support line to get help.

These difficulties affected clinical practice in multiple ways. If pipettes arrived late, clinics had to halt inseminations for a month. If catheters weren't delivered on time, clinicians had to improvise with general-purpose syringes. If the lab ran out of certain cultivation media, they had to transfer embryos back into patients on day 2 instead of day 3, the optimal time. Ecuador's remoteness also affected practitioners' ability to stick to international protocols and norms for IVF. The quantity of hormones used to stimulate a patient's reproductive cycle, the amount of time between aspiration and transfer, the number of times sperm should be spun in the centrifuge, and the temperature of gametes and culture media were tightly specified in the protocols brought back to Ecuador by physicians trained abroad. Yet these standards were often altered when IVF was practiced in *nuestra realidad.*

Doctors routinely noted that bodily states, such as the experience of IVF side effects, vary across national borders. The most common acute side effect, and one that IVF physicians tend to underemphasize to patients, is ovarian hyperstimulation. IVF involves overstimulating a woman's ovaries so that more than one follicle ripens. The process can enlarge the follicles to the point of causing abdominal cramping, excessive swelling, and dehydration, symptoms that in some cases require hospitalization. Diego explained to me that Brazilian and Ecuadorian thresholds for diagnosing hyperstimulation differed. In Brazil, the definition of hyperstimulation was the development of sixty mature follicles. In Ecuador, it was anything over twenty-five follicles. This difference was due to both economics and biology. In Ecuador, patients received lower doses of hormones because of the cost, and their bodies were smaller because of a collective history of malnutrition. Twenty-five follicles represented a hyperstimulation response to a lower dosage. Bodies in *nuestra realidad* are different from bodies elsewhere. There is no universal body and no normative experience of embodiment. Differently situated bodies can suffer from different afflictions, given that material conditions vary. Bodies in *nuestra realidad* are specific and malleable. Both of these attributes have a history.

Under the Spanish Real Audiencia of Quito (which had jurisdiction over most of modern Ecuador and southern Colombia from 1563 to 1822), designations of difference organized labor hierarchically. People were divided into categories that determined who would build, farm, serve, rule, administer, and minister to the empire. One of the most important means of making these distinctions was by designating the quantity of a person's Christian "blood purity." This was not a biological designation—the biological sciences did not exist yet—but instead a genealogical and religious means of enacting a person or group's relationship to labor. Over time this designation became the *casta* system, which distinguished criollos,

Indians, *peninsulars*, mestizos, *coyotes*, blacks, and *zambos*.[8] When designations of *casta* transformed into *raza*, in the nineteenth century, a greater emphasis was placed on biology, but labor remained embedded in the designation. To this day, *raza* is enacted through profession, language, and level of education.

Of central concern to Andean political elites and social reformers in the nineteenth and twentieth centuries, particularly after Ecuador achieved nationhood in 1822, was the mixture of *razas:* most people spoke different languages and were uninterested in becoming individual citizens with allegiance to the larger national collective. The "tribalism" of Indians was seen to impede the progress of a cohesive Ecuador. The solution was to try to make a lighter and whiter nation filled with educated citizens through the process of *mestizaje*, encouraging more mixture between the descendants of the conquerors and the conquered. While the "hybrid vigor" of the new mestizo race has at times been celebrated on its own terms, the project of elites has always been that of *blancamiento*, whitening the nation through mixture in both national and private contexts (Larson 2004; Lyons 2006; O'Connor 2007; Stutzman 1981; Swanson 2007, 2010; Weismantel 1997).

Proponents of these racist programs of *mestizaje* were "race optimists" rather than "race pessimists," more common in Europe, who sought to impede the reproduction of undesirable groups (Cadena 1995, 2000). Race optimists strove not to excise whole groups but rather to enfold them into a "better" race. Doing so meant guarding the borders of whiter families and encouraging illegitimate offspring between whiter men and darker women. Racial optimism assumed, and still assumes, the malleability instead of the intractability of race and the ability to effect racial betterment within one generation, even within already living individuals. The central targets of this betterment were Indians, who through the cultivation and interventions of public education and state-funded medical care, could change their race and become mestizos. This national whitening project also took place in ostensibly private spheres, including the agrarian hacienda: although it appeared to exist outside national jurisdiction, it was ruled by the elite nation builders. The whiteness of elite families was preserved through the guarding of its whiter women in order to make legitimate children, while criollo and mestizo patrons and overseers made lighter mestizos through the sexual domination of darker peon women. The practice of seeking out lighter skin in a sexual partner persists today.

This racial and racist history is essential for understanding IVF in Ecuador. IVF allows its participants to be actively involved in the national whitening project through mixture. Many IVF practitioners spoke about their work as directly contributing to that project through the selection of egg and sperm donors who would *mejorar la raƷa* (better the race). This explicit race optimism differed from the underlying racial presumptions at work in the United States, where IVF practitioners work to maintain racial sameness (Thompson 2001).

Less explicitly discussed were the ways in which the private medical care and assistance provided to IVF patients also served to whiten them. The racially optimistic practice of cultivating a person's race through medical care is analogous to that of transforming Indians into mestizos through education. Initially public education and health care were expected to lighten Indians into mestizos, but after more than a century of state neglect and corruption, these institutions enact their students and patients as Indians, that is, those who don't have the resources for private care. Like public education, the public health system in the Andes has a fraught history as a site of intervention among indigenous groups, especially indigenous women (Ewig 2010). In private medicine, with its paternalistic relations, as opposed to the harsh bureaucracy of public facilities, patients were whitened through the very fact of their care there. In millennial Ecuador, private medical care exemplified desirable care relations and forms of governance that marked patients not as part of the proletariat, managed and mistreated in public medical facilities, but as privileged intimates of their fatherly physicians. Along with dress, occupation, and language, the kind of medical care received makes race. The ability to enter into these personal relations of medical care emphasizes the ability to evade state institutions, and, as we'll see in the cases of abortion and adoption, sometimes to evade the law as well.[9]

The women and men participating in assisted reproduction within *nuestra realidad* shared in a sense of the material and biological world as malleable, shaped through configurations of people and things, including money and the care it can buy. These private medical care relations, like education, language, and profession, are capable of making *raƷa*. The changes are corporeal and material. Defying perceptions of genetically determined race, they reveal how *raƷa* is materially enacted. These practices acknowledge the manipulation of the material world through mixture while continuing to valorize racial hierarchies. The common phrase "money whitens" (*el dinero blanquea*) is accurate (Lau 1998). Money allowed for participation in IVF, a practice that served the ongoing national project of whitening by making whiter IVF patients and children. Patients derived pleasure from discussing how much it cost to produce children through assisted reproduction. Their pleasure derived from the way in which, within the thick relations of hierarchy and inequality in everyday urban life, the expenditure made them favored recipients of care by powerful patrons: private IVF doctors and God. Because IVF doctors offered their care largely outside the regulation of state institutions, patients weren't so much targets of the whitening project as actors in making their own whiter children for the nation. In Ecuador, then, assisted reproduction, which takes place in the private sector, also assists whiteness.

The ability to change and cultivate new material states of being is an ontological, shape-shifting power that anthropologists, sociologists, and feminist scholars in science and technology studies have associated with hybrid postmoderns, who partake in the latest that technology has to offer as they modify their bodies and cross the modern borders between nature and culture (Chen and Moglen 2007; Roberts and Scheper-Hughes 2011; Ticktin 2011).[10] These social-science approaches to the material world resonate with contemporary developments in the natural sciences, where new paradigms like epigenetics, neuroplasticity, and ecological developmental biology examine how living shapes the brain, and the environment shapes organisms. This is a more plastic vision of nature than the biological and genetically deterministic paradigms prevalent in the twentieth century (Paul 2010; Siok et al. 2004; Wall, Xu, and Wang 2002; Franklin and Roberts 2006; Landecker 2007; Daston 1992).[11] It is similar to Andean as well as Amazonian frameworks that assume the malleability of reality and the possibility of shaping it through practice (Descola 1994; Kohn 2007; Raffles 2002).

The Ecuadorian IVF laboratories I observed were materially different from those located in major U.S. cities. In the U.S. clinics, supplies were accessible. Patients were readily available and could pay. Practitioners had easy access to information and exchange with other scientists, researchers, and clinicians who shared the excitement of constantly changing and improving protocols. The reality in IVF clinics in Ecuador was less certain and more malleable. Practitioners seemed alternately annoyed by and resigned to obstacles in *nuestra realidad*. As physicians of private, high-end medicine, trained at better-appointed clinics in Spain, Brazil, and the United States, these practitioners did not see themselves as resembling the Dominican "bare-handed doctors" described by Ana Ortiz, who cultivated "cowboy personas" as they practiced public medicine in the face of extreme shortage (Ortiz 1997). They lamented their country's failure to achieve the infrastructure of a modern nation-state, where supplies might be produced domestically and customs officials were not so corrupt. But for most of them, practicing IVF within the material disadvantages of *nuestra realidad* contributed to the malleability of the material world, as opposed to the more hardened and immutable environment of places with better resources.

THE STUDY: IN ECUADOR

After studying assisted reproduction and surrogate motherhood in California in the early 1990s, I became interested in how biomedical technologies are used in the global South and the specific kinds of IVF patients and babies they produce, especially in the context of Catholicism, the only major world religion that completely condemns assisted reproduction.[12] With flourishing IVF industries in nearly every nation (except Costa Rica, where the practice was illegal from 2000 to 2011), Catholic Latin America was obvious terrain for my research. Additionally, I wanted to explore how assisted reproduction in Latin America would be taken up within the context of historically racialized programs of population control and sterilization, as well as the more recent debates over juridical and moral stances toward abortion and the rights of women and the unborn. Despite the near-total illegality of abortion across the continent, Latin America has some of the highest rates of abortion in the world. The continent also has very high surgical female sterilization rates and close to the highest cesarean section rates in the world. These statistics indicated a particular embrace of surgical medical intervention in women's bodies. I wondered what a study of IVF might tell us in relation to the reproductive policies and practices that constitute "reproductive governance" in Latin America (Morgan and Roberts. forthcoming).

The shifts in life debates and reproductive governance were connected to vast economic changes throughout the region, many carried out under the banner of neoliberal structural adjustment, which led to the increased privatization of health care. The practices and policies of neoliberalism and the ideology of free trade sought to limit the scope and activity of state governance as well as state responsibility for social programs (Ong 2006). Practices of neoliberalism have also contributed to the formation of new subjectivities that posit individuals as the fundamental units of society. With regard to health care, this view posts good citizens as self-reliant, educated, and entrepreneurial consumer patients who need very little from state institutions (Rose 1999).

These economic shifts are also linked to the increasing power across the continent of evangelical Christianity, which champions the moral and economic responsibility of individuals for themselves and for their families. Evangelical Christianity is a central player in the life debates, with its specific focus on the juridical rights of the individual unborn. Individual rights claims are also a feature of neoliberal governance, which encourages different constituencies to pursue their claims in courts, as actors separate from and often antagonistic to the state (Harvey 2005).

These political and economic processes helped shape Ecuador's IVF industry in the early 2000s. At the time, Ecuador had nine clinics, which initially seemed to me a high number for a poor nation with a reputation for Catholic conservatism, increasing right-to life-activism, and a history of population interventions (despite the fact that Ecuador never officially had an overpopulation "problem"). But the proliferation of expensive, private-sector "elective" medical treatments like IVF is symptomatic of medical landscapes in fiscally devastated developing nations that "never had the resources of a Keynesian welfare state" (Sharma and Gupta 2006).[13] In Ecuador, neoliberal ideologies and policies that deemphasized the responsibility of the state for citizens' welfare enhanced the status of these practices. Thus, although there was no Ecuadorian golden era of social services, public health care in the 1990s and early 2000s arguably worsened along with economic conditions after the country adopted the U.S. currency and removed trade barriers.[14] Simultaneously, private medicine in Ecuador flourished, fueled by a glut of doctors and low levels of health care spending by the state.[15] This landscape has been changing yet again since the election of Rafael Correa in 2007. His post-neoliberal call for a "citizens' revolution" arguably has increased social welfare provisioning.[16]

One of the surprises of my research was how many working-class and lower-income families made use of assisted reproduction. This heterogeneity came to make sense as I saw how even poor and working-class families spent large amounts of their own resources on private healers (from biomedical as well as alternative and indigenous treatment modalities) in order to avoid public services. At the start of the twenty-first century, all Ecuadorians officially had access to free or low-cost health services, but more than 50 percent of health care spending came directly out of individuals' pockets, with even 42 percent of the poor turning to the private sector rather than using free or low-cost public services.[17] The most expensive private clinics had the latest technologies and techniques, but even the more moderately priced and inexpensive clinics provided a level of personalized patient care impossible to find in public facilities, where there were few supplies, crumbling buildings, and a high rate of iatrogenic (clinically induced) infection.

Ultimately, I found that assisted reproduction must be understood in the context of Ecuador's racial divides. These divides informed the kinds of personalized care people sought, as well as how they went about making children and attempting to whiten their families and make sure their racial boundaries stayed intact. In Ecuador, then, even though debates over abortion and birth control had become more heated through the proliferation of evangelical Christian groups, IVF babies and embryos did not appear to be part of them. Instead I found an expanding IVF industry staffed and supported by enthusiastic Catholics, who involved God in the process and were whitened through their participation, activating a "complicated paternalism" with historical resonances refueled by neoliberal political and economic shifts (Biehl and Eskerod 2007, 157).

The research for this book centers on a year of fieldwork in Quito and Guayaquil in 2002–2003, with preliminary and follow-up research trips from 1999 to 2007. During my year in residence, I observed in seven of the country's nine IVF clinics, concentrating mostly on five. I was able to compare practices among these five clinics and follow patients from all of them. I also interviewed egg and sperm donors through several other clinics. Additional interviews with priests, lawyers, bioethicists, and health officials helped me understand the legal, religious, and economic ramifications of Ecuadorian IVF. I supplemented these discussions with analysis of popular-media accounts of assisted and non-assisted reproduction.

I spent the bulk of my weekdays in IVF clinics and the homes of patients as they recovered from IVF procedures. In the clinics, I spent time in the waiting room and recovery rooms with patients and auxiliary staff, on the OR and clinic rooms with physicians and clinic directors, and in the dark and stifling laboratories with the laboratory biologists. I helped with small tasks during aspirations and transfers: bringing pipettes filled with follicular fluid into the laboratory, reporting to the clinicians on the number of eggs that the biologist had found in the lab, helping set up equipment to make videotapes of embryos, and holding patients' hands during transfers. Sometimes I was called on as a record keeper, as my notebook contained information about the size of a woman's follicles, the number of eggs retrieved, and the quality or cell count of particular eggs and embryos. Watching laboratory practices over time allowed me to note the differences in practice between the clinics in Guayaquil and those in Quito.

I also noted differences in the backgrounds of the staff. IVF doctors and clinic directors tended to come from elite families and to be men, whereas laboratory biologists tended to come from middle-class or modest backgrounds and to be women. Observing and talking with these practitioners over several years allowed me to observe their ongoing efforts at entrepreneurship in Ecuador's competitive private medical marketplace. Most medical technicians' and even private physicians' salaries are still too low to keep up with inflation, and the majority of the physicians I met in the private IVF clinics worked in two or three clinics or hospitals, both private and public. One physician worked in the mornings in an IVF laboratory, making life, and in the afternoon as a pathologist at the local state-funded police hospital, dissecting death.

Besides following the clinic schedule, I followed the schedule of women's IVF cycles, the most intensive part of which lasted about a month, with a cluster of clinical procedures in the middle and subsequent bed rest. I conducted more than one hundred interviews with IVF patients in the clinic or at home after a procedure. These were often collective affairs, with male partners, sisters, cousins, known donors, and *empleadas* gathered around the bed, along with an image of a household saint or the Virgin Mary keeping watch, all assisting the patient in cultivating her body to accept the embryos and become pregnant. I began my interviews with some basic demographic questions. Then I asked patients to tell me the story of their involvement with IVF. These stories lasted from thirty minutes to four hours. From 2003 to 2007 I revisited several patients who eventually had children, with or without clinical assistance. Women who had children usually wanted to maintain our connection, to share their narrative trajectory. Women who didn't get pregnant often didn't want to keep talking to me about their participation in IVF. They saw themselves as literally having nothing to talk about.

I was surprised by the variation in the class backgrounds of IVF patients. Twenty percent of the patients I encountered came from households with combined salaries of less than $500 a month. Ninety percent of the patients I came in contact with considered themselves middle class: this self-definition turned out to encompass a huge salary range, from $200 to $2,000 a month. Such identifications demonstrated a pervasive desire to identify as middle class—connected, I think, to that unifying discourse of *mestizaje,* a nation characterized by people in the middle. Salaries rarely represented all of a patient's assets, because many also had informal work that brought in more income. Additionally, to finance their treatments, many were adept at gathering resources from family members and employers and even made credit arrangements with doctors. Even patients with higher incomes sometimes took out small loans to pay for IVF.

The effects of the economic crisis of the 1990s and the early 2000s were evident in the professional lives of Ecuadorian IVF patients (Portes and Hoffman 2003). Infertility is commonly linked to delayed childbearing in women working in white-collar professions, but in the United States the connection does not necessarily prove empirically causative. In Ecuador, it was even less relevant as a causal factor: very few female patients were in white-collar professions, although almost of all them engaged in some sort of income-producing activity, often sewing or taking care of children. This work was considered more flexible than their male partners' labor. Because few had to follow an employer's schedule, undergoing IVF was somewhat less stressful than for the few professional Ecuadorian women I met in the clinics.[18]

My observations in the clinics and my interviews with IVF participants revealed regional divides between the tropical coast and the dry and cool sierra. Quito, Ecuador's administrative center and the capital of the country, is located in the Andes and has long been marked by its relative inaccessibility to the coast and other trade thoroughfares (map 1). The humid port city of Guayaquil, located on the river Guayas near the southern coast, was founded to serve Ecuador's Pacific trade. It's larger, more commercial, and more prosperous than Quito. IVF participants constantly called my attention to the differences between the residents of these two regions. According to Guayaquileños, Quiteños are educated, hardworking, conservative, closed, reserved, cold, and hypocritical, experts in false compliments. Quiteños characterize Guayaquileños as open, forward-thinking, loud, relaxed, brash, and fast talking.[19] There was a racial tinge to these attributions: Indians commonly live in the sierra, while Afro-Ecuadorians live on the coast.

Though unremarked upon by IVF participants, it became apparent that variations in the practice of assisted reproduction in these two cities, especially in regard to gamete donation and embryo disposal, were related to co-constituted historical and economic differences, especially with regard to the organization of labor. These histories in turn affected religiosity, relatedness, and personhood. Differences between the two cities and regions widened in the nineteenth century, when contestations over various modernization projects, like national railroads and national education, came to be understood as part of the geographical divide between coastal progressives (proponents of free trade, made rich from the cacao trade based in Guayaquil) and conservative, land-holding elites from Quito (Clark 2002; Kasza 1980; Larson 2004).

In the sierra, a history of agrarian patron-client labor relations produced a corporate collective labor system and family structure. In contrast, on the coast, labor relations since the nineteenth century have been structured around the sale of individual labor, and the notion of individual personhood has come to be stronger there than in the sierra. Coastal liberal reformers battled against what they saw as the entrenched patron-client relations endemic to sierran agrarian society, which they understood as preventing the development of free trade (Clark 2002). These different economic positions became regional and religious subjectivities as well, with sierrans tending to engage in more materialistic and personal exchanges with God, while coastal residents established a more doctrinaire relationship with a more distant God.[20]

These divides resonated in the relationships that IVF practitioners had with God. I came to think of the majority of IVF practitioners (fifteen out of twenty) and patients that I met as "materialist" Catholics, whose God existed close at

MAP 1.
Ecuador. In 2002–3 there were nine IVF clinics in Ecuador:
seven in Quito in the Andean sierra, and two in the port city
of Guayaquil.

hand. These practitioners mostly resided in Quito, where there were more clinics. Although they did not subscribe to contemporary Church doctrine, their laboratories were filled with emblems of God's presence: crucifixes and religious images acknowledged their faith in his assistance. The God of these materialist Catholics played an active role in their daily affairs. He and his intermediaries were seen as deeply involved in personal, interdependent relationships that altered the material world.

Of the five remaining practitioners I spent the most time with, two were atheists, and the other three I came to think of as "spiritual," as opposed to materialist, Catholics.[21] Those three all lived in Guayaquil. They denied God's influence on clinical outcomes, making statements like "God is not a puppet master" and "Faith does nothing." They told me that they had no dealings with individual saints, only with Jesus Christ, echoing longstanding Protestant and evangelical criticisms of the idolatry involved in regarding individual saints as mediators rather than communicating directly with an immaterial God. The practitioners in Guayaquil were somewhat more devout and doctrinaire in attempting to fit their IVF practice within Catholic strictures, and their laboratories and clinics displayed fewer overt material and mediated signs of Catholicism than the ones I observed in Quito. But when working with patients, everyone—even the spiritual and atheist practitioners—invoked God at specific moments of the IVF process. They were not yearning to be fully secular subjects or to be fully autonomous from God's assistance.[22]

These different religiosities directly shaped IVF practice, especially in terms of personhood, kinship, and care. For instance, materialist Catholic practitioners in Quito avoided the cryopreservation of embryos, while IVF practitioners in Guayaquil tended to embrace it. This difference is based in the labor history in Ecuador. The practices of free labor and free trade on the coast produced specific relations between God and persons, and more recently between God and embryos. In that context, people (and embryos) are seen as individuals who can circulate freely, whereas within the peonage hacienda systems in the sierra, people and embryos are seen as embedded in groups. Thus Quiteños believed freezing embryos would facilitate their circulation outside families and racial boundaries, which they saw as undesirable. Guayaquileños, on the other hand, envisioned embryos as individuals with the right to a future less dependent on their family of origin. These are regional and religious differences influenced by economic practices within Ecuador's material reality.

STORIES OF ASSISTED REPRODUCTION

Every time I left Quito, my transcriber, Maritza, slipped a small farewell gift in with my tapes: packets of herbs that she mixed herself to make *aguitas*, medicinal teas that she knew I could not get in the United States. This was one of many ongoing exchanges—tapes, words, money, herbs—that characterized my fieldwork. Maritza had transcribed interviews for many of my North American colleagues— fellow anthropologists as well as geographers, historians, and political scientists who work in Ecuador—mostly on topics like agrarian reform, water rights and indigenous political struggles, so she had an acute sense of the kinds of social-science research North Americans do. Once she mentioned, in an offhand way, how much she liked working on my tapes. Until she started transcribing them, she had no idea that egg and sperm donation, IVF, and surrogate motherhood were going on right there in Quito, among urban mestizos just like her. "Your tapes are just like *telenovelas*," she said.

I was thrilled by Maritza's interest, but her compliment—comparing my tapes to soap operas, perhaps the most popular form of entertainment in Latin America besides soccer—played into some of my anxieties about the project. My nervousness came from the value-laden distinctions made between macro and micro, public and private, high and low culture, masculine and feminine, the political front page and the human-interest stories in the women's section (dualisms that were disregarded by the Ecuadorian women and men involved in assisted reproduction).[23] Agrarian reform, water rights, indigenous political struggles—these seemed like the important topics, politics writ large, history in the making. Ultimately, however as so many scholars who have traced the coproduction of "private" and "public" life in the modern world have shown, the stakes of IVF for all participants—with regard to their value as people and to the nation—link assisted reproduction to these front-page issues.

Maritza's assertion about the power and interest of individual stories informed the organization of this book. Before each of the analytic chapters I include a narrative account of a particular patient's experience with IVF. These stories offer more intimate accounts of a woman's relationship to various family members and to God. Each narrative is related to the ideas discussed in the chapter that follows. Cumulatively, they link up with the book's larger arguments about reproductive assistance and the malleability of the material world. Additionally, I hope they provide insights into what Maritza found compelling in the interview transcripts.

Several women I met in the clinics had first heard about assisted reproduction from a *telenovela* like *El Clon* (The Clone), a popular Brazilian show dubbed into Spanish. These women were amazed to be a part of something so current, so seen-on-TV. *Telenovelas* intertwine romance and family with the fractious history of Latin American nations. Their storylines about illegitimate unions across race and class lines echo stories of IVF in Ecuador. It's no accident that the stories I tell in these separate sections tend to be about less privileged women and their relations. The IVF experiences of poorer and browner patients were more fraught because of their position within the national whitening project.

Notably, all but one of the women in these stories ultimately bore children through IVF. In reality, IVF only works in about one-quarter to one-third of attempted cycles. So these stories are about patients who, as they sometimes put it, had "won" a child. But winning an IVF baby did not guarantee an easy life. After these patients underwent IVF and produced a child, their lives became even more complicated. Their economic situations usually worsened. Sometimes their husbands left them; sometimes they had aging relatives to care for as well as an infant; often they had various problems with their children. These children were part of a complex set of relations. Although children often gave people something to live for—a cliché, of course, but one with some truth—a child didn't always save or even improve these women's varied relationships.

These stories also resemble *telenovelas* because they are domestic dramas involving a quest to have children, who are ultimately produced through and despite racial struggle, bitter inequalities, and a mixture of secrets, care, betrayal, love, and money. They aren't morality stories; they're morally ambiguous. There are some happy endings, but even when the domestic drama ends with a child, the characters rarely live happily ever after. These stories demonstrated a rather simple truth. While undergoing an IVF cycle is an important moment in anyone's life, within all the relational complexity of these women's lives, it was certainly not a defining moment.

Of course these stories differ from the plots of *telenovelas*. For one thing, Latin American *telenovelas* often revolve around the dyadic relationship of a heterosexual couple. The IVF stories I present here involve a variety of relationships, which are often obscured by biotech romance narratives of sperm meets egg (Martin 1992). They explore key dyads within an IVF relationship: between a woman and her egg donor (who might also be a business partner or niece) and between medical practitioners and God. These stories reveal ways in which a woman's encounter with IVF is also an effort to gather assistance from care relations and how that assistance changes her corporeality.

The following chapters explore different aspects of these care relations. Chapter 1 considers the nature of reproductive assistance provided by private clinicians and God in relation to the Catholic Church and the Ecuadorian state. Chapter 2 addresses the ways in which race is constituted through IVF procedures and other sexed medicalized care practices, like surgery, hormone treatment, and bed rest. Chapter 3 looks at how the practice of anonymous gamete donation is configured within Ecuador's racial hierarchy. Chapter 4 examines how intrafamilial egg donation reinforces relationships between female family members.

And chapter 5 discusses embryo cryopreservation, analyzing regional variations in practice and the relationship of the technology to family formation and personhood. Overall, I explore the ways in which care relations in Ecuadorian IVF clinics assist in the reproduction of families as well as, problematically, in whitening the nation.

Corporeal Punishment: Sandra

Llamas grazed in the crumbling median strip of the road outside Sandra's tiny cinderblock house in northern Quito, near a decaying public hospital. In her bare and chilly kitchen, Sandra told me about the illegal abortions she had undergone as a teenager. At fifteen, she had fled to the city from the south to escape the sexual abuse of her mother's new boyfriend. She found work in a canning factory and met Luis, a truck driver, twelve years her senior. After her third abortion, when she was seventeen, she landed in the hospital. The pregnancy had been ectopic (a dangerous condition in which the embryo lodges in the fallopian tube instead of the uterus), but the abortionist had no way of knowing that without an ultrasound scan, a procedure performed only in upscale clinics. Sandra almost bled to death, and her fallopian tubes and uterus were permanently damaged.

Nearly two decades later, in 2003, Sandra underwent IVF with Luis's participation. I met her in Dr. Molina's clinic on the day of her embryo transfer. Women need to have a full bladder for the procedure, and Sandra was about to explode. Although she was uncomfortable and nervous before the transfer of the four embryos, she felt wonderful afterward, "calm and beautiful from the hormones." She told me how her skin had been soft, her breasts full, as they had been after an earlier surgery when doctors removed some uterine cysts, and afterward, she "put on high heels and nice clothes and went out again after years of sorrow."

Sandra was obviously lonely. She was out of work. She looked older than her thirty-five years. Luis, still a truck driver, worked fifteen days on and fifteen days off. Sandra's mother-in- law lived across the courtyard, but her own family was far away, mostly in Loja, a city in the south of Ecuador, or in Europe, and she didn't have many friends left from her factory days. Their children were painful reminders of her own childlessness. She also linked some of these friends with her infertility, since they had given her the address of the *obstetriz* (medically trained midwife) who performed her third abortion. "I was so silly. I never wanted to be pregnant. My friends in the factory had been pregnant, so they said, 'So have an abortion.' One of them gave me the address. My husband told me this was normal. That we were very young and we would marry afterwards. I went to this place, and it was fast. She did it. Good. Done. Over. I was happy I didn't have to give this problem to my family."

Sandra soon became pregnant again, and this time she went to a doctor who gave her an injection "to make my period come." To convince him to administer the shot, she told him that she had been raped and that she lived with her aunts, who would kick her out of the house if they discovered her pregnancy. When she became pregnant a third time, Sandra went back to the *obstetriz* who performed the first abortion. She took a taxi home by herself. But within a day, she was in terrible pain. Her twelve-year-old sister, who had just traveled north to keep house for her, tried to help, but there wasn't much the sister could do. Sandra stayed in bed for eight days, bleeding, before her sister was able to track down Luis, who was away on a long trucking job.

Luis took Sandra to the Voz Andes, a Christian hospital, where the doctors told her she had an ectopic pregnancy and would need surgery. The operation was too expensive there, so Luis took her to the Andrade Marin, a public hospital. The doctors at Andrade Marin also diagnosed an ectopic pregnancy and operated immediately. The growing embryo had caused one of her fallopian tubes to burst soon after the abortion, which it turned out hadn't aborted anything at all. When Sandra's mother and some other relatives came from the south, she told them that she was suffering from uterine cysts so that they wouldn't know she had been sexually active. She had lost so much blood that her friends and her boss from the factory came to donate their own. After the doctors removed her damaged tube. "I was covered with scars. I was never the same," Sandra told me. In that month alone she went from 105 to 75 pounds. She was skin and bone.

When she went back to work, all she did was cry. "I regretted everything. I was such a coward. I didn't think I could have had a baby. It seemed too difficult. I didn't want to be a single mother." She and Luis got married and tried to have a child right away. For ten years Sandra took hormones, pills, and herbs. Nothing worked. Eventually she had an exploratory laparoscopy to diagnose her difficulty in conceiving. Crying a little as she remembered that time, Sandra recounted that the surgeon said her surgery at the public hospital had been poorly done: "He had never seen so many scars in his life. Scars everywhere."

Early on in her treatment Dr. Molina told Sandra that her chances for pregnancy were in "God's hands." This comment, which practitioners nearly always made to reassure patients, had been especially painful because she was sure that her infertility was God's punishment for the abortions. She worried that if she did get pregnant, there would be something wrong with the child, another punishment from God. When Sandra finally told her sister about the abortion, her sister cried and said, "God has forgiven you. God even pardons criminals that have killed." But Sandra wasn't sure that God had forgiven her. "I think about it all the time. What if I hadn't left my mother's house? . . . What if my friend hadn't given me the address? I would have a young son now."

Like so many Catholics I met in Ecuador undergoing IVF, when Sandra first heard of IVF, she thought it sounded wonderful, and she wanted to do it right away. The Church's condemnation of IVF made no sense to her. It seemed so *antiguo* (old-fashioned) to Sandra when "God was giving the scientists a way to make babies." But Luis's car had just been stolen, and they didn't have much money. They saved for six years for the IVF cycle. During the cycle Sandra had been hopeful, dreaming of a baby to keep her company when Luis was away. After the embryo transfer, when Luis left for his fifteen-day shift, he was happy too. Sandra thought that when he came back, "He would see the cradle and my belly. I knew if I got pregnant with IVF I would shout out to the world about it. Tell everyone! I was so hopeful, until I began to bleed early. My hopes are lost now." She had prayed to God and the Virgen del Cisne (from Loja) while she waited. She made promises to give orphans candy at Christmas. But it hadn't worked, and now she wondered if they should try again. They had spent more than $10,000. Another cycle would cost about $5,000. Their car had been stolen again. Luis was making about $600 a month—a good salary, but not much compared to the cost. They could borrow more money. Or maybe she should start trying other things again, like a guinea-pig cure with a healer in Loja.

I met several women like Sandra in Ecuador, women without much money who showed up at IVF clinics years after abortions gone awry. And I never could think of anything to say, especially when they talked about their infertility as God's punishment. This was not about their "right to choose." They saw their efforts to conceive a child as a negotiation with God that could end badly. For these women, infertility caused by a botched abortion became a scarring form of corporeal punishment that they had to suffer alone.

Sandra wished she had told Dr. Molina at the IVF clinic about the abortions, thinking it might have helped him make a better diagnosis or offer a more effective treatment, but she had been ashamed to tell him. Luis also didn't want anyone to know. Sandra asked me to tell Dr. Molina about her history. But when I did, he showed little interest in my report. It would have made no difference, he said. Damaged tubes are damaged tubes, regardless of the reason. He wouldn't call her to reassure her, either. Maybe she wasn't a patient worth retaining: it was obvious she couldn't pay again. But I don't think disapproval of her abortions was the reason for his neglect. Most of the doctors I met in Quito condemned abortion in the abstract, like most Ecuadorians, but didn't really condemn the women who got them, "those poor things."

I called Sandra to relay the news: there was nothing to be done. Feeling helpless, I offered her the phone number of an acupuncturist who worked with women having problems conceiving. One woman told me it had worked for her. Sandra seemed eager to try something new. When I contacted her four years later, Sandra was still childless.

ONE · Private Medicine
and the Law of Life

OF POPES AND PRESIDENTS

On April 19, 2005, Cardinal Joseph Ratzinger was elected to succeed John Paul
II as pope. Pope Benedict, as he is now known, was, in the decades before his
ordination, the theologian primarily responsible for framing the Church's position on reproduction and the dignity of human life. In his address on behalf of the
Congregation for the Doctrine of the Faith, titled *Instruction on Respect for Human
Life in its Origin and on the Dignity of Procreation* (Ratzinger 1987), Ratzinger reinforced the Vatican's position against abortion and birth control and laid out objections to new reproductive technologies like IVF. This document provided Catholic
theologians with the framework to oppose the oncoming tide of embryonic stem-
cell research and cloning made possible by assisted reproductive technologies.

The day after Pope Benedict's election, Lucio Gutiérrez, the beleaguered president of Ecuador (and one of only two elected presidents in a decade), was ousted
after months of protests.[1] Widespread dissatisfaction with the incompetence of his
administration, along with outrage over his capitulation to IMF–mandated austerity measures, had plagued his presidency since his election two years before.
During his administration, Ecuador's congress ratified a new civil code that prohibited "the manipulation of human life after conception," which in theory could
have restricted some practices within Ecuador's expanding IVF industry. The civil
code, along with the 1998 constitution, which declared that "life begins at concep-

tion," were shaped within the emergence of evangelical Christianity as a powerful force in Ecuador and throughout Latin America.

The near-simultaneous election of Pope Benedict and the toppling of Gutiérrez can inform our understanding of individual reproductive histories like Sandra's (see "Corporeal Punishment"). Both the procedures Sandra underwent, abortion and IVF, are of intense interest to church and state actors in sustaining the demographics of the faithful and of the nation-state. In Ecuador, the officially distinct but intertwined institutions of church and state impose restrictions that claim to protect unborn human life. The law against abortion is flouted by women of all classes (and by men, as partners and practitioners) but it is significantly more difficult for women without *recursos* (resources) to access safe clinical abortion. Sandra's misfortune was to be young, a recent migrant to the city, and lacking in familial assistance or monetary resources. She probably didn't feel able to "manage" her sexual encounters. Sandra didn't have the resources to seek out private clinical gynecological care for an abortion. She didn't think of herself as an individual with rights. She was a client with a patron—God—who didn't agree to her bargain. And when she entered the IVF clinic, she wasn't a consumer with rights either.

Surgical abortion can be an extremely safe procedure with few side effects. In Ecuador, despite the law, women with money can undergo safe abortions in clinical settings. The women I met who had had clinical abortions or who had the money to leave the country suffered no complications. But the devastating effects of unsafe abortions on poorer women can have repercussions for decades. Sandra's abortion history, ectopic pregnancy, and poor hospital care made her infertile. Years later she sought out IVF in an expensive private clinic that theoretically should have been governed by the same church and state politics that outlaw abortion. But although Catholic doctrines and state policies scarred Sandra internally, they did not follow her into the private IVF clinic.

As Cardinal Ratzinger, Pope Benedict was a famous hard-liner on the question of the protection of nascent human life. Vatican condemnation of IVF, as dictated by Ratzinger, is based on two main arguments. First, the research, development, and practice of IVF involves the destruction of embryos. The Church regards this practice as "destruction of human life," equivalent to abortion. Second, by engaging in assisted reproduction, humans are interfering with a process that should remain under God's dominion (Ratzinger 1987). Globally, much of the controversy surrounding assisted-reproduction technologies has come from religious institutions; but within Islam, Judaism, Confucianism, Hinduism, and most forms of Christianity, adjustments have been made to facilitate the fertility procedures of their adherents (Bharadwaj 2002; Handwerker 1995; Inhorn 2003; Kahn 2000). Catholicism remains the only major world faith that unequivocally condemns the use of IVF. Although the Vatican has influenced many of the debates over IVF in different parts of the world, this has not meant that all or even most Catholics heed its denunciation of this technology. In Ecuador, for so-called traditional and religiously conservative Catholics, an ongoing relationship with God has taken precedence over Church doctrine.

In Ecuador, despite the 2003 legal code that bans the manipulation of life after conception, the law has had no impact on private reproductive medicine. It remains to be seen whether or how the views of the current president, Rafael Correa, an anti-abortion leftist who is implementing health-sector reform, will affect Ecuador's IVF industry. So far, IVF practitioners have ignored the strictures that might limit their practice. They see state regulations as largely irrelevant to their private medical practices and don't see the Church as speaking for God in its condemnation of IVF. Church and state institutions in Ecuador rarely interfere with the business of the elite men who tend to be the directors of private IVF clinics. These clinics appear to exist outside or above state and church oversight or regulation.

REPRODUCTIVE GOVERNANCE

In this chapter I explore how IVF clinics are situated relative to Ecuador's church and state institutions. Both are seen as impersonal bureaucracies that can be evaded by elite male clinic directors and patients with adequate resources within paternalistic private clinics. Church condemnation of assisted reproduction means little when patients and doctors invoke God's help in the undertaking. Both patients and practitioners turn to God to arbitrate questions of life, and practitioners literally place responsibility for IVF in God's hands. Likewise, state governance means little when patients turn to private clinics, largely outside state control.

Sandra's trajectory through illegal abortion and into an IVF clinic was embedded in various forms of what Lynn Morgan and I call *reproductive governance:* the mechanisms through which different historical configurations of actors (such as state institutions, churches, hacienda owners, private doctors, corporate actors, donor agencies, and NGOs) use legislative controls, personal interactions, economic inducements, moral injunctions, and ethical incitements to produce and control reproductive behaviors and practices (Morgan and Roberts, forthcoming). As several commentators have noted, Cold War–era population programs have been quite effective in bringing birth rates down across Latin America (Leite 2004). I had imagined that studying the arrival of assisted-reproductive technologies in a developing nation would offer a means to examine the lasting effects of population-control efforts in Ecuador, along with the effects of abortion politics. Like most developing nations, Ecuador has been the target of international family planning programs for half a century, even if by no one's account has it ever been "overpopulated." Private organizations began conducting family planning programs in Ecuador in 1966. State programs partially funded by the United Nations Fund for Population Activities began in 1975 (Ruilova 1974). And indeed, family-planning campaigns appear to have been successful in Ecuador: more than 66 percent of women with male partners use some form of birth control (CEPAR 2000). As of 2007 the total fertility rate (TFR) in Ecuador was 2.71; the U.S. rate was 2.07.[2] It's debatable, though, whether this lowered birth rate is an effect of these campaigns or of shifting economic realities.

Currently, reproductive governance in Ecuador tends to center on rights and the sanctity of life; however, assisted reproduction and the urban experience of childbearing is also enmeshed in the midcentury modernity of fertility control, small families, changing gender roles and shifting consumption habits. Almost all reproductive-aged Ecuadorian urbanites I met, across class lines, felt that they could afford no more than two children, although they usually longed for more.[3] Economic conditions make large families untenable. One young woman undergoing IVF told me that her husband had nine brothers and sisters. Her mother, on the other hand, had only three children. "My mother is maybe more modern," she observed. Her husband added, "My mother is from an older time, more traditional. In this time they were accustomed to have nine, ten, twelve, fourteen [children]." Although government policies on population have shaped reproductive practices in Ecuador, IVF patients rarely mentioned them. The necessity for small families, which, among other advantages, allow parents to invest more in their children's education, is now normalized.

Abortion politics came up more than population politics in Ecuadorian IVF practice. The Catholic focus on the idea that life begins at conception took shape in the nineteenth century, in conjunction with the development of the biological sciences and the rise of nation-states—developments that could not (and still cannot) be divorced from a eugenic agenda. As in Western Europe and the United States, abortion became illegal in most Latin American countries only in the late nineteenth and early twentieth centuries (Mohr 1978). Despite the continued illegality of on-demand abortion in Latin America, except in Cuba and now Mexico City, it is the region with the world's highest abortion rates (Browner 1979; Htun 2003; Scrimshaw 1985). But until recently, there has been no move to decriminalize abortion. In her survey of reproductive and family law in Latin America, Mala Htun argues that because clandestine abortion is available and relatively safe for those with money, there has been little impetus for legalization (Htun 2003; see also Mooney 2009, 51). Recently abortion was legalized in Mexico City, and in Colombia, feminist activists and lawyers have succeeded in decriminalizing abortion to varying degrees. Their arguments for decriminalization center on a right to public health rather than the North American concept of the right to choose (Morgan and Roberts 2009, forthcoming).

In Ecuador the legislature and the judiciary are intensely engaged in abortion politics, as exemplified by their positions against legal abortion and for the protection of life from conception. Clandestine abortion is nevertheless ubiquitous and relatively easy to obtain. The WHO estimates that 95,000 abortions take place in Ecuador every year, a rate of 30 per 1,000 women of fertile age. Each year 20,000 to 30,000 women are admitted to clinics and emergency rooms with complications arising from botched abortions, and abortions cause 18 percent of maternal fatalities in Ecuador. This rate might start to fall as the use of misoprostol, a medication officially used for the treatment of peptic ulcers but also effective as an abortifacient, becomes more common throughout the region.

Like several researchers, I found that most urban Ecuadorians I surveyed had ambivalent attitudes toward abortion (Morgan 1998). Most thought it was wrong but deemed it acceptable in individual situations, especially for young women, in cases involving rape or a damaged fetus. In these cases, my informants believed, women could negotiate with God for pardon. One IVF patient told me that when she developed toxoplasmosis in an earlier pregnancy she had an abortion because of the possibility of birth defects. Her priest told her that God forgave her. Another IVF patient reasoned with me, "If a woman has an abortion, she is in debt to God."[4] These were not rights-based arguments that assume discrete, rational individuals but a rationale embedded in relational exchanges (the kinds of exchanges that were encouraged in private IVF clinics). Most women knew at least one friend or relative who had undergone an abortion. Only a few women and men involved with IVF thought abortion was always wrong: a few told me it was "assassination" in all cases. In general, urban Ecuadorians didn't want to appear extreme on the issue.

During my year of resident fieldwork in 2002–3, I scanned the newspaper every day for articles related to assisted reproductive technologies, population issues, abortion, and family planning. I found several every week. On a return trip in 2007, I discovered an explosion of articles in response to a legislative battle about the morning-after pill. At the same time, graffiti about abortion, condoms, and the morning-after pill appeared on street walls throughout Quito. Various groups, including local and transnational right-to-life and feminist organizations, were gearing up for a fight about the new constitution, which was ratified in the fall of 2008. The final draft of the constitution guaranteed the right to "take free, responsible, and informed decisions about one's health and reproductive life and to decide how many children to have" but continued to outlaw abortion (in Article 66, Number 10). No one was happy with this outcome. The Catholic Church denounced the constitution as anti-life, while feminist groups denounced it as a threat to reproductive health. President Rafael Correa, who backed the constitution, remained on record as opposing legal abortion.

Throughout the 1990s several Latin American legal codes were revised to define life as beginning at the moment of conception, not at birth. Ecuadorian state and church institutions participated in a newly energized mandate to protect human life promulgated by the globalized right-to life-movement, through rights-based arguments. In recent legislative battles, the reproductive rights of individual women have been pitted against the right to life of the unborn. As in other Latin American nations, laws and policies on abortion have become more restrictive at the same time that laws providing free maternity care have been enacted under the banner of the right to reproductive health (Hermida et al. 2004). In Andean nations, the resources for free maternity care tend to be channeled into public-sector health care, not social security, which provides for the employed middle class—once again making poor and indigenous women the targets of intervention and reproductive governance (Ewig 2010).

The shift in the discourse of reproductive governance, from issues of population and race to those of rights and life, was manifested through a host of complex material and political forces in Latin America. Internationally, rights-based discourses have flourished in the context of economic policies that promote the expansion of private-sector medicine, and they have pitted citizens against states in the legal arena, where rights can be debated. Under these political and juridical conditions, rights have been allotted to previously unrecognized groups: the landless, women, indigenous people, and, increasingly, the unborn. Although granting rights to the unborn is a hotly debated issue, the idea that embryos and fetuses might have rights is fostered by medical technologies that make it possible to see inside, measure, and manage human bodies, especially women's. Through this visualization of women's insides, fetuses and embryos have become increasingly personified (J. Taylor 2008a).

U.S.–based right-to-life groups are working in Latin America to shape the debate. These groups are finding fertile ground in many nations where the Cold War legacy of the Left's alignment with the Church has created alliances between newly elected leftist administrations and the local Catholic episcopal conferences. At the same time, international feminist health organizations are working to promote women's rights. In Latin America they frame their arguments in terms of the right to health, rather than the right to autonomy or reproductive freedom: they thus cast illegal abortion as a public health problem (Morgan 1998). The language of rights that currently frames reproductive practice in relation to the rights of women and the rights of the unborn also produces consumers with rights for the flourishing, privatized medical sector throughout Latin America (Radcliffe and Westwood 1996; Rose 1999).

THE CODE OF LIFE

The Child and Adolescent Civil Code enacted while Lucio Gutiérrez was president states: "Boys and girls and adolescents have the right to life from their conception. . . . Experiments and medical and genetic manipulations are prohibited from the fertilization of the egg until birth" (Congreso Nacional, Función Ejecutiva, Ecuador 2003). Some of the techniques used in IVF, particularly embryo cryopreservation, could be interpreted as medical manipulation after fertilization. In this process, embryos are mixed with a cryoprotectant fluid, allowing them to be stored at very low temperatures without damage. Below I describe how three lawyers with different agendas and positions—Marco Andrade, Ricardo Rabinovich-Berkman, and Sonia Merlyn Sacoto—responded to this code.

The code was most likely intended to reinforce the illegality of abortion and ward off the specter of embryonic stem-cell research and genetic engineering. To find out whether the code was directed toward assisted reproduction, I visited one of its primary authors, Marco Andrade (a pseudonym), an attorney and law professor at a Quiteño university. We met soon after the code was passed in 2003. Andrade carefully explained how the language of the previous code had been revised. The 1992 child protection code used the word *experimentation* in relation to interventions in embryonic life: it was replaced with *manipulation*. He and the other authors wanted the new code to be more precise, "like it is in Europe, England, and the United States. . . . The idea is to incorporate regulations gradually, linked to the new scientific advances and technologies. Because . . . well, yes, the country is not in a condition to use the technologies to the point of genetic engineering. But it is necessary to incorporate what is happening with these technologies in the conscience of our community's humanity."

Andrade thought this code would allow Ecuador to enact preemptive legislation that would anticipate and govern emerging scientific technologies. But Ecuador's private assisted-reproduction industry was farther along than Andrade knew. When I asked him how embryo cryopreservation would be interpreted under this new code, he replied, "Well, they don't freeze embryos in Ecuador." When I informed him that cryopreserved embryos had existed in Ecuador since 1998, he seemed a bit flustered. He responded that he had thought freezing embryos was against international law. But there are no international laws governing assisted reproduction.

I asked again if embryo cryopreservation would be considered "manipulation." "Yes," he replied, but then he began to reconsider: "Manipulation is an intervention, and here [with freezing] there is no intervention. It does not provoke a change. One could say then that freezing is not a manipulation. No, for me personally, it's not manipulation because there is no intervention in the embryo, but maybe the law might need to become more precise. The radical question is to define what manipulation is."

Andrade explained that a motion had been proposed to regulate reproductive technologies in Ecuador. The motion failed in Congress "because of conservatives and the Church."

"They don't want a law?" I asked.

"They don't want assisted reproduction. They don't want man to interfere in the phenomenon of life. So they attacked the idea."

"But then the doctors can do whatever they want," I pointed out.

"Well, they have a policy to look the other way. . . . We don't see it. We don't look at it. We prefer to not see. They say, "If we accept these rules, it signifies that we have to look and take a position,' and this is what they don't want."

Toward the end of the conversation, Andrade told me he did not personally oppose abortion. This was an extremely uncommon position for anyone in Ecuador to acknowledge out loud, but he gave me the sense that several other legal scholars privately shared his opinion. It seemed that he and his colleagues had averted their gaze from IVF while drafting the law so that issues of embryonic life could remain out of sight, a strategy that Andrade claimed the Church employs as well.

Over the next few weeks, I took a copy of the new legal code to the IVF doctors at the clinics where I observed. None of them had heard about it. For the most part, they were uninterested, and they became even more dismissive after seeing the actual language. It seemed the words of the code were not precise enough for them to feel threatened. I began to think that this newly ratified code possessed juridical power only in the minds of North Americans like me.

A year later, I witnessed another foreigner try unsuccessfully to press these practitioners to consider the juridical import of the civil code. In the fall of 2003, SEMER (Sociedad Ecuatoriana de Medicina Reproductiva) organized a national congress of infertility specialists, sponsored by several pharmaceutical companies and the Ministry of Public Health. Ricardo Rabinovich-Berkman, a lawyer and historian from Buenos Aires, gave a talk about recent legal changes in many Latin American nations that have mandated juridical protection from conception, not birth. He declared with fervor, "What's inside the uterus must be protected." He appeared not to have considered that IVF involves conception outside, not inside, the uterus, a crucial distinction for many of the IVF patients I had met in the local clinics (see chapter 5).

Near the end of his presentation, Rabinovich brought up the Adolescent and Child Civil Code that I had discussed the previous year with Andrade. Rabinovich told the assembled Ecuadorian clinicians that their new code "makes cryopreservation illegal" because it bans manipulation of the embryo from the moment of conception. When he finished speaking, there were no questions from the audience. It was easy to approach him afterward: no one else wanted to be near him. A few doctors I knew even tried to chase me away from him with frantic hand motions and raised eyebrows. Rabinovich invited me to sit with him at lunch, and when he picked a table, the people already seated there became immediately quiet. He murmured that he had grown up partly in England and suggested we speak in English, which most of the people at the table would not understand. This suggestion seemed to relieve our tablemates as well.

As we talked, it became clear that Rabinovich held complicated views. He called himself a militant Catholic, but he did not oppose IVF, as long as all embryos produced were transferred back into the woman's body. He didn't agree with the lawmakers who, in 2000, had succeeded in banning IVF in Costa Rica, the only nation in the world to do so. (The ban was reversed in 2010.) But he was vociferous about what he saw as the negative ethical consequences of cryopreservation. He told me that although Argentina has had a law defining life from conception since 1871, he was envious of Ecuador's new, "more precise" code, remarking, "Ecuador is now ahead," an unusual sentiment for a cosmopolitan Argentinian. Rabinovich hoped his talk would accomplish two things: assert the need for law and lawyers to adjudicate issues of life, and force Ecuadorian IVF specialists to "wake up" to the fact that some of what they do is now illegal. He said rather dolefully: "Sadly, my talk ruined nobody's lunch, and it should have. The thing is, someone will prosecute a doctor here for freezing embryos. This will happen because it's such a Catholic country. The power of the Church is very potent in the sierra. There is a very strong possibility this will go to court. And they will find a sympathetic judge and put the doctor in jail. But no one is aware of it. They are walking a tightrope and don't know it."

After lunch another Argentinian spoke: Dr. Carlos Carizza, a well-known IVF specialist from Rosario. Carizza's talk concerned ovarian function, but he finished with a defiant outburst toward Rabinovich: "We know those cells are not human beings, since we know it can be a molar pregnancy or a vacant embryo.[5] This man should not be telling us what to do!" These words received a huge round of applause. When I introduced myself to Dr. Carizza later, he told me that although in Argentina Rabinovich is marginalized by the medical establishment, he appears on the radio and TV all the time. "He is part of a group of extremists, but he doesn't have power."

For the next day and a half, there was tumult in the conference halls. I spoke with several doctors and biologists about Rabinovich's presentation, and a few doctors sought me out, as I had mentioned the code to them the year before. Other doctors said they had never heard of the law before the talk. An IVF laboratory biologist joked that she would be working from jail now. Most practitioners dismissed Rabinovich as a fanatic or "Opus Dei," an epithet referring to the ultraconservative, secretive lay Catholic organization with international membership. One geneticist looked worried and suggested that doctors who cryopreserve embryos should be careful. When one doctor suggested that SEMER set up a committee to decide what to do about the new law, I offered to give him Andrade's phone number, but he did not take it. By the last day of the conference, the issue seemed dead. Rabinovich was consigned to the margins as an extremist. His efforts to ruin lunch had failed, perhaps because his understanding of the powers of church and state seemed to have more to do with Argentina than with Ecuador.

Eight months after Rabinovich's harangue at the SEMER conference, I was back in Quito. That week the national paper carried several advertisements for

IVF centers as well as four articles about IVF. One was an in-depth story in the "Futuro" section of the paper about the availability of cryopreservation in Ecuador (Comercio 2004). Several of the doctors with whom I had worked were interviewed or described in the article. Apparently Rabinovich's warnings about the new Child and Adolescent Civil Code had not hampered these practitioners' desire to publicize their services. Most doctors told me nothing had changed in the last year.

When I brought up the subject of Rabinovich with Diego, one of Dr. Molina's sons, he said, "Oh yes, the guy who said that we're criminals."

"But why not try to change the law?" I asked.

"Because the government does not know that this is done. It would be a waste of time to get involved."

"But do you ever worry about what happened in Costa Rica?" I asked.

"No. This law doesn't have any power here, because infertile patients are going to keep doing treatment here, or leave for Colombia or Peru."

When I talked about the impact of the civil code with Linda, the biologist at Dr. Padilla's clinic, she grinned: "In our country all the laws are made to be broken. We are accustomed to do what we want and to evade all laws. Laws could be good in the sense of protection of clinics and the couple, because the problem is that we are not prepared to follow laws that they give us. We always violate them. I don't believe that they would come now and tell us to stop."

Linda showed me an invitation for a dinner for IVF practitioners at a luxury hotel hosted by SEMER and sponsored by the pharmaceutical company Organon. The printed invitation stated that after dinner there would be a preliminary meeting "to establish norms of concern to the infertility clinics of Ecuador."

Even though Linda knew that the law in question concerned the life of embryos, she was concerned with how treatment protocols might be standardized across clinics, not whether specific techniques should be allowed in the effort to protect unborn life. But at the dinner, which I attended with Linda, the topic of "legal norms or normative protocols" never arose. Instead, more immediate concerns took precedence, like establishing legitimacy and territory within the small pool of potential Ecuadorian IVF patients.

IVF practitioners in other parts of Latin America have been much more concerned about the entwined national powers of church and state (Htun 2003). In Costa Rica, Catholic lawmakers succeeded in dismantling the IVF industry by outlawing the practice from 2000 to 2010 (Poblete 2002). In Chile and Argentina, which both have large IVF industries, clinicians have attempted to forestall church interference by regulating the practice themselves. In Chile, IVF doctors use the term *pre-embryos* for two- to three-day-old embryos to exempt them from legislative debates that would involve Church representatives. In Buenos Aires, some Catholic laboratory biologists freeze all extra embryos, regardless of quality, out of respect for their "life potential." Except in Costa Rica, any move toward explicit regulation of IVF in Latin American nations has been self-directed, conducted quietly in meetings of technical elites, out of public or government view. Overtly attempting to influence policy would mean negotiating the minefield of official Catholic and state censure.

One Ecuadorian IVF doctor was concerned with Rabinovich's predictions about the law and embryo cryopreservation. When I visited with Antonia and Dr. Castro at Dr. Hidalgo's clinic, they told me that Dr. Hidalgo had decided to stop talking to the press so that he could "stay under the radar." He had also decided to use the term *pre-embryo* instead of *embryo* when talking with patients. I asked them what they thought of the new legal code. Antonia replied bitterly, "Congress makes laws of shit, because there is no consultation with the right people, specialists in the field." She began to regale me with examples of the ways laws were not followed in Ecuador. Dr. Castro added: "This is more or less how we function. There could be laws but here, the whole world passes above the law [*aquí, todo mundo pasa por encima de las leyes*]. This is how we are, in this phase of maturation."

On a later visit in 2007, the practitioners at Dr. Molina's clinic were excited to tell me about Sonia Merlyn Sacoto, a lawyer who had conducted research at the clinic a year earlier. Sacoto's book about assisted reproduction and the law in Ecuador had just been published, and the clinic was featured prominently in her discussions. I was confused by their excitement. Wouldn't more legal attention affect their practice for the worse? But I was excited too, looking forward to speaking with someone who could help me understand assisted reproduction with regard to legislative and juridical processes in Ecuador.

Sacoto arrived late for our meeting and began talking a million miles a minute. She taught at a few private universities around Quito in addition to running a private practice. As a French Ecuadorian, she had ties to other places, just as Andrade and Rabinovich-Berkman did. As she saw it, Article 20 of the Child and Adolescent Civil Code, prohibiting manipulation from conception, should have prevented embryo freezing, but it hadn't. Sacoto had learned from her observations in Quito's IVF clinics, just as I had, that all of the clinics that could freeze embryos did so, ignoring the law. She was frustrated that it didn't appear to have had any effect on the practice of IVF in Ecuador.

It was exhilarating to argue with Sacoto about embryo freezing, abortion, and Ecuadorian law, given her absolutist moral sense of how the law should work, which was very different from the attitudes I had usually encountered in Ecuador. "Embryos are human life and should not be killed," she told me. "Abortion is wrong. . . . Law should prohibit these practices." Much of Sacoto's thinking about frozen embryos had been shaped by none other than Ricardo Rabinovich-Berkman, her most formative mentor, whom she thanked profusely in the acknowledgments of her book (Sacoto 2006). Like Rabinovich, Sacoto did not think IVF should be banned. But she was dismayed by Ecuador's legislative imprecision:

> Conception needs to be defined precisely in law. Last year the president declared March 25 El Dia del Niño por Nacer [Day of the Unborn Child], without defining what conception is. Inexplicably our lawmakers guard a silence about the topic. There are too many gray areas. The law is mestizo, a mixture. The laboratories work in gray areas. Things need to be black or white for the security of society. What if I am older and am divorced and want to have more kids? And I want to know what's possible or not? I need to know if what they [the IVF clinics] are doing is legal. Law is security for patients. It is security for doctors.

Sacoto brushed aside my observation that few of the older, divorced women I met in the IVF clinics—or any other patients for that matter—had articulated any of the concerns about the law that she ascribed to them. In fact, none of them had ever mentioned or seemed concerned about the legal status of assisted reproduction in Ecuador.

Underlying Sacoto's argument was her mission to uphold the rights of embryos, shaped by the liberal discourse of individual rights that informs both pro-life and pro-choice arguments. She took me through the changes in Ecuadorian legal view of life. In 1861 Ecuador adopted Chile's civil code, which established that a person's legal existence begins at birth. In 1938 abortion was made illegal. In 1967, with a new constitution, life was defined as beginning at conception. This definition was reiterated in the constitution of 1998. Then, in 2003, with the Child and Adolescent Civil Code, the embryo gained even higher status, moving from being entitled to protection to being a rights holder, *titulado*. According to Sacoto, Ecuador's was "one of the most modern codes in Latin America," with modernity predicated on the notion of individual rights. Sacoto argued that "law should reflect society." I tried to pounce on her argument, asking, "Then why should abortions be illegal, since so many women in Ecuador have them?" She countered:

> I never understood why so many women get abortions here when they say they are against it. Lots of my friends have had abortions, and I don't condemn them. I'm Catholic. But I'm not Opus Dei. I'm not a fanatic. I am not that religious. But most Ecuadorian women are not really in favor of abortion. Most think that if they get an abortion they are killing something. It's not just a bunch of cells. Their boyfriend makes them do it. Or they think, if he is not going to marry me, then I'll have an abortion. I don't believe that in our Ecuadorian reality women can immerse themselves inside this mentality: I have the right to my body. They don't think of the conceived as only cells. No. I believe, to the contrary, a woman who aborts is not a woman who is culturally immersed in Ecuador. They are more like my European friends.

According to Sacoto, it is Ecuadorian to protect the right to life, including the life of the unborn. It's European to think about abortion in relation to the rights of the individual woman. Most frustrating from her viewpoint, it is also Ecuadorian to make contradictory laws about rights. Through all of Ecuador's changes, the original civil code of 1861 has not been superseded. Thus, technically, rights begin at birth, although constitutionally the "conceived" are subject to protection. Within the Child and Adolescent Civil Code, the conceived have individual rights. The penal code of 1938 made abortion illegal, in contradiction to the civil code of 1861, which grants protection under the law only at birth. Sacoto found the contradictions between these different expressions of the law immensely vexing.

Within the gray areas of Ecuador's legal landscape, IVF clinics flourish. As Sacoto saw it, Ecuadorian law was born through *mestizaje*, the colonial process of race mixture. She felt "things should be more black and white":

> The law here is a mixture, mestizo. Everything we have came from somewhere else. . . . It all originated with what came from the West. We don't have adequate norms for our daily reality, without falling on the traditional schema of importing [from other nations] before producing it ourselves. *Mestizaje* for me is the assemblage of various cultures. The penal code of 1938 was inspired by the Belgian penal code, but it left certain penal institutions that are, in reality, legal monstrosities. For example, abortion is criminal except for two cases: the first is therapeutic, and the second—which is a horrible mixture—is the case of an idiot or demented woman. That's completely taken from the Belgian penal

code of the last century. It has nothing to do with *nuestra realidad*. . . . It would be excellent if it reflected who we are. But there is just a lot of mixing. So for this we are in a legal crisis. People feel that the law is made to be violated. People believe that the law is only a written thing.

I could not imagine how Sacoto planned to prevent embryo cryopreservation. Invariably, IVF procedures result in extra embryos that can't be transferred in case they produce unwanted multiple births. I drew little diagrams of embryo counts per aspiration and asked what she thought should be done. "If ten eggs are retrieved and eight fertilized, how many should be transferred? What should be done with the rest?"

"There should be a strict limit," she argued. "Only three eggs should be fertilized, and all three should be transferred. The rest of the eggs should be frozen."

"But that's not realistic," I argued back. "They aren't freezing eggs in Ecuador. And even in places where they are freezing eggs, it's not very successful. Egg freezing doesn't really work yet."

Sacoto's solution was to change the reality. "They are doing it in Peru. They just won't do it here because it's cheaper and easier to freeze embryos. But they could, and they should. And it's the law. The patients and the doctors should be conscious of the juridical implication of creating human life."

I knew that Sacoto's concern for embryos was not in line with the views of most Ecuadorian IVF practitioners and biotech professionals. The difference was made abundantly clear at a biotechnology conference held in Quito in 2003, called Trascendiendo Fronteras en Medicina (Transcending Frontiers in Medicine). Among a group of prominent European and American biologists and genetic engineers invited to speak, the star attraction was Ian Wilmut, the Scottish embryologist credited with cloning Dolly the sheep. His movements around the country before the conference were tracked like a rock star's. Newspaper headlines screamed: "Ian Wilmut in the Galápagos!" "Ian Wilmut in the Centro Historico!" "Ian Wilmut at the volcano!" Wilmut's lecture was the finale of the conference at a luxury hotel. He talked about the state of stem-cell research and cloning to a packed crowd of more than a thousand Ecuadorian biotech professionals, most wearing simultaneous-translator headsets. During the question period, a man stood up and asked about the ethics of destroying embryos.

Wilmut replied with a hypothetical scenario resembling a parable: "You are in your lab, and you have a child with you. And you are working on a petri dish filled with human embryos, and a fire breaks out. Who are you going to grab and run for the door, the child or the embryos? You would grab the child!" For this he received a thunderous round of applause, howls of delight, and a lengthy standing ovation, the sound of the pent-up frustration of a mass of assembled biotech professionals working in a nation officially committed to protecting embryonic life.

I don't think Sacoto would have been clapping, even if she agreed that she would grab the child rather than the embryos. Given her commitment to embryonic life, she was contemplating doing something more legally proactive in the future, perhaps asking the Ministry of Health to carry out a census of embryos—literally counting all the frozen embryos stored in IVF clinics around the country.

The three lawyers I describe here had different views on the power of the Catholic Church and the rule of state law in Ecuador. All three assumed that abortion would remain illegal and that legal codes were written to protect the unborn as rights-bearing individuals. Dr. Sacoto, a French Ecuadorian, was deeply frustrated that embryos were still not protected from destruction. Her interactions with the various clinics had not influenced them to change their practices. Her passion for abstract and transcendent principles of law felt alien to the Ecuadorian sensibility I was used to, and in some ways alien to her own call for laws tailored to *nuestra realidad*.

Dr. Rabinovich's view was the most oblivious to Ecuadorian legal realities. Although he is an accomplished Church historian and scholar of comparative Latin American law, he assumed that the situation in Argentina, where church and state have more direct influence on the regulation of medicine, was similar in Ecuador: that religious conservatism in Ecuador would lead the Church to combine forces with state powers to prosecute doctors who froze embryos. Rabinovich overestimated the power of these institutions and actors to assert their agenda in Ecuadorian IVF clinics directly. IVF practitioners in Ecuador do almost nothing to ward off the regulative powers of church and state, as clinicians do in other Latin American countries: they do not need to.

Dr. Andrade, from the Southern Cone, who had lived and worked in Ecuador for decades, had the most grounded view of the Church's ability to assert itself through the level of the state and the state's ability to enforce law. Of the three lawyers, only Andrade had had a hand in shaping the Ecuadorian legislation, and he was the most pragmatic about the disconnect between the law and the conduct of Ecuadorian citizens, especially elite doctors in private medical practice. By the summer of 2007, the civil code had been in effect for four years; yet the approach of the Ecuadorian IVF practitioners to IVF, embryo cryopreservation, and questions of life had remained nearly unchanged, and their willingness to publicize their activities had actually increased. Of all the IVF doctors in Ecuador, only Dr. Hidalgo had been concerned about the potential for state intervention, and his concern proved temporary: he was back to advertising like all the other IVF specialists in Ecuador.

PASSIVE CATHOLICS

On the last night of the 2003 Quito SEMER conference where Rabinovich gave his unpopular speech, the Grünenthal Group, a German pharmaceutical company that markets birth-control pills, hosted a dinner for the conference participants in the convent of San Francisco, the largest, oldest and most celebrated church complex in Ecuador.[6] The IVF doctors, lab biologists, pharmaceutical executives, their spouses, and I ate our dinners under monumental paintings of Franciscan history and larger-than-life crucifixes carved by members of the sixteenth- and seventeenth-century baroque Quiteño school of religious art. San Francisco de Quito is controlled by the local episcopal conference, and, as part of colonial Quito, has been deemed a UNESCO World Heritage Site. I couldn't help thinking it was noteworthy that this convent was hosting an assortment of professionals dedicated to promoting nonreproductive sex and asexual reproduction. One doctor joked that he hoped to find some egg donors among the nuns.

The conference events included a bus tour of Quito's Centro Historico, on which we passed the convent of Santa Catalina, which houses the seventeenth-century bench of an especially pious nun, Sister Catalina de Jesús Maria Herrera. When I had visited the convent the previous year, one of the nuns had told me that about twenty years before, a woman came to visit the convent. She sat on the bench crying because she couldn't get pregnant. The woman's sister, a resident nun, suggested she pray to Sister Catalina. Soon after, the woman's doctor told her she was pregnant. She went on to have six children. Since then almost one hundred women have come and prayed to Santa Catalina on the bench and become pregnant. When I related this story to Dr. Molina, who was sitting next to me on the bus, he wanted to know "if the nuns get pregnant too?" He told me, "There are tunnels under the churches here in the old town where the priests and nuns meet, and [people] have found the remains of babies there." I had heard this tale of subterranean sex and infant disposal by priests and nuns before, but never from a doctor with his own role in facilitating an illicit sort of virgin birth.

Dr. Molina's anticlerical humor and his IVF practice exemplified how the Catholic Church has failed to indoctrinate its constituents, at least in Ecuador, into compliance. Many narratives circulate about the Church's inability to enforce its dictates on a wayward flock. Conversational remarks often point out the hypocrisy of Ecuadorian Catholicism: "Look how the churches are empty." "Look how everyone uses contraception." Social scientists such as Michael Taussig and Weston LaBarre have noted the Church's failure to enforce piety among Andean peoples (Taussig 1980; LaBarre and Mason 1948). However, Ecuador has also been described as "the most religiously conservative nation in the Andes, perhaps in all of Latin America" (Lane 2003, 92). Throughout my research I pondered these two seemingly contradictory claims.

Ecuadorians tend to express antipathy toward extremism, religious or otherwise. When I asked doctors, patients, and other citizens if they were religious, the responses were often along these lines: "I'm Catholic. I'm not a fanatic, though. I don't go to mass." This sort of response came even from urbanites who made yearly pilgrimages to Catholic shrines. The cultivation of the antifanatical self was evident in nonreligious forums as well. When I asked a friend if he was worried about the newly elected president being overthrown, he replied, "Don't worry. We are *not* a tropical people. We are not fanatics." The phrase "We are not fanatics," or "I am not a fanatic," recurred frequently in discussions of abortion, homosexuality, and politics: "I don't believe in abortion, but I'm not a fanatic. I understand some people have them, poor things." "I think it's wrong to be homosexual, but I'm not a fanatic. My children know some of *los gays,* and they might be accepted here someday. Just not now." No one should believe too fervently, lest one become a fanatic. The implication that going to church is fanatical suggests that it is the rule-following Catholics whose zeal must be curtailed, while those who participate in personalist exchange relationships with God and saints view themselves as tolerant moderates.

Rocio, a lab biologist, explained that Ecuadorian Catholics, including herself, are "mas pasivas" (more passive), using birth control, never attending mass, ignoring Vatican doctrine. Even though her tone and the word *pasiva* sounded derogatory, this derision was nothing compared to the scorn she reserved for "Catolicas mas activas"(more active), linked to right-wing movements like Opus Dei.

Rocio's distinction between passive and active Catholics is similar to the distinction between spiritual and materialist Catholics I draw in the introduction. Materialists and passive Catholics pay little attention to doctrine; they devote themselves instead to the cultivation of relations with God and the saints. In these formulations, IVF practitioners are passive and materialist Catholics. By disavowing their own agency, IVF practitioners effectively countered the Church's claim that IVF is a godless practice and the law's claim that IVF manipulates human life. Humbly giving over their laboratories to God, and to a relationship of material exchange, effectively allowed these practitioners to stake a claim to a legitimate practice.

In addition to claiming not to attend mass, Ecuadorians also distanced themselves from fanaticism through their rhetorical references to Opus Dei. The organization is rumored to have made powerful inroads in Ecuador. The label *Opus Dei* functioned as shorthand for fanatic, or what I would call a spiritual Catholic. With its emphasis on infusing daily life with Catholic idealism and spiritualism, Opus Dei resembles typical Ecuadorian Catholicism in its infiltration of everyday activity; but unlike typical Ecuadorian Catholics, Opus Dei supporters adhere strictly to a conservative reading of Church doctrine. Criticism of Opus Dei is a criticism of Catholic doxa. In the minds of many Ecuadorians, Opus Dei is anathema to the personal relationships they have established with God, which emphasize negotiation rather than conformity to seemingly arbitrary rules.

Most of the patients I met in the clinics had a vague sense that the Church disapproved of IVF, but very few struggled with the issue. Most dismissed the Church as out of date and selfish for trying to deny them children. Several patients related that despite the Church's official condemnation, they sought and received a blessing for their IVF cycles from their priests. One woman told me she confessed to her priest about the IVF origins of her child. He reassured her that "her child was brought into being with love." I don't know if the priest was aware that the church's stance against IVF is derived from the idea that the practice represents a threat to embryonic life.

Another couple, Ximena and Victor, had a similar experience with their parish priest: "We went to talk to the priest at our parish, and we told him what we are doing. And he was not against it. We told him everything, and he said that it was fine. And what's more it is a decision that he could not deny. He said that he didn't know what it was like to lack [children]. It was good. He gave us his blessing. People get married and everything the Church says to do. But the population will diminish [from infertility], so that we will end up with no one."

For Ximena, as for many patients, the Church's official stance against IVF is inexplicable, especially when their own priests bless their use of IVF. It was not the Church they had to answer to for their reproductive practices: it was God.

GOD'S HANDS

IVF practitioners' invocations of God in the laboratory are a way of declaring his sovereignty over matters of reproduction, above the Catholic Church and state policies that protect unborn human life. Clinical practitioners are keenly aware of the fact that the Church finds IVF objectionable, and as Catholics, this is a conflict with which they have to grapple. Their rebuttals took two basic forms: first, they argued that they were not playing God but rather were God's helpers; and second, they reasoned that if God had given them the ability to do this, he must approve. Both of these rebuttals focus on Vatican objections to the artificiality of IVF and sidestep the charge that IVF exterminates human life, an objection that both Ecuadorian practitioners and patients, and even many priests, often overlooked.

Many practitioners had practiced responses to church condemnation of IVF's artificiality. One clinician told me, "The Church thinks only God can create life, and I agree. I'm not creating a life. I'm just giving a hormone. I'm not playing God." Most commonly, practitioners told me that IVF conception takes place "in God's hands." Hands were one of the central images that practitioners used to establish the difference between their limited capabilities and God's expansive capabilities. Linda talked about holding the cells of life in her hands, but she explained that making life was not within her power: "To know that I had these cells in my hands—I checked them, I manipulated them, and now there is a precious baby. In reality, it affects me when the patients don't become pregnant, but we do that which is in our hands. Outside of that we can't do anything. God helps so that all will go well."

Antonia was keenly aware of the right way to present her work in relation to God's work. Like Linda, she addressed the power to manipulate gametes but insisted that she did not have God's ultimate power to create life: "I joke sometimes that I am one of the few people who is similar to God. But this I say as a joke. [It] is not something I say to the patients. I always say to them that the only thing I do is present the sperm to the eggs. That's all. If they don't fertilize, it is in divine hands. There is a difference between God and me."

Silvia portrayed her role in the laboratory in a similar way:

> The church believes that we are trying to be God. But from my point of view,
> I don't see it like this. I believe that I help the couple to complete a desire, to
> realize a dream. I have a friend who is a nun, and she says to me that she is not
> in agreement: "It's like wanting to do what God does." Then I say to her that
> I am only a human that learns to do. We are helping, but no more. Because,
> for example, when I transfer the embryos, we have to wait twelve days to see
> if they implant or not. If then, in this lapse of time, these embryos implant and
> give a pregnancy, it's because God gives us a hand and said this couple deserves
> to have a baby. If the patient doesn't get pregnant, it's one test more.

These laboratory biologists made crucial distinctions between God's hands and their own. While all three seemed deeply satisfied with the act of holding reproductive cells in their hands, they emphasized that fertilization and implantation can occur only in the hands of God. This humility differed greatly from the more autonomous sense of practice I encountered among IVF doctors in the United States (Roberts 1998a, 1998b).

Rather than ignoring Church claims that God condemns IVF, Ecuadorian IVF practitioners believed that, on the contrary, God directly supports the practice and is the main actor in determining IVF outcomes. These assertions are made in the specific context of a religiosity in which religious observance transpires through personal, material relationships with God and the saints, instead of through adherence to abstract rules. Dr. Molina articulated it this way: "Many times in interviews in radio and television, they have asked me if in the laboratory you are not playing with life, playing God. And I have answered, 'God is in the laboratory.' We are nothing more than assistants. We are only putting our small grain of sand in to get results."

When I asked priests why the Church is opposed to IVF, they most often framed the issue as one of artificiality. They objected to the idea of the laboratory replacing nature or conjugal sex in the production of children. They asserted that children would feel terrible if they found out about their "unnatural" origins. In this regard, they differed from the majority of IVF patients, who imagined that when they told their children that they were IVF babies, they would feel more loved, when they knew about the efforts their parents made and the assistance their parents received in order to have them. For these, patients the asexuality of IVF was of no concern, as they were still following the God-given script for producing life.

Another priest told me dismissively that praying to God in an IVF clinic is like Colombian assassins praying before a killing, or doctors praying before performing an abortion. In effect, he framed the issue as a moral contest between IVF practitioners and the Catholic Church. Are IVF practitioners acting as false gods, as killers, or are they God's helpers, as they themselves claim? These priests emphasized God's primary role as the creator of natural laws, not as an entity with a material presence on earth. When I told one priest that IVF practitioners saw God's handiwork in IVF clinics, he countered by dismissing the idea of divine intervention and identifying psychological forces, such as relaxation, as the real causes of apparently miraculous clinic results.

In the priests' view, only very occasionally does God intervene on earth. One priest told me, "God doesn't break his own natural laws." This is an Enlightenment attitude, reflecting the view that God is no longer engaged in the everyday affairs of humans. Nevertheless, he had known one infertile woman who become pregnant after praying on the miraculous bench at the convent of Santa Catalina. Another knew of a woman who went to Europe forty years earlier to have fertility treatment without success, but who became pregnant with twins after returning to Ecuador and having a vision of a light shining through the monstrance at the Corpus Christi celebration. This contrast between IVF practitioners claiming God's intervention and priestly denial of this possibility enacts a centuries-old quandary for the Church. While Church representatives must clearly distance themselves from the mainline Protestant view of a God separate from earth and acknowledge the possibility of divine intervention, they also must prevent the populist faithful, who claim God's constant earthly intervention, from determining the public face of Catholicism (O'Connell 1986). This historic and contemporary struggle to determine control of the miraculous has usually been characterized as a conflict between educated clergy and humble peasants. In the case of Ecuadorian IVF however, the conflict involves educated elites and middle classes in contestation with the Church.

THE EDGES OF CHURCH AND STATE

To understand the flourishing of IVF clinics in Ecuador, it's crucial to understand the history of church and state in relation to elite and indigenous groups. Church and state institutions have developed separately from each other, through official separation of the two, and from certain elite domains, like haciendas. that ostensibly remained outside state governance. Elites had paternalistic authority over their families, workers, and Indians who resided in the realm of the hacienda. In the early days of the republic, the architects of the state were these same elites, and thus the interests of the nation and these elite domains overlapped extensively. Private medical clinics are similar to haciendas in that the relations are paternalistic (not consumer-oriented) and, although effectively outside state governance, the goals of doctors and patients resonate with broader national agendas. Additionally, the regimes of church and state are enacted through daily experiences of their failure to regulate ("look how the churches are empty," "look at all the abortions") and, with regard to state institutions, to provide services. The ineffectiveness of state institutions at providing services leads people to avoid them, especially given the historic association of marginalized groups with governance enforced through state services. This avoidance reinforces the popularity of private medicine as well as private education and security. Private IVF clinics are direct beneficiaries of this avoidance.

Recent social-science literature argues that the state is not a "given and immobile" entity but a name for a way of "tying together, multiplying and coordinating power relations, a kind of knotting or congealing of power" (Ferguson 2006, 282). We can also track what the Church is and how it is constituted by documenting how it has historically played an integral role in the governance of population, race, and life. Although the Ecuadorian state is officially secular, the origins of the nation are thoroughly intertwined with the Catholic Church.

Ecuador became a nation-state in 1830, one of the three nations that emerged from the collapse of the Gran Columbia republic formed by Simón Bolívar. The new nation survived postindependence turmoil with its colonial highland aristocracy relatively intact and was considered the most politically and socially conservative of the Andean states (Larson 2004; O'Connor 2007). Ecuador had the highest percentage of Indians of all the new Andean republics, providing a social and demographic basis for adapting colonial practice and ideologies to the postcolonial national order.

In the highlands, this order was carried out within haciendas, landed estates for herding or agriculture, granted at first to elite men by the Spanish Crown. The *huasipungeros* (debt peons) living on these estates worked the land, providing the *hacendados* the wherewithal to pay tribute to the Crown. During the colonial period, the Crown attempted to control indigenous labor, trying to prevent independence movements by colonial landed elite. These efforts ultimately failed. By the late 1700s, indigenous people began to flee chiefdoms for the haciendas, allowing the colonial elite to gain primary control over indigenous labor and resources. With independence, the Creole landed elite began to manage the newly formed state to advance their interests, free of interference from the Spanish Crown (Lyons 2006). Within these reorganized relations, *hacendados* came to control the labor of Indians.

The interplay of liberalism and perceived radical otherness and inequality in the Andes fostered the creation of exclusionary nineteenth-century "republics without citizens" (Larson 2004). Nation making for postcolonial Creole elites in the Andes was motivated more by fear of the native masses than by the desire for political freedom and free trade. To mitigate the "Indian problem," elites arrived at authoritarian republicanism rather than representative democracy, in a very clear rejection of liberal ideals of egalitarian citizenship (Larson 2004, 38). The hacienda system, with coercive debt peonage, was more widespread in Ecuador than in any other Andean nation. Labor policies were designed to manage subjugated groups, especially highland Indians on haciendas, relying on long-standing templates for marking difference to justify hierarchical structures and inequality. These templates, especially the program of whitening the national racial stock through *mestizaje* (mixture), were also part of state institutional practice within ideological, medical, and pedagogical domains (Sommers 2002). On their own estates, *hacendados* participated in whitening as well, aligning the private domain of the hacienda with the national projects of education, medicine, and the law, while making the two seem to remain separate from each other (Guerrero 2003). Elites did not see the state as separate from themselves but instead as kind of "booty," a perception that persists today (Torre 2008, 268).

Before the 1850s, Indians were defined as a specific population for legal purposes and governed through the colonial practice of tribute. When this practice became unacceptable with the wider spread of liberal political theory in the mid-nineteenth century, Indians were declared to be equal under the law and were designated as taxpayers. In fact, tax paying became one of the defining features of Indian identity. Most of Ecuador's tax riots have involved mestizos protesting the imposition of taxes: in their view, only Indians should pay taxes. To this day in fact, only a very small minority of mestizos and whites pay taxes. Christopher Krupa argues that this history demonstrates a long-standing relationship of Indians to state institutions. Tax paying is a form of "active citizenship" that has contributed to indigenous people's entitlement to make claims on the state. Mestizos continue to distinguish themselves from Indians by avoiding state institutions and services, a pattern of behavior that I observed in IVF clinics (Krupa 2010).

One of the solutions to nineteenth-century mestizo tax protests was the official handover of the designated pastoral care of Indian groups from the state to the *hacendados*, who were themselves lawmakers and state actors (Guerrero 2003). This handover had the effect of separating the *hacendados* from the state. On the haciendas, the indigenous populations, *huasipungeros*, were managed through the patriarchal and patrimonial care of the *hacendados*. In this period Indians as a designated group disappeared from national documents, but they continued to be mentioned in hacienda, valley, and regional documents, as well as those of parish churches (Guerrero 1997, 558).

Since Ecuadorian independence, the Catholic Church has exerted varying degrees of explicit power in shaping state policy. Gabriel García Moreno, president from 1861 to 1875 (with a nominal break from 1866 to 1869), was born on the coast but schooled in the sierra and Europe. He envisioned the state as "a truly Catholic nation" (Williams 2001). Moreno strengthened the ties between church and state, which had become officially separate after independence from Spain. He was labeled conservative even though his involvement with Church institutions facilitated a modernizing agenda of nation building, including railroad construction and standardized national education (Clark 2002). García Moreno's national project enacted Enlightenment ideas and imperatives of material "progress" through colonial forms of exploitation (Larson 1999), an approach termed "Catholic modernity" by historians (Williams 2001). His theory of state modernization differed from that of northern European seventeenth- and eighteenth-century thinkers, who argued that religious belief could not "provide an institutional basis for a common morality" and who thought religion and religious experience should be a domain separate from society and the state (Asad 2003, 205). Moreno's effort to strengthen the connection between the state and the Catholic Church thoroughly enmeshed the Church in his state-building projects, bringing its institutions more under state institutional control than ever before. During Moreno's terms in office, Catholicism became a requirement of citizenship: it was seen as the "only remaining bond" in a country "so divided by the interests and passions of parties, regions and races" (Williams 2001, 149).

After Moreno's assassination in 1875, his successors oscillated between conservative and liberal policies until the coastal liberal José Eloy Alfaro, who held anticlerical views, came to power in 1895 and dismantled the official ties between church and state that Moreno had built. Alfaro mandated civic marriage and wrested the keeping of vital records from Church control. Alfaro's official program of separation remained in place even after his murder in 1912, which initiated a tumultuous civil war. Church and state relations in Ecuador since then have remained contentious, but at present the official separation between the two is considered one of the most marked in Latin America (Aguilar-Monslave 1984). State policy regarding human life and reproduction, however, has always been thoroughly informed by Catholic doctrine.

García Moreno's nation-building policies pushed yet more indigenous people into the hacienda system of labor and debt, of which he was a part. During the nineteenth century, work relations on haciendas came to be understood as conservative and traditional, whereas coastal elites assumed a liberal and progressive mantle as they fought for the right to "free" labor, involving contractual arrangements between individual parties understood to be equal. On the haciendas, disputes were mediated by a sovereign, the *hacendados,* and God, rather than treated as differences between equal parties under contract law. *Hacendados* worked with local priests to keep their peons in line, but they themselves were rarely subject to Church censure for their actions. Daily life on haciendas could seem isolated, divorced from the transnational economic and labor relations that initially produced the hacienda labor-extraction system. This system was built on violence and the threat of violence, although the violence often took place between peons and the mestizo majordomos who ran the estates, allowing the patrons or *hacendados* to appear benevolently paternalistic (O'Connor 2007).

Controlling Indian agrarian labor was a reproductive project as well. The children born of this labor force replenished the labor supply. Additionally, many children born to subjugated women on haciendas were the illegitimate sons of the whiter *hacendados* and overseers, contributing significantly to the national project of *blancamiento*. Although the interests of the new state and the elite landholders were not identical, they converged in a variety of ways. Elite landholders were effectively a part of state institutions that maintained their territory and cultivated a population of unequal groups within it.

On haciendas, divisions between races were reinforced by assigning different work to different kinds of bodies: peons performed agricultural and field work, mestizos worked as overseers, and Creole whites were owners. Women were not part of this official gradation. Indigenous women were considered extensions of their husbands and provided agrarian labor as well as household service (O'Connor 2007). They also provided reproductive labor, bearing children both for their peon husbands (thus increasing the labor supply), and for their Spanish, criollo, white, and mestizo patrons, thus furthering the national project to *mejorar la raza* (Harris 2008; Leifsen 2009).

The forms of governance developed on haciendas resonate with the relations found in Ecuadorian IVF clinics today. I am not arguing that relations in IVF clinics precisely mirror hacienda relations but rather that hacienda relations provided a template for the institutions that seemed in the early 2000s to stand outside the state in Ecuador, private IVF clinics among them. State-funded services, such as medicine, education, and security, have always been used to dominate certain subordinate subject populations, making their recipients into devalued citizens. For patients, patron-client relationships modeled on hacienda systems of labor relations were preferable, because relational paternalism allows for personalized instead of impersonal, bureaucratic care.

Ecuadorian IVF clinical directors are in many ways similar to agrarian *hacendados*, who were able to circumvent the law because they were its makers. Like *hacendados*, elite physicians, usually from powerful families, can shield their clinics from state oversight.[7] In the domain of the clinic, the IVF director is sovereign: he answers only to God, with whom he and his staff and patients are in constant negotiation. State oversight is minimal. Except for the logistics of getting supplies and equipment through national customs, the occasional concern about laws like the new civil code, and a yearly, perfunctory sanitation inspection by the Ministry of Health, the question of state regulation never seemed to surface in the clinics. Ecuador has no self-governing board of medicine that can issue or revoke licenses to practice. The doctors I spoke to could not remember being investigated for any matter beyond sanitation issues. Functionaries at the Ministry of Health confirmed that surveillance of private clinics was rare.

Nor are IVF clinic directors accountable to any other formal institution. The documents signed by practitioners and patients are not legally binding. Physicians' clinical practices are not scrutinized by insurance companies because patients pay out of pocket. There is no such thing as malpractice insurance.

Within the walls of their private clinics, then, doctors have nearly complete autonomy, just as the *hacendados* who controlled and managed the life of their *huasipungeros* carried on with no state oversight. Relations are often familial: indeed, several of Ecuador's IVF clinics are family-run businesses. The dynamic is personal and paternalistic, especially for patients with *bajos recursos*. It involves ongoing asymmetrical debt relations that keep patients in the physicians' care. Through displays of generosity, doctors gain the acquiescence of patients to continue treatment, sometimes treatment they cannot afford. Patients are like a doctor's daughters. Sometimes the doctors play favorites.

Like haciendas, IVF clinics mark the boundaries of state and church. With respect to reproduction and assisted reproduction, state and church are defined by their absence and by narratives of their failure. The gap between state law and Church doctrine with regard to IVF was narrated all the time by people like Antonia and Dr. Castro. when they told me how people pass above the law, and Dr. Molina, when he told me about the illicit sex of priests and nuns in subterranean chambers under the city center, or Sonia Sacoto, when she invoked *nuestra realidad* directly. These narratives allow Ecuadorian urbanites to experience themselves as participants in a reality with a state and church that are seemingly easy to circumvent. The routine nature of these circumventions are similar to what Sharma and Gupta describe in arguing that proceduralism—the routine repetitive practices of rule following and violation—is central to the way the state is imagined, encountered, and reexamined (Sharma and Gupta 2006).

In Ecuador, violation of state rule and Church doctrine is an experience shared across classes—although, as Sandra's story shows, its consequences are unevenly distributed. Popular confidence in the Ecuadorian government was extremely low in the 1990s and early 2000s, especially after the toppling of Gutiérrez, the eighth president in less than eight years. The ongoing gap between the services, rights, and protections guaranteed by law and those actually delivered keep confidence low as well. The law in most Latin American nations, including Ecuador, is based on the French Napoleonic civil code. Civil law tends to promote an ideal vision of society, even if attainment of that vision proves difficult. It's a more abstract, less procedural form of law than English common law, which is based on precedent, developed by court decisions, and subject to legal interpretation (Edmonds 2010). In Ecuador the idealism of the civil-code tradition guarantees universal social welfare and specifies the state's obligations to citizens, but the vast majority of residents cannot rely on these guarantees.

The less affluent classes are continually entangled with state institutions because they need the services the state purports to offer. The Ecuadorian state and its programs do not serve the poor as promised but rather govern them as they seek services. Indeed, the Ecuadorian state was partially created through programs that intervened in the lives of indigenous people, particularly women (Ewig 2010). It employed mostly mestiza women to carry out a civilizing mission among poor and indigenous women, simultaneously asserting governance and building the state (Clark 1998).

For those who need public services, mostly urban poor and working-class citizens, the state is a potent bureaucratic force in everyday life, and it disciplines them in order to reinforce their devalued status. In Ecuador, prosaic activities that I never gave much thought to in the United States—paying utility bills, replacing a lost driver's license, registering for public education, even entering a public swimming pool—represent an absurdly large drain on the time and emotional resources of poorer people. They do not have the resources to avoid numerous bureaucratic hurdles, such as employees who can stand in line for them. They can't afford *tramitadores* (paid paperwork processors) to deal with the required paperwork. Deborah Poole observes that in the Andes, poor and indigenous citizen subjects are made to learn the "gap between membership and belonging" (Poole 2004). The disenfranchised are forced to stand in line to await distribution of unequal resources, while the well-connected jump ahead, are ushered into back rooms, or don't require these services at all. Evading state institutions and passing above the law both serve to distinguish the evader from Indians, who are subject to state governance.

ADOPTION AND "CUNNING WHITENESS"

The desire to avoid entanglements with state institutions extends to the adoption of children. Extralegal circulation of children is widespread in Ecuador, resulting in a very low official national adoption rate. Although legal adoption is relatively uncommon (there were seventy-five cases in 2001, up from thirty-four in 1998), informal or extralegal adoption among mestizos, especially on the coast, is much more common than in North America (Leifsen 2009). For people without sufficient economic resources or steady employment who want children but have had trouble conceiving, legal adoption is seen as an impossibility: this is one state service that appears to be reserved for those with stable resources.[8] Private IVF physicians don't require proof of income to take on patients, just a willingness to pay (which often means that patients become entangled in debt).

When an IVF cycle did not succeed, physicians would often help the couple find a child through extralegal means, another form of evading state authority. The doctor would sign the birth certificate with his clients' names, erasing all legal links to the birth mother and father. Often the birth mother was a young woman who had sought an abortion from the practitioner. He would talk her out of the abortion, as he could place the child directly with an IVF patient whose cycle had failed.

These practices are not the same as informal child circulation, whereby relatives provide children to childless couples and the children's birth provenance is not necessarily hidden (Bloch and Gugenheim 1981; Charney 1991; Davila 1971; Leinaweaver 2008). In the clandestine adoptions arranged by these physicians, there is no state record of the transfer, and ties are severed between the child and the birth mother. At the same time, the relationship between the doctor and the recipients is strengthened. As with abortion, the ease of clandestine adoptions that circumvent state institutions in effect prevents the need for adoption reforms. They do not seem necessary when it is so easy to procure a child through other means.

Dr. Vega, the psychologist at Dr. Vroit's clinic, spoke about the obstacles to adoption.

> Here in our country they have to work so hard [to adopt]. It has to be people
> over thirty-five with money in the bank. This can be very hard to achieve.
> Adoption seems to me to be a resource that is very interesting, and God willing
> would be more common, because there are so many children that are born
> that are abandoned. It seems to me that adoption is very poorly managed here.

There should be a promotion. Instead there are a series of requirements and protocols and blocks . . . that they put in place. It's perverse. There are good and simple human beings that want to care for children.

Jorge, an IVF patient from Guayaquil with few resources, told me that he and his wife, Consuelo, wanted to legally adopt a child (see "Crazy for Bingo") but decided they shouldn't even try, because even his much wealthier aunt had been thwarted: "Adoption seems very interesting, if it could be done. But in our circles it doesn't happen, because when one goes to the institution there are many requirements, and they see the economic situation, the level of work, the level of education, they do questionnaires, everything psychological. They deny the request. There are lots of children available, but they deny it. My family experienced this. I have an aunt that is sterile, and she [tried to adopt] and they denied her. Yes, and her husband makes a very good salary."

Jorge's uncle made $1,500 a month, in contrast to Jorge's monthly salary of $100. Because legal adoption wasn't an option, his aunt pursued a clandestine adoption: "She found [her adopted daughter] through a friend. It is a crazy environment. It's like wandering at a fair and picking. My aunt picked a little girl only a few months old. And my aunt and her husband decided to do it, but with documentation and everything [meaning they obtained a false birth certificate]. Because here in Ecuador, as is commonly said, what reigns is *viveza criolla* [cunning whiteness]. The mother might say, 'I give her to them to raise her, because when she is big I take her back again.' My aunt and uncle selected the child, and they gave her their last names."

The term *viveza criolla* has a historically rich, complex meaning. At its most basic, it means putting one over on someone else, flouting the rules. It can be said admiringly or resentfully. *Criollo* means Creole: it suggests links to ancestry in Spain and thus whiteness. *Viveza* signifies the ability to get the upper hand, to pass above the law. *Viveza criolla* makes it possible to skip the line at the bank or the utility company or to get a driver's license without the usual difficulties. Jorge, a poor brown man, imagined that the birth mother of his aunt's child possessed the "cunning whiteness" to put her child up for adoption and then try to reclaim her. Jorge's aunt might also be said to have displayed *viveza criolla* in evading the adoption laws, as flouting certain laws signifies whiteness. The law in this case is for the darker-skinned. If they flout it or violate it, they're accused of hindering national progress. When wealthier and whiter people evade the law, they can be admired for their *viveza criolla*.[9]

In Ecuador, the state is made real by the evident gap between the promise and the reality of services, and through the elite's ability to stand above and outside its institutions, its services, and its governance. Across classes, people look for ways out of forms of governance that involve bureaucratic and impersonal relations. They use their cunning and their connections, or they pay to enter the private, unregulated realms of medicine, adoption, education, and security, where relations are marketized and hierarchical but intensely personal and relational as well. Going into debt in order to pay for services from patrons and private doctors makes sense as an alternative to the humility and frustration, not to mention the ineffectiveness, of seeking public services. Receiving private care and patronage while circumventing state institutions and the law can make the recipient whiter. But not all private or clandestine care is equal. The effects of Sandra's third abortion demonstrated her lack of cunning whiteness.

INTO THE REALM OF PRIVATE MEDICINE

Although I disagree with her position on abortion, I do agree with some of Sonia Sacoto's observations about women's experiences of abortion in Ecuador. Most women view abortion in the context of relational and material circumstance, not as an overarching right. They do not see themselves as free individuals with a right to choose what's best for their bodies and their futures, or as individuals subject to transcendent principles like the right to life. After her experience with clandestine abortion, Sandra talked about the lies she told her doctors and family members to prevent them from knowing about her sexual activity and her abortions. She talked about her relationship with God. But she never discussed abortion in the context of rights or laws. She was hoping that her life circumstances—her poverty, her youth, her abusive stepfather—would mitigate the sin of her abortions in the eyes of God. As she saw it, God had decided that she deserved punishment. She didn't include popes or presidents on the list of those responsible for her infertility. I wish she had.

As with abortion, the staff and patients at IVF clinics didn't talk about IVF's murky legal status or the Church's condemnation unless I asked them about it directly. The important question was not the state's laws or the Church's doctrine but the judgment of God. IVF was a part of people's ongoing dependency on God, whereby decisions are based on contingent circumstances rather than transcendent doctrines. The only people I encountered who talked about IVF in legal terms were lawyers themselves. Only priests described IVF in terms of Church doctrine, and even then their focus was quite different from the Vatican's.

Although the legal and doctrinal status of both IVF and abortion are conspicuously ignored in Ecuador, the two procedures are governed differently. When seeking her abortions, Sandra was subject to the governance of state institutions and laws that have been influenced by Church teachings. When seeking IVF, she was subject to the governance of the private medical clinic. The domain of private clinics is protected, and thus so are their patients, whereas poorer women seeking abortions evade the law at their peril. The effects of illegal abortion on women *sin recursos* can take the form of corporeal punishment. When I encountered women suffering from botched abortions, I told them, "If abortion was legal, this wouldn't have happened." I came to realize that a more accurate statement would have been "If you had more money, this wouldn't have happened." But for a woman like Sandra, who grew up thinking that abortion was shameful and that she must suffer the consequences alone, I doubt that either hypothetical scenario would have provided much solace. It was too late to renegotiate her punishment with God.

Sandra's life circumstances illustrate how the policies of church and state institutions affect certain bodies more than others. When Sandra violated the law by seeking an abortion, she was intensely affected. More than a decade later, when she sought IVF treatment, her experience of the law was very different. By walking through the doors of Dr. Molina's clinic, Sandra became a client with a patron, Dr. Molina. In his domain, the laws of church and state did not intrude. Elite IVF doctors were free to ignore Article 20 of the Child Civil Code and continue freezing embryos. They could reap the benefits of policies that press people toward private medical care. They went safely about their business, manipulating life in plain sight, feeling no need to influence lawmakers to change the laws governing IVF. They could rise above legal mandates to protect embryonic life, especially when the Church could not enforce its position. While these clinicians remained unaffected, women like Sandra bore the brunt of the uneven reach of church and state.

Sandra moved from being a devalued citizen, affected by the life politics of abortion and sub-par social services, to being enmeshed in and managed through patron-client relations in the clinic. The failure of her negotiation for a child with Dr. Molina was less devastating to her than her failed negotiations with God.

Crazy for Bingo: Consuelo

Consuelo was an out-of-work medical technician, and her husband, Jorge, was a janitor who left school when he was fourteen. He made $100 a month, almost poverty-level wages. The couple had the lowest combined income of all the IVF patients I met in Ecuador. At twenty-seven, Consuelo got pregnant with twins through an IVF cycle with Dr. Jaramillo in Guayaquil. When I visited her for the first time in 2003, she immediately apologized for the shabbiness of their home. It was a windowless, hot cement room partitioned off with blankets. The walls were peeling and moist—and this was the cool rainy season. It was hard to imagine what the place was like during Guayaquil's sweltering summer. When I asked about their income, Jorge answered, "Ni media ni alta" (neither middle nor upper), making him one of the few Ecuadorian IVF patients I met who did not claim to be middle class. It helped that their rent was free because Jorge's grandmother owned the apartment.

The pair told me how they ended up at Dr. Jaramillo's clinic. Years before, when Consuelo began to menstruate, she felt terrible pain. She went to see a private doctor who gave her injections. Eventually he told her she had cysts that would make it impossible to have children if she didn't do something about them. He advised surgery to remove the cysts as well as a nonmedical prescription: "Get married, because the cysts will grow again. They will obstruct your ovaries, and you won't have children. If you marry and have children, they will go away." She and Jorge had just started dating, and this advice prompted them to marry. Jorge said he wasn't concerned about Consuelo's fertility because "I always knew that what will happen is what God wants, and more than anything, I loved her so much."

The pair never used birth control, but six months passed, and Consuelo didn't get pregnant. She went back to the doctor, who said the cysts were now so large she definitely needed an operation to remove them. She went in for surgery, but the doctor couldn't find any uterine cysts. Forty days later, Consuelo began to experience a terrible burning pain near her kidneys. The same doctor performed an ultrasound, but he couldn't see anything. He thought she might have a urinary tract infection. Then the pain got worse, and he operated again. This time the doctor explored Consuelo's "whole organism," and he found the cysts in her kidneys.

While Consuelo was still under anesthesia, the doctor left the operating room, carrying the cysts in his hands. He showed them to Jorge and Consuelo's mother, telling them, "Look. This is what she had. And it has the look of cancer. You have to be prepared for anything." The doctor recommended that as a precaution they immediately take out Consuelo's fallopian tubes and ovaries, leaving her uterus in place. Jorge and his mother-in-law acquiesced, but they didn't tell Consuelo about the removal until a few weeks after the surgery, when she began to go into premenopause. "I was drowned with sweat, had hot flashes, headaches, my mood changed, and I didn't understand why, because they hadn't told me anything. It was like the entire world was talking only to each other, away from me. Finally I asked, what happened?"

When Jorge told her what the doctor had done, Consuelo felt horrible. She believed "that all women long to have children. And we had recently been married, we had been married for a year." She was worried Jorge would leave her. Jorge, however, was committed to staying with Consuelo. He thanked God that she didn't have cancer.

Consuelo recuperated slowly from the news. "Thanks to God, it went well, very well. We are young. We had to continue forward. This is what God wants, for this to be," she said.

A year later a friend recommended that Consuelo visit Dr. Jaramillo to deal with her menopause symptoms. At that point she had given up her hope for children. Dr. Jaramillo examined her and explained that IVF could help her have children even without ovaries and tubes. Consuelo hadn't heard of IVF before. After she understood the process, she was enthusiastic about the possibility. She asked Dr. Jaramillo how much it would cost. He explained that he ran IVF cycles in groups, so he could offer it for $1,500 instead of $2,500–$4,000. Still, Consuelo and Jorge didn't have enough money to participate in the next group cycle. They could not take part in the following cycle either, because just beforehand, Jorge was robbed, beaten and left unconscious by a gang of men. When he recovered, Dr. Jaramillo advised them to start looking for an egg donor in preparation for the next group cycle, seven months later. He suggested they find someone with whom Consuelo and Jorge had very good relations.

As Consuelo began to launch into the story of their search for an egg donor, I interrupted to ask about Jorge's sperm, expecting they would tell me that it was fine. Instead, Jorge told that me early in Consuelo's attempts to get pregnant, a pharmacist friend ran a test on his sperm. Consuelo looked at the sample through the microscope herself. She didn't want to believe her eyes. "I saw one spermatozoid. I realized that there was not one single sperm more."

Jorge took medicine to try to increase his sperm count, but it had no effect. So Dr. Jaramillo convinced them to use a sperm donor. He asked Jorge to bring in a photo of himself to make a donor match. Jorge worried that Dr. Jaramillo would not be able to find a suitable donor, "dark, like my skin."

Meanwhile Consuelo and Jorge also needed to find an egg donor, a woman under thirty-five, but not a virgin. (The process was understood as involving "penetration.") Consuelo couldn't think of anyone in her family who fit the bill: her aunts were too old, and she didn't think her nieces were sexually active at fifteen and sixteen. Consuelo then thought of her childhood friend Juliet, who had a small daughter. She approached her carefully. "I didn't say to her, I want you to be my donor. No. I said to her, I need a donor." Juliet immediately offered to help. Consuelo explained, "She gave me everything that I wanted because we have a very high level of friendship. We have loved each other since high school."

But when Juliet approached her husband about the procedure, he said, "No way are you are going to hand over an egg that is part of you to someone else." Consuelo portrayed Juliet's husband as an old-fashioned simpleton, "like parents that live in the country." Juliet told him that she wouldn't go through with it, but then told Consuelo she would donate her eggs in secret. She confided, "He said no, but I am myself. I say it's my body, and I will give them [my eggs] to you."

Dr. Jaramillo had wanted Juliet's husband's permission, but he agreed to carry on without it, despite his concern that it might be difficult for Juliet to abstain from intercourse during the IVF cycle with an unknowing and uncooperative husband. (There was a high chance of pregnancy during this stage of the process because of the hormonal stimulation Juliet received.) The doctor began treating Juliet with the necessary hormones as well as administering a hormonal treatment to Consuelo to make her uterus receptive for the embryo transfer.

Consuelo and Jorge thought that once they had finally borrowed enough money for IVF, things would get easier. But the complications were legion. The retrieval was set for a Sunday night, the worst possible time for them because Juliet's husband wasn't at work then. Dr. Jaramillo said that the procedure would be quick, taking fifteen to thirty minutes. Consuelo and Jorge waited anxiously outside the operating room from 6:30 until 10:00 p.m. Consuelo was terrified because Juliet had told her husband she would be home by 8:00 p.m. Finally, a nurse came out and told them the visiting doctors still weren't done, because "in women who are short, and a little bit fat, it's harder to get the eggs."[1]

To make matters worse, the receptionist told Jorge that the bill for the aspiration was now $600 instead of $300 because the visiting specialists charged by the hour. It had been hard enough for Consuelo and Jorge to scrape the $300 together. When they were finally done aspirating Juliet's eggs, the staff did not want Consuelo and Jorge to leave the clinic until they had paid the additional amount. Consuelo began crying, imploring the staff to let them go because they had to get Juliet home. Eventually, Consuelo called Dr. Jaramillo, who arrived to settle the matter. He agreed to let them go without paying but claimed he'd explained beforehand that he charged for the operating room by the hour, while Jorge argued that he had told them they would only have to pay a set fee. It was after 11:00 p.m. when they finally got Juliet into a taxi for the forty-five minute ride home. Fortunately, her husband had spent the evening out. He arrived just after she slipped into bed.

The visiting physicians aspirated four eggs from Juliet, fewer than they had hoped. Three were fertilized, and two were transferred to Consuelo's uterus. Two weeks later she got a positive pregnancy test. Consuelo told Juliet that she was pregnant, and Juliet immediately declared that she would be the godmother. Soon after, when Juliet's husband found out that Consuelo was pregnant, he demanded to know if his wife had donated her eggs. He was suspicious now because he and Juliet hadn't had sex for a few weeks around the time that Consuelo would have conceived. Juliet denied the donation. She told Consuelo, "No one will ever know. I am content that I helped. I won't ever do it again. I did it for you and no one else."

This seemed like a conclusion to an especially harrowing and complicated tale. When I exclaimed, "¡Que historia!" Consuelo laughed and said, "Well, there is more to tell. We are now entered into a tremendous debt." They owed money to countless relatives. Consuelo had hoped to sell her one asset—a piece of land outside of Guayaquil—to pay for everything, but so far no one was buying.

Jorge was worried. "The people that lent us the money, they are charging us interest. Some came from family, and we have waited since April to pay it back, and the other day my aunt called me and said she needed the money. With the interest it's more like $1,000. We are late on the interest."

Most perplexing to Jorge was that Dr. Jaramillo ordered Consuelo to be calm and not worry about anything, but then his office called constantly about their unpaid bills. Consuelo was desperate to find the money to pay him. She kept taking trips to borrow money from her aunt, who lived in the country, where it was very hot. One night after a long bus ride, she began to bleed. Frightened, she called Dr. Jaramillo, who told her, "You cannot move. If you move from place to place, you will miscarry." He prescribed bed rest for the duration of her pregnancy.

As Jorge said, with some pride, "She will be lazy." Consuelo seemed happy that Dr. Jaramillo was so concerned. She got up to eat what her relatives cooked for her. Otherwise, she stayed in bed. Consuelo realized it would be much cheaper for her to switch her prenatal care to a public facility, but Dr. Jaramillo strategically lowered his prices, trying to keep Consuelo as a patient. Consuelo and Jorge were now thinking about where she would have her cesarean section when it came time for the birth of her twins. Dr. Jaramillo's services were more expensive than going to the public maternity hospital or even to another private clinic. Though he had offered to discount the fee for the birth as well, his price would still be beyond their means as their debts continued to accrue.

Jorge reminded me, "I only make $100 a month. We can only have faith in God." Consuelo and Jorge's plan to convert land into money hadn't succeeded. "Now only God can provide."

Consuelo's twins, Nicole and Brian, were born in early 2004, after six and a half months' gestation.[2] They both weighed less than three pounds, but by the summer of 2007, when I saw Consuelo again, they were skinny, high-energy three-year-olds. Consuelo wanted me to see them, but it was difficult to arrange a meeting. I couldn't come to her house because she now lived in the same complex as her in-laws, and she didn't want them asking questions about a visit from a gringa. They did not know the twins had been born through egg and sperm donation. Finally Consuelo decided we could meet at one of Guayaquil's new playgrounds on the Malecon 2000, the city's gleaming new river promenade. Consuelo's mother, Juana, came along. She was the only other person who knew about the twins' origins. Juana greeted me warmly and told me almost immediately that Consuelo's father had left her after Consuelo was born. Now her two grandchildren were making up for the additional children she had always wanted. Juana watched Nicole and Brian play on the swings and slides while Consuelo filled me in on what had happened since I'd seen her last.

Consuelo gave birth at the public maternity hospital. But, like so many women I met in Ecuador, she was terrified of what could happen there. The hospital had recently started providing three different classes of service. It was still possible to have a low- or no-cost birth there, but patients could also opt for *pensionada* (full-service) or *semi-pensionada* (half-service) birth. She and Jorge paid for the half-service, which included a cesarean section.

Consuelo had been extremely anxious at the thought of the public maternity hospital. "I said to Jorge, please don't put me in there. I don't want to go for all the things you hear sometimes. Those babies are born dead. I was traumatized by this. We made all the effort, and I was put in the *semi-pensionada*. You don't pay as much as a private clinic for the same care."

Consuelo blamed the premature birth of the twins on the IVF hormone injections: she experienced placental abruption that caused hemorrhaging, sending her into preterm labor. She bled so much that she didn't wake for days after the C-section. She only remembers begging the obstetrician to save the babies. Because Nicole and Brian were kept in incubators for a week, Consuelo could not breastfeed them. At home they needed to be incubated in a room that only she and her mother could enter. Jorge was too frightened by their fragility to go in. The pediatrician told her to feed the babies taro milk. They drank a jar a day for seven months, at $8 a day. Though the pediatrician gave her a discount, and Jorge began making twice as much money, the cost of the taro milk put them into debt.

Consuelo and Juliet were still very close, but they had never talked about the egg donation. While Consuelo was pregnant, they hadn't seen each other. But Juliet is the twins' *madrina* (godmother), and when they were born, she bought them a beautiful double stroller. With Juliet as *madrina*, her husband became Nicole and Brian's *padrino*, and he held the babies at their baptism. He didn't say a word about his suspicions. Soon after, he and Juliet separated. Consuelo made a point of explaining that her children don't resemble Juliet. "People say that Nicole looks like Jorge, like a *sambo*, with his curly hair. And she has A-positive blood like her papa. And Brian has O-positive, just like me."

Consuelo and Jorge didn't want Nicole and Brian to know they were born from egg and sperm donation, so they weren't planning to tell them about the IVF procedure at all. Though many patients I encountered wanted to tell their children that assisted reproduction had brought them into being, they often felt different when nonfamilial gamete donors were involved. When female family members donated eggs, usually the whole family knew. But eggs from an outsider might call their parenthood into question. Consuelo was happy that Juliet was the donor, instead of an anonymous woman, but she didn't want people to know. Jorge had almost asked his brother to donate the sperm, but decided against it, because then the whole family would know. The couple wanted to avoid what had happened to Jorge's aunt when she adopted a child from a woman in her neighborhood. Everyone knew the birth mother, and they never stopped talking about it. Jorge's aunt wished she had kept it a secret.

Because no one knew how difficult and expensive it had been to have the twins, people were constantly asking Consuelo and Jorge if they planned to have more children. Consuelo wanted to, but she was out of debt, and didn't want to rack up more expenses. When the twins were a year old, she was finally able to sell her land for $3,500. The proceeds paid off most of the bills for the IVF cycle, the drugs, the operating fees, and the pregnancy care to the IVF clinic and relatives, which amounted to around $6,000. But nothing was left to pay for the babies' long stay in the hospital after their premature birth. An aunt who had migrated to Spain sent some money, and Jorge's janitorial company took up a collection, which covered a little of the bill. But it took a night of bingo for the couple to pay off the rest of their debt. Consuelo is, as she put it, "loca por bingo" [crazy for bingo], so she organized an event with food and prizes where friends and family paid to play. It brought in $400.

Consuelo talked in terms of winning and losing. She reflected: "Imagine all the people who have money and do IVF again, and lose again. From the moment that I began to do the treatment, we prayed to God, so that he would stick two [embryos]. And two stuck. The bottom line is to have enough patience, and above all to have faith in God. It's thanks to God that I left debt."

TWO · Assisted Whiteness

This chapter is a tour through some of the care practices and relations that make up assisted reproduction in Ecuador and which cultivate a woman's whiteness. These include surgical and medical invasions like cesarean sections and IVF, the kindly authority male physicians wield over their female patients, the administration of hormones, the economy of bed rest, and collectively organized bingo games. This chapter is in part about class: that is, the ability of women and their supporters to access medical care through material and symbolic capital. It is also about whiteness, which is both a physiological and an economic state.

Class involves labor relations, which in Ecuador have historically been racially and regionally differentiated. In the highlands, labor was embedded in the paternalism of the hacienda. Constitutive race relations between Spanish and Indian, and later between Indian, mestizo, and white women and men, determined the role of workers in the labor hierarchy. This chapter examines reproductive labor relations, which involve both women and men, although women are the main and sometimes only targets of reproductive interventions. Through IVF, women can become whiter reproducers not through education or professional advancement, but through being cared for the way whiter women are cared for. IVF physicians are invested in these women's reproductive potential and care for them like indulgent fathers. Patients are shielded from the indignities of impersonal, state-provided care by the clinic staff. Patients understand well the "crucial economic and moral significance of care relations, in which life chances are forged" (Biehl and Eskerod 2007, 110).

Consuelo's harrowing experience trying to have children was both alleviated and exacerbated by her rejection of public medical care and embrace of private clinics (see "Crazy for Bingo"). Her story sheds light on practices like reproductive surgery and hormone treatment in Ecuador. These forms of care emphasize, first, the perceived fragility of a woman's physiology, and second, the way private care in turn emphasizes whiteness. As potential mothers of offspring that contribute to the nation's implicit whitening project, whiter women both receive the best in paternalistic care and are penetrated and scarred by expensive surgical interventions. When IVF patients with limited material resources go about financing and gathering assistance for their reproductive projects, they become whiter. Both reproductive dysfunction and attempts to alleviate that dysfunction are physiological and economic markers of whiteness.

In urban Ecuador, biomedicine that involves physical care relations contributes to making the race of its participants. The aspirations of Andean urbanites toward an "elusive yet possible social whiteness" has been well documented by social scientists (see Cadena 2000). This struggle for whiteness describes how participants move along a relational continuum between the oppositional poles of Indian and white rather than remaining subjects of fixed race. Spending time with Consuelo and Sandra (as well as Teresa, whom I describe in the next chapter), I found that the dynamics of private care entailed a similar struggle for whiteness.

The explicit term for whitening, *blancamiento*, is not often used for the care relations I describe. In the Andes, whiteness is spoken of in terms of education and cultivation. Whites, or whiter people, are *gente decente* (decent people), *vecinos* (neighbors). They are town dwellers, in comparison to uneducated, *mal criada* (poorly raised) rural Indians (Cadena 1995, 2000). The fact that these terms mark race is often lost on foreigners (Weismantel 2001). Public education and medicine are for browner, Indian, and devalued citizen-subjects, whereas private education and private medical care make and mark whiteness (Clark 1998). Although scholars have demonstrated that race in the Andes is constituted by education, clothing, language, and occupation, my research documents that it is also enacted through corporeal relations within biomedical care. Collectively, I refer to these care relations as "assisted whiteness," tracing how attributes of whiteness are inscribed, however discreetly, within the interventions and care practices of assisted reproduction.

FEMALE REPRODUCTIVE DYSFUNCTION

State planners, elite pundits, medical professionals, and eugenicists have long associated infertility and other reproductive afflictions with the hypercivilization and education of elite women, while at the same time linking fertility, especially hyper-fertility, to poor, uncivilized women. These are constitutive associations redolent with the practice of marking racial difference (Stern 2006). In Northern Europe and the United States, these associations became part of the divide between tradition and modernity dating from the industrial revolution. The separate spheres of modern life shaped a "traditional" family, in which, ideally, middle-class women did not engage in wage labor outside the newly privatized bourgeois home. In Japan, Italy, and China as well, practices of modernity, industrialization, and progress inspired fears of pathologies that threatened the ability of middle- and upper-class women to reproduce and carry out wifely and motherly duties in the domestic sphere (Handwerker 1995; Horn 1994; Lock 1993; Nouzeilles 2003; Sawicki 1991).

Fertility problems were, and still are, attributed to the deleterious effects of modern behaviors, like working outside the home, studying, premarital and promiscuous sex, stress, smoking, drinking, drug use, strenuous exercise, delayed childbearing, abortion, and industrial and environmental damage. In the early nineteenth-century United States, the diminished reproductive capacities of elite women were perceived as a threat to a nation's progress, a form of "race suicide" (*Literary Digest* 1917). This perception is still alive and well in media stories about "black welfare queens," "deadbeat immigrants," and "anchor babies."

Similar sentiments were expressed in Latin America. Starting in the late nineteenth century, middle- and upper-class women in new nation-states came to be seen as responsible for improving the national racial stock (Zulawski 2007). Anxieties about declining or unfit populations led to state institutional programs to protect women's and children's health as well as programs organized by elite eugenicists concerned with "racial degeneration" (Leifsen 2010; Stepan 1991). These programs didn't perhaps achieve their goals of encouraging the right kinds of births and discouraging the wrong kinds, but they did reinforce racial distinctions between right and wrong reproduction. In turn-of-the-century Argentina, physicians linked an epidemic of hysteria among middle- and upper-class women to the potential for racial degeneration. One physician argued: "Science undeniably proves that the degeneration, like the perfecting, of the race always begins with the female sex. Because of her organization, women in all climes and races, because they are more subject to external influences, offer more plasticity to biological transformations" (quoted in Nouzeilles 2003).

Hysteria was the dark side of progress. While most of the women treated for hysteria were in fact lower class, the moral panic about the hysteria epidemic concerned the whiter, upper-class *porteñas* (female residents of Buenos Aires), the repositories of the destiny of the national race. Treatment for the epidemic sought to promote reproductive fitness among elite women.

Eugenic practices in the early Andean republics were aimed at addressing an urgent "Indian problem." The reproductive capacity of elite and upper-class women remained jealously guarded to preserve purity. Such women had delicate constitutions and had to be sheltered from public life and the harshness of the marketplace (Cadena 2000). Browner, Indian women were "known" to have more savage physiologies and constitutions than whiter women (Icaza 1968). Darker women's bodies were characterized as strong and rugged. These "strong brown" women were said to give birth in the same fields where they labored: they could withstand both manual labor and the labor of giving birth, unlike fragile whiter women, whose delicate reproductive capacities required special protection. Throughout the twentieth century, the perceived strength and overfecundity of poorer and darker women made them subject to greater reproductive governance. Public health and social-service programs were designed to manage them and lower their fertility. Interventions on wealthier, whiter women were managed in the private sphere, through careful guarding of their virginity until marriage (Clark 1998; Ewig 2010; Harris 2008).

Efforts in the Andean republics to improve the nation's racial stock and combat racial contamination were incorporated into internationally funded Cold War–era overpopulation programs, even without much evidence that the Andes had a population "problem" (Morgan and Roberts, forthcoming). With the cooperation of Andean state institutions, international aid and development organizations promoted fertility control as a means of improving public health, economic security, and regional stability. Less explicit agendas involved reducing family size as a way to combat the spread of communism, increase consumption of consumer goods, and, most nefariously, reduce the number of darker-skinned people. Aid agencies and state administrations, and even occasionally the Catholic Church, engaged in concerted efforts to make modern contraceptive methods available (Mooney 2009; Necochea López 2008).

In contemporary epidemiological studies, subfertility and infertility are clearly associated with poverty and disease. Nevertheless, the popular media portrays infertility as a complaint of elite women. Critics of IVF and other forms of assisted reproduction have well-justified concerns that the existence of these technologies leads women and their partners to seek expensive and invasive treatments before their infertility is established and to disregard nonclinical solutions for having children (Arditti, Minden, and Klein 1984; Corea 1988; Inhorn 1994; Thompson 2002). In Ecuador, I found prevalent "anticipatory infertility" among middle class women. Considering the historic construction of whiter women as possessing a more fragile fertility, claiming to be reproductively dysfunctional is to claim the care and resources reserved for Ecuador's most desired reproducers.

In the clinics, when people spoke about the causes of infertility, the problem was almost invariably represented as female in nature.[1] The specific economic and physiological histories that have made women (especially whiter women) the targets of reproductive medicine are so entrenched that it can be very difficult to imagine an alternative view. Middle-class women are primed to accept that their reproductive capacity is in disarray and that measures should be taken to fix it: pills swallowed, drugs injected, surgeries undergone.

I was viscerally reminded of how women are made the "natural" patients in reproductive medicine when the body on the surgical table changed sex. Male reproductive procedures were relatively rare in Ecuador: I observed only two near the end of my fieldwork, both for PESA (percutaneous sperm aspiration), the surgical removal of sperm directly from the testes for the treatment of male-factor infertility. I was unprepared for how jarring it was to walk into the OR and confront an unconscious, naked man with a shaved crotch stretched out before me. He just simply seemed the wrong body on the table, too big and too flat. Instead of seeing a woman's unconscious body, feet up in stirrups, I saw a man sprawled supine and expansive, his flaccid penis lying to one side. Obviously this was not a matter of course for the practitioners either. Both male and female practitioners made crude jokes as they cut into the patient's testicles in search of viable sperm. I never heard jokes about female patients undergoing a surgical procedure. A woman on the table was business as usual.

The young, childless, middle-class women I encountered in Ecuador had almost all undergone some sort of surgery (such as diagnostic laparoscopy or fibroid removal) or had intensive hormonal treatments to address female functions gone awry. These women were often sure that they could not have children because of strange or troublesome menstrual symptoms. When they did get pregnant, the interventions they had already undergone primed these women to expect the pregnancy to end with a cesarean section rather than a vaginal birth. The use of assisted reproductive technologies in Ecuador reinforced the assumption that these fragile bodies would fail under the ordeal of delivering a baby. Even for Consuelo, with her meager resources, the cure for reproductive dysfunction seemed to lie in private IVF clinics, where she could be treated as a whiter woman, delicate and in need of specialist care.

For most of the Ecuadorian middle-class women I encountered, these multiple surgical procedures required great financial sacrifice. They also often left the women with the scars of invasive surgery. If an IVF pregnancy resulted in an early miscarriage, the woman would most likely undergo a dilation and curettage (D&C), paying to have taken out what she and her family had paid so dearly to have put in. If a woman stayed pregnant, she might undergo cerclage (temporarily stitching the cervix closed to prevent preterm labor), followed by the nearly obligatory C-section, which would leave a scar demonstrating her dysfunctional and whiter physiology.

IN THE CUT

One day during my observations at Dr. Molina's clinic, while sperm was settling in the centrifuge inside the lab, I waited on the bench outside with Silvia, an IVF biologist. As we were passing the time, she showed me a tiny layer of fat on her abdomen. Silvia planned to have it removed that weekend by liposuction, a procedure that would be performed by one of the traveling Argentinian plastic surgeons so common in Quito after the 2001 Argentinian economic collapse.

This seemed noteworthy in a nation where highland Indians live in fear of the *pishtaco*, a white stranger who sucks fat. The ethnographic literature describes the *pishtaco* as a spectral male figure, usually urban, rich, and white. He roams rural areas with a knife hidden under his coat, waiting to cut the fat out of Indian women and men who cross his path, thus weakening them to the point of death. The story of his cut is told by Andean Indians as a way to distinguish themselves from those who engage in the immoral, impersonal, profit-taking exchanges of mestizos and whites. It makes them more Indian by affirming the right kind of personal reciprocity (Canessa 2000; Mannheim and Vleet 1998).

A plastic surgeon is also usually urban, rich, and white. He roams cities with a scalpel, waiting to cut the fat out of the mestiza women who pay to lie down before him. The story of his cut is told by mestizas as a way to distinguish themselves from those who engage in degrading, impersonal, bureaucratic exchanges of public medicine. Whereas a *pishtaco*'s unwelcome invasion into a rural woman's body with a knife produces an Indian woman (Weismantel 2001), a physician's expensive surgical cut produces a whiter urban woman.

What does either sort of fat cutting have to do with Consuelo's experience of reproductive malfunction and IVF? As with plastic surgery, IVF in Ecuador allows its participants, even those of *bajos recursos*, to experience privatized care relations, thus cultivating whiteness. Silvia and Consuelo would be cut into as white women. Consuelo's entrance into Dr. Jaramillo's private IVF clinic marked her reproductive dysfunction. The care she received there, as well as from family, friends, and God throughout her pregnancy, demonstrated her ability to address that dysfunction.

Cesarean birth is very common for middle-class women in Ecuador. According to the public health literature, Latin America has some of the highest rates of C-section in the world, involving 30 to 35 percent of all deliveries (Althabe et al. 2004; Belizán et al. 1999).[2] Marian Catholicism values female suffering, but the pain of vaginal childbirth is too closely associated with the bodies of animals and Indian women. A woman who can stand that pain is considered *bruta*, like a mule. The fact that pain medication isn't widely available in public hospitals reinforces this notion.

These views are further reinforced by standard practices for delivering IVF babies. After the expensive, delicate, and emotionally fraught procedures of IVF, cesarean delivery is generally recommended to avoid the risks to these hard-won children posed by vaginal delivery. Ana, a poorly paid young physician who worked in a public hospital, got pregnant through an IVF cycle in a private clinic in Guayaquil. She supposed she would try to have a *parto normal*, a vaginal birth. But none of her friends had had normal births, and her mother (echoing widespread beliefs about the fragility of female elites) suggested she had better have a C-section too, because she wouldn't be able to stand the pain. Ultimately, Ana's IVF doctor convinced her to have a C-section by reminding her of the preciousness of her IVF child. So she gave birth to a son, Isaac, by C-section.

When Ana told Isaac his origin story, she showed him the scar on her belly and said, "This is where they removed you. . . . I suffered a lot to get you in there. We waited a long time, wanting to have a baby, and the doctor put you there." The scar represented not only the invasive C-section but also the invasion, the effort, and the expense of IVF: what it took to get Isaac into Ana's belly, as well as what it took to get him out. Six years after her first child was born, Ana had another baby—this time without IVF but again by C-section, now obligatory, the scar made fresh again.

In Ecuador, the cesarean scar is a bodily marker of a woman's participation in private medicine, her assisted whiteness. With cesarean scars, women can distinguish their bodies from those of poor and rural black or Indian women. A scarless, blank abdomen on a mother is the sign of a poor woman who can't afford to be cut and has to open her legs. A C-section allows women to avoid opening themselves to the indignities of state-funded care. The scar inscribes their privatized worthiness literally on their bodies. Theirs is a specific kind of desirable skin, skin that has been obviously cared for with a cut. These visible scars are different from the invisible, internal scars Sandra received at the hands of public surgeons after her botched abortion.

Although they can sometimes save lives, C-sections are major surgery and are associated with increased maternal death, injury, and infection, as well as a host of problems for the infant. To combat the rising worldwide rates of cesarean births, the World Health Organization has declared that a safe target rate for C-sections is no more than 15 percent of all births. This recommendation has produced a multitude of public-health intervention programs in Latin America. Policy authors call the high incidence of C-sections in Latin America "a symptom of a perverse logic," in which the procedure has become "a consumer good," a status symbol of superior medical care (Rattner, 1996, 19; see also Barros 2011). They paint a portrait of greedy doctors and frivolous, status-obsessed women "too posh to push," while feminist authors cite concerns about the effects of unnecessary surgery on women's bodies. Although it's the private clinics that have the highest C-section rates, the targets of programs to reduce the number are generally practitioners and patients in public hospitals and clinics. Reproductive governance in the shape of state or NGO intervention does not enter the domain of private medicine. Once again, it's poorer women who are subject to intervention.

In her research on C-sections in Pelotas, Brazil, the anthropologist Dominique Béhague found that poorer women who gave birth in public hospitals recognized that the option of a C-section was being withheld from them. They saw cesareans as unfairly distributed resources, given that wealthier women have them as a matter of course and that the procedure involved attention from more thoroughly trained doctors. Some women approached labor strategically in order to obtain their own C-sections at public hospitals. While in labor, they would emphasize their physiological or psychological inability to go through labor and birth: "I can't dilate," "I'm in too much pain," "I don't have any contractions." All of these strategies contradicted the racist view that poorer, browner women are better at giving birth. Béhague also argues that given poorer women's overall poorer health, they are in fact much more likely than affluent women to need C-sections (Béhague 2002). In this context, public health authors' portrayals of women who seek C-sections as "perverse" or "frivolous" is ill aimed. If C-sections are seen as evidence of superior medical care, it's understandable that poorer women will pursue the procedure.

The urban Ecuadorian women I came into contact with were also well aware of the radical differences between public and private, urban and rural birth, which is why Consuelo wanted to pay for the *semi-pensionada* birth service. In the tier of service she wanted, the C-section rate is estimated to be between 70 and 90 percent. In publicly funded clinics and hospitals, it's less than 20 percent; in rural areas, it's about 8 percent. Although these overall rates are lower than in some other Latin American nations, like Brazil, Venezuela, Chile, and Argentina (Althabe et al. 2004), they still illustrate a high level of surgical intervention in birth.[3] Costing anywhere between $300 and $1,500, a C-section scar is affordable for most urban Ecuadorians.[4] The vast majority of middle-class women of childbearing age whom I spoke with did not know any women of their generation and social class who had had a vaginal birth. Their *empleadas* (domestic servants) might have had vaginal births, but not their peers. Every woman in my study who got pregnant via IVF gave birth with a cesarean, even those women who had given birth vaginally before.

Despite the prevalence of cesarean births among middle-class Ecuadorian women, vaginal birth is still referred to as *lo normal,* suggesting that a woman who has a C-section deviates from the norm. Poor urban woman, Indians, rural *campesinas,* and black women are apparently able to give birth normally, in public hospitals or elsewhere. These women's bodies don't seem to malfunction like those of whiter women, for whom conception is difficult, menstruation is troublesome, pelvises are misshapen, and childbirth pain is unbearable. Some of these women told me they had wanted a normal birth but that their doctors advised against it, claiming their pelvises were too small and the baby would get stuck, that they wouldn't be able to endure the pain, or that their history of heavy periods would make them unable to give birth without heavy blood loss (a counterintuitive argument given that surgical procedures such as C-sections generally involve a higher risk of heavy blood loss). Again, such fragility conveys whiteness. Pathology is a sign of achievement for a newly normative body (Canguilhem 1991), a whiter body that can afford to be corrected through surgical intervention.

CESAREAN SECTION AND THE FAMILY DOG

In Quito I often stay with Marta in her multi-unit, multigenerational family home. Marta has five adult children and six grandchildren. All of her children were born vaginally; all of her grandchildren were born by C-section. One evening in 2002, one of Marta's sons, Esteban, was over for his nightly visit with his wife, Keti, who was about to have their first child. We spent the evening talking about Keti's upcoming C-section. Keti explained that her doctor said her pelvis wasn't shaped right: "He said I'd get to seven centimeters [dilation], and my labor will stop. I will never get to ten." Almost blithely she added, "It's all *plata* (money). They just want to charge more."

Esteban nodded. "The doctor doesn't think that she will progress, and she will be checked every two hours. And he doesn't want to wait around in the hospital all day. He wants it to take ten minutes. Money and time. Money and time."

We all started to speculate about how much money Keti's doctor made per month. Esteban estimated that he made at least $4,000. Marta estimated $20,000. I added that it must be a lot, noting that every middle-class woman I had met in Ecuador had a C-section. Marta protested. She reminded us that Maria, her long-term *empleada*, had told us the day before about her daughter Rosa's labor at the public hospital. She did not have a C-section.

Esteban turned to Marta excitedly: "Mama! Mama! Middle class! Middle class!" Marta conceded. Rosa was certainly not middle class. Keti remembered one friend who had a vaginal birth. She was waiting to be prepped for her "medically necessary" cesarean, was "begging for one," in fact, but the baby came out before they could begin the surgery. She was the only friend or relative any of them could think of who had a vaginal birth, and it was by accident.

We went back to talking about the impending birth of their child. Esteban said he'd be allowed in the operating room so that he could take photos. He would only have this time, and possibly one other chance to take pictures, because "you know if you have two C-sections, you can't have more children." In Ecuador women are told that they risk uterine rupture with a third C-section; this advice effectively limits most urban women to two children.[5]

A bit later Keti and I were having our dinner of coffee and rolls in the kitchen. Esteban barreled into the room, followed by Marta. They had been arguing in the living room about Tulo, the family dog. Their cousin wanted to perform a vasectomy on Tulo. She was in veterinary school, and the surgery would allow her to pass her graduation exam.

Esteban exclaimed, "I feel bad for the dog, bad for the dog! How he will suffer!" Marta countered that Cuca, the female dog, was pregnant again: "She is old, and the puppies she has keep getting smaller and smaller. She shouldn't have any more puppies."

Esteban was indignant. He asked his mother, "Is this a *casa social?*" meaning a brothel. "Here, have my father. Have my brother-in-law. Do surgery on them. My mother is so generous." Esteban continued, "What would have happened if Esteban Sr. [his father] had had a vasectomy?" Marta and Keti both turned away from Esteban. I asked the two of them about the pros and cons of female sterilization versus vasectomy. They both thought this was a funny question. Laughing, they agreed that it's much more common for women to be sterilized in Ecuador. Yet Marta had heard that it was much safer for men than women.

A few days later, I asked Marta what had happened with Tulo, and she told me that Esteban had called his cousin's father and convinced him to forbid his daughter from using the dog for the surgery. I was disappointed that Esteban had prevailed over his mother, who lived with and cared for the dogs. For once, it had seemed that a male body might be targeted for intervention out of concern for a female body.

During that evening our conversation had stayed on topic the time, though the sex and species under discussion had changed. We moved from the discussion of Keti's inevitable and uncontroversial reproductive surgery, which reinforced her status as a whiter middle-class mother, to a debate about possible reproductive surgery on a male dog. Esteban felt that his mother was pimping Tulo to further his younger female cousin's professional ambitions, thus threatening the masculinity of males in the family. By calling his mother's home a *casa social*, Esteban implied that its borders were open to the promiscuous and indiscriminate invasion of a surgical knife that targeted the male body. He was unconcerned about Keti's surgery, which would limit her fertility rather than his. Keti, as a woman, was seen as the proper subject of surgery. Bodily invasion is frequently coded as emasculating (Cohen 2004; Gutmann 2003).[6]

It would have been unlikely for Marta and Keti to link their sexed fate to that of a dog, however, as most middle-class urban Ecuadorian women found comparisons with animals odious and redolent of association with Indians, who birth "naturally," without surgery. This association also emerged in my observations in gynecological clinics. A few years after the birth of her last child by C-section, Linda, the laboratory biologist at Dr. Padilla's clinic in Quito, convinced him to allow her to watch a woman attempt a *parto normal*, a vaginal birth, a rare event at the clinic. For Linda, the experience was horrifying and traumatic, like "watching torture." The woman screamed explosively and acted like "an animal, like a savage wild woman, like an *auca*." (An *auca* is less than human, a jungle dweller.) In the end the woman had a cesarean section anyway. Linda asked me rhetorically, "What was the point?" Linda saw the attempt at a *parto normal* as degrading: in her view, the woman became animal, savage, tied to darkness, Indianness, and blackness.

For working-class and poorer women like Consuelo, C-section scars are aspirations of upward mobility. Their scars, red at first, eventually turn white. In turn, the scars whiten them, serving as proof of multiple claims to higher status: that they were too delicate to reproduce "normally," that they had the means to overcome their dysfunction, and that they weren't subject to state neglect or treated like savages in public hospitals.[7] Their whiteness and their children's whiteness were cultivated in a private clinic by a doctor who cut them tenderly, like a patron or father, not a *pishtaco*.

CARE AND CULTIVATION

Marilyn, a woman from the United States who worked as a consultant for a nongovernmental organization in Ecuador, went through an unsuccessful IVF attempt at Dr. Cabeza's clinic in Quito.[8] She later underwent an second unsuccessful IVF cycle at a clinic in Los Angeles. A year after the second cycle she became pregnant without any medical assistance and carried the baby to term. For the most part, Marilyn felt positive about her care in Dr. Cabeza's clinic. She found the attention she received to be exemplary, particularly Dr. Cabeza's kindness and the staff's understanding of her desire to be a mother. She liked the fact that the clinical staff and physicians were "less businesslike than in the United States."

Nevertheless, there were several things Marilyn did not like about her care. At the time, the clinic performed IVF procedures on groups of women, synchronizing their cycles in preparation for treatment by a visiting specialist. She wasn't happy about undergoing the cycle in a group, and she was sure the other patients also felt dehumanized by this approach. However, the women I met who had undergone group cycles at Dr. Jaramillo's clinic had never complained about the process and in fact seemed to enjoy getting to know the other patients. There were few opportunities for interactions among the female patients in the clinics that conducted individual cycles. Marilyn was also unhappy about the long waits for appointments at the clinic—an experience I knew well, as I often waited with patients for up to three hours to see their doctors. Yet most Ecuadorian patients I encountered didn't complain about the waits. The exceptions were professional women who felt rushed to get back to work. According to the clinical staff, their impatience indicated that "career women" were too "stressed" to undergo IVF successfully.

Marilyn had also been annoyed by the psychologist brought to Dr. Cabeza's clinic by the visiting specialist. When all of the patients were lying on cots after the aspiration, the psychologist walked among them and spoke in an "overly calm voice." She told the patients, "You will all become pregnant. You must think of yourselves as pregnant." Marilyn was appalled; in her mind, the role of an IVF psychologist was to help patients manage their expectations, not feed them.

I'm not sure the other patients found this practice troubling. When patients were undergoing a cycle, the Ecuadorian practitioners I knew focused on the positive, reassuring patients that they would become pregnant and telling them that God would help them. The practitioners saw it as their duty to envision positive outcomes, an approach that patients seemed to appreciate. If a patient had a negative outcome, practitioners helped them cope in ways that might seem extraordinary to a North American. They had the patients come in for extra visits and followed up with phone calls. Sometimes they even made house calls. One patient told me that after three failed IVF cycles, the laboratory biologist came to her house over the weekend, and they talked for several hours. The biologist made the patient and her husband feel "cared for and relaxed, like family. It's what God intended for now." The couple decided to try again after six months.

Marilyn's impressions exemplify some of the fundamental characteristics of paternalistic private medicine in Ecuadorian IVF, in which physicians are construed as all-knowing, powerful men, and patients viewed as young girls.[9] Gradually, I came to see what this kind of medical care had to offer. The IVF patients I met in Ecuador knew less about the medical details of the procedures than those I met in the United States. Although I would hesitate to suggest that knowing less is a beneficial approach to medical treatment, it did seem that these patients were, on the whole, more relaxed and positive about their experience than their counterparts in the United States, because of the faith they had in male doctors and a male God.

The waiting rooms of IVF clinics in the United States are filled with pamphlets and other publications explaining procedures and services. Very little information was available in the lobbies of Ecuadorian clinics. Printed paper is expensive in Ecuador, and it wasn't expected that patients would read material if it were available. I frequently explained procedures to patients who knew little about what to expect during their treatment.[10] They did not think in terms of percentages, statistical success rates, or risks, except for the risk of failure. Patients often hoped for twins, and sometimes even larger multiple births, but they believed it was all up to God. They usually knew little about the possible complications for mothers and multiple fetuses.

Instead of being saturated with information, patients were enmeshed in various personal interactions. Male doctors greeted patients with kisses and endearments, patting them before and after procedures. IVF physicians talked about patients as their daughters, and they often characterized these *hijas* as ignorant and lacking in discipline. Occasionally, patients' reluctance to take their medications as directed, their tardiness in showing up to time-sensitive appointments, or their ignorance about what was being done to them would inspire lengthy diatribes. Practitioners linked their patients' failings with what they saw as the chronic failure of most Ecuadorians to behave as disciplined adults. These frustrations notwithstanding, they continued to treat most of their patients like beloved, wayward daughters.

Women in Ecuadorian IVF clinics did not tend to imagine themselves as consumers of medicine, and they didn't feel the need to be experts on their own care. Patients could call doctors and other staff at any time of the day or night and receive in-depth attention. They expected doctors to tell them what to do, and they followed those orders somewhat haphazardly, expecting doctors to accommodate their lack of understanding of the process. Doctors served as fathers and husbands who cared for their daughters and wives by protecting them from having to know or worry too much.

The care patients received from physicians was akin to care from God. The halls of the clinics were lined with photos of babies born to patients after IVF, as well as commemorative engraved plaques, offering thanks to the doctors, sometimes calling him "our scientific papa." These plaques were similar to the ones found at religious shrines throughout Ecuador, left in gratitude to God and the saints for healing miracles. Patients who had positive things to say about their doctors—and most did—described how the doctors' ministrations soothed them, especially the advice to have faith in God. Their faith in the doctor's ability to enact God's will meant that patients might do things they wouldn't necessarily have chosen to do on their own. They would undergo amniocentesis and then terminate a pregnancy if the doctor told them to. Patients also talked about their faith in doctors' ability to pick the best embryos for transfer. They felt they could trust doctors to dispose of the bad embryos, and this mindset enabled them to avoid thinking of this process as abortion or the killing of potential life.[11]

Repeatedly, patients told me that what they looked for in a doctor was professionalism. This meant not high success rates or ability to perform the latest procedures but "charisma" and "humanity." When patients found these traits lacking, they often switched to a new doctor without notice. Tatiana was effusive on the topic of her doctor's professionalism. He had the ability to anticipate her and her husband's needs, framing IVF for them in a positive way: "The doctor is professional, supremely professional. He knows what you need each time he helps you. . . . He comes singing at the beginning of each day. He lifts your mood and gives you hope."

Roxana was equally happy with the treatment she received at her clinic. She connected especially well with the laboratory biologist: "She gave us courage. Every day she injected me and she asked, 'Are you hurt, my dear?' And the doctor called me 'My little one, you are the littlest one of all my patients.'" For many patients like Roxana, IVF was seen as emotionally difficult, especially the process of waiting, but being under a "professional" doctor's care produced a calming effect.

When I asked about the statistical likelihood of pregnancy, God was often a part of a patient's equation. One patient explained that her doctor told her she had an 80 percent chance of pregnancy. Although she didn't get pregnant, she and her husband remarked that they adored their doctor because he was "scientific" and because he told them to have faith in God. One patient reported that at the aspiration the nurse told her to have faith in the Divino Niño, a popular Colombian version of the Christ child. When she was only one of three patients out of fifteen to get pregnant that month, she attributed the success to the nurse's encouragements and the blessing of the Christ child. The two other women later miscarried. The clinic staff repeatedly reminded her to maintain her prayers. She went on to give birth and remains a devotee of the Divino Niño.

The patients' tremendous faith in the ability of the private doctors and clinic staff to get them pregnant undoubtedly created a strong sense of hope, leading them to spend money that they would not have spent otherwise and to undergo procedures that were invasive, arduous, and sometimes dangerous. These forms of care situated patients in the valued interconnected space "of biomedical production and consumption" (Ackerman 2010, 406), a space inaccessible to patients of public-sector medicine. The relations between patients and their care providers were similar to relations on haciendas between privileged wives and daughters and their patron husbands and fathers, relations bound up in the project of whitening the nation.

HORMONES

The importance of care relations in Ecuadorian IVF practice was especially notable in connection with the hormone treatments that are part of the IVF cycle. They are administered to regulate and stimulate follicle production and enhance uterine receptivity. Hormones did not seem to have the same effects in Ecuador as they do in the United States. Women I encountered in both countries found the experience of IVF to be emotionally tumultuous; but in Ecuador, women tended to perceive the tumult as resulting from the shifting dynamic of care relations, whereas in the United States the feeling of instability was attributed to discrete external agents, hormones. By contrast, many Ecuadorian women perceived the hormones they received in IVF in a positive way, saying the treatment made them feel calmer and more womanly. The hormones exemplified the resources and care that went into making their bodies more reproductive.

In the early 1990s, I conducted research with IVF patients, surrogate mothers, and egg donors in the United States (Roberts 1998a, 1998b). The hormones used throughout IVF cycles and the emotional states they caused were a common topic of conversation among the participants. They described the hormones as making them feel as if they were on an emotional roller coaster or as if they were crazy. Similar findings have been reported elsewhere in the anthropological and sociological literature on IVF in the United States. One woman had this to say about Lupron, one of the hormones commonly used to regulate a woman's menstrual cycle in preparation for IVF: "Lupron is like going into madness. I get on Lupron and I get this agitated depression, really severe. I have never felt so suicidal in my life. . . . You kind of know on some level it's just the chemicals. I'm not looking forward to it, especially with the agitation on top of it. . . . So in some ways, the Lupron is just this little shot in your thigh, it seems so benign. But it's not. The depression seems like such a common response to Lupron" (Becker 2000, 88).

This woman could take comfort in the fact that this response to Lupron is common among women undergoing IVF, at least in the United States. In this context, IVF hormones are seen as ontological biological agents with universal effects (Oudshoorn 1994; Rosenberg 1979; Temkin 1977). They are perceived as intensifying the already volatile emotions associated with a woman's reproductive cycle (involved in puberty, premenstrual syndrome, and menopause). In the United States, hormones are seen as biological agents that produce predictable responses in most women.

To be clear, I'm not arguing that women in the United States have simplistic and unitary understandings of their IVF experiences. Certainly, in longer conversations with North American women about their experience of IVF, I've heard women attribute their emotional and physiological states to factors other than hormone treatments (see also Becker 2000; Thompson 2005). But it's clear that in the United States, hormones are often viewed as agents of emotional instability, representative of the physical and emotional experience of IVF. In my own investigations, however, I never specifically analyzed the discussion of hormones, perhaps because it was so ubiquitous in the United States that I barely noticed it (the very essence of hegemony). I only noticed hormones when they disappeared from the conversation.

In Ecuador, doctors sometimes discussed hormonal effects with patients, but patients rarely mentioned them except when I raised the topic directly. They would then talk about their hormone treatments, but differently from women in the United States. As the majority of women in IVF clinics saw it, hormones could help them reach a normal equilibrium. Infertility signified the failure of their female bodies; the hormones made many women feel more feminine. My sense is that hormones were perceived as a form of care. The emotional tumult that accompanied IVF was attributed not to biochemical effects but to the complex state of women's lives, related to childlessness and the stress of combining their customary responsibilities with the financial, physical, and existential demands of IVF. This view reflects what Owsei Temkin calls a physiological understanding of affliction, which presupposes that disease stems from a body in flux that encounters a shifting material and social environment. Unlike ontological models of disease, this model does not presuppose a universal and fixed body (Temkin 1977).

In Ecuador, a woman's failure to get pregnant was often attributed, by both patients and clinicians, to nerves, stress, and anxiety. Several women told me they were so anxious after their transfer that their nerves caused the embryos not to implant. Several others who had completed two rounds of IVF told me they'd gotten pregnant the second time because they were able to relax, as they now knew what to expect. Doctors shared this view, telling patients to relax after the transfer, "so the embryos will climb." Relaxation was a frequently cited cure for infertility. I heard countless stories about women who, after one or two IVF treatments, took a vacation (most often a trip to the beach) and returned pregnant. (The ability to take a vacation from work of course involved a level of class privilege unavailable to most Ecuadorian women, an issue I examine in more depth in the next section.)

The widespread and ready assumption that nerves and relaxation affect reproductive outcomes contrasts with the way such explanations are regarded in the United States. A recurring complaint in Internet chat rooms, support groups, and self-help books for infertile women in North America centers on well-meaning but thoughtless friends, relatives, and strangers who suggest that all they need to do to become pregnant is calm down or relax. These women feel that they're being told their failure to conceive is all in their heads. Until recently in the United States, an observation of this sort served more as an accusation of somatic psychosis than as a legitimate explanation for a problem like infertility, because the distress of the sufferer was not based on a material, and thus "real," biological cause. This view has changed somewhat in the last quarter century, as *stress* has become a shorthand explanation for some, but not all, forms of corporeal distress. But even though the mention of emotional stress has become acceptable in discussions about one's physiological condition, many U.S. women undergoing IVF attribute emotional fluctuations to hormonal treatment.

Ecuadorian IVF patients, by contrast, didn't find it necessary to mark distinct borders between biology and emotion, and so there was little stigma attached to the idea that moods, events, experiences, and the environment affect a woman's physical state. In Ecuador, hormones were occasionally used to explain depressive states, but for the most part they were invoked only in conjunction with the social environment of the woman using them. Although many women described experiencing irritability, nerves, and stress during IVF treatment, when I asked them directly whether these feelings were due to the hormones, the usual response was a blank look or something like Roxana's reply as she was undergoing IVF for a second time: "Nothing affected me. Because the doctor told me that it might put me in a bad mood. But to me it wasn't that. I had this feeling that if I was going to get pregnant, that nothing was important. I suffered a little from the injections, when they put them in the *pompies* [slang for buttocks]. How strange it was. That hurt, yes, but moods, no. . . . With all the things together—school, the house, the husband—there are always problems."

Even though Roxana's doctor prepared her to view her moods as hormonally related, she saw them as indicative of a larger set of problems. For Roxana, undergoing IVF entailed time away from other obligations revolving around school, work, and her husband. Like Roxana, the vast majority of Ecuadorian IVF patients rarely relied on substances or biological agents like hormones to explain their shifting moods.

Tatiana, a patient in Dr. Padilla's clinic in 2002, was an executive at an accounting firm—one of the few professional women I encountered in the clinics. She was also one of the only IVF patients I met in Ecuador who attributed some of the tumult of her IVF cycle to the hormone treatments. The female practitioners in the clinic wouldn't let her blame her feelings solely on the hormones, though. They made sure she saw her erratic moods as related to her stressful work life, causing her to reevaluate how her career as a finance executive affected her ability to become pregnant. During the follicle stimulation phase of Tatiana's cycle, her follicles grew rather slowly. This became a central concern for Dr. Padilla and Linda and subsequently for Tatiana and her husband, Tomas. Dr. Padilla increased her hormonal dosage several times and decided to have her follicles monitored via ultrasound every day instead of every other day. After days of hormone increases and monitoring, Tatiana's follicles still hadn't grown. As Linda was administering her hormone injections on day 10, Tatiana suggested that perhaps the follicles hadn't grown "because I have so much pressure at work." She'd had an awful headache the day before, and she couldn't work because of it. "Maybe it was the hormones," Tatiana ventured. Linda asked, "Are you tense, maybe?" Tatiana nodded. On her way out of the clinic, she told Dr. Padilla that she was going to take some time off work.

On day 13, the tide turned. Tatiana showed up looking different. She usually wore a suit to the clinic, but today she was wearing jeans and a T-shirt. She had been off work for two days. We all gathered in the exam room, and when Padilla inserted the probe, he exclaimed, "¡Que lindo! ¡Lindo! ¡Sacamos!" (How beautiful! Let's take them out!) He read off the numbers, which were now on target.

Beaming, Tatiana asked, "They have grown?"

Padilla nodded. "This is the result of patience," he said. When Tatiana reminded him that she had taken the week off from work, he said, "That's why the follicles grew."

Tatiana and I walked out together into the waiting room. She seemed to be bubbling over with energy, bouncing on the balls of her feet. She asked the lab tech, "Is it normal to feel so agitated, and for my heart to beat so fast?" The lab tech replied, "Of course. You're worried you might have eight babies."

Tatiana's aspiration took place a few days later, and Dr. Padilla retrieved twelve eggs. Eight fertilized, and three embryos were transferred. Afterwards, Linda counseled Tatiana to stay in bed. Tatiana did until the pregnancy test, which turned out to be negative. A few months later, she took a longer leave from work for a vacation and came back pregnant.

By 2007 Tatiana had a toddler and a baby, both conceived without the assistance of IVF. She talked with me in her new gated house outside Quito as she nursed her baby. Her *empleada* bustled around us, vacuuming, sweeping, and making lunch. Tatiana attributed her temporary infertility to her stressful job and her first pregnancy to an extended beach vacation. Tatiana mused that her *empleadas*, who were all from the countryside, never experienced problems conceiving. One had given birth to eight children, a fact that horrified and fascinated Tatiana. "It all seems easier for them," she said. She explained that her *empleadas* didn't share her preoccupations with eating right during pregnancy, making sure her children grew up in a healthy environment (she and Tomas had moved outside Quito for that reason), finding the right day-care center, or balancing the demands of motherhood and work.

Tatiana is certainly not the first upper-middle-class woman to wildly minimize the hardships of her domestic servants' lives. She was dead wrong in her assessment that poorer rural women have more carefree reproductive lives. Besides having the economic wherewithal to take a lot of time off from work, including significant savings and a husband with a good income, Tatiana had the resources and the help she needed to lie in bed for two weeks while she waited for the results of the pregnancy test. She had *empleadas* to cook and clean and tend to her physical needs and relatives nearby to bring her what she needed. And after she had a child, she was able to work part-time. Tatiana "needed" these ministrations and care to successfully reproduce, whereas her *empleadas,* who toiled nonstop, were able to have eight children without ceasing. Had she linked her jumpiness and moodiness only to hormones, that would have stopped the chain of associations that accounted for her slow follicular growth. Through the encouragement of the clinic staff, she linked the problem instead to her stressful career and was able to place herself in a position to receive more care.

Both U.S. and Ecuadorian approaches to understanding the emotional distress brought about by IVF could be fashioned into critiques of the power of medicine and the pharmaceutical industry conjoined within the IVF apparatus. When U.S. women blame hormones for their erratic emotional states during IVF, this might signal distrust of the pharmaceutical industry, which promotes powerful drugs: patients are effectively paying to act as guinea pigs in a massive, largely unregulated experiment. The tendency among Ecuadorian women to point to life circumstances, rather than hormone treatments, as affecting emotional states and fertility might serve as a critique of biomedical attempts to define and simplify the boundaries of bodily disruption. While both these modes of experience effectively organize distress, they are apolitical, unless they are juxtaposed in order to denaturalize powerful, universalizing claims about the hormonal body and the immutability of biological processes. As Ecuadorian IVF patients attest, fertility hormones do not have the same effects everywhere. For these women, the quality of the care they receive from doctors, husbands, female relatives and servants, and the care they must give to others, do much more than hormones to affect their emotional and reproductive states.

It's not as if North American women's typical experience of IVF hormones is false—a social-constructionist argument. Or that IVF hormones have the same effects on women in Ecuador as in the United States, but Ecuadorian women just don't notice them—a realist argument. Or that Ecuadorian women's experience of care relations is more holistic—a culturalist argument. These arguments presume a divide between nature and culture, with one side dominant over the other. I am arguing instead that in both places, hormones are real and have effects, but the effects are different. In both places, care relations are real and have effects, but the effects are different. When IVF hormones produce tumult, they also produce individuals who experience that tumult from within, physiologically and emotionally, as irritability, depression, or even madness. This tumult is experienced as a price worth paying for the reproductive project of a woman and her supporters. When care relations are disrupted or activated in the IVF process, they reveal a woman embedded in care relations, whose body can be cultivated and altered through the experience of those care relations.

AN ECONOMY OF BED REST

Care relations were most obviously activated in Ecuadorian clinics right after an IVF cycle. Clinics held different views about what a woman should do after an embryo transfer, while waiting for her pregnancy test. Patients tended to want to take to their beds, as Consuelo did after a miscarriage threat and Tatiana did after her ultimately failed IVF cycle. At Dr. Molina's clinic, patients spent a few hours in the recovery room, followed by three days of bed rest at home. After Dr. Molina's son Wilson returned to his father's clinic from a year's advanced medical training in Spain, this policy underwent a rapid transformation. Taking his cue from recent North American and European studies showing that bed rest did nothing to augment pregnancy rates, Wilson decreed that women should rest for fifteen minutes after the transfer and then leave the clinic soon after. He had a difficult time persuading patients and staff of this approach, however, and I observed him on several occasions practically chasing patients out their beds, admonishing them to return to normal life. Nearly all of the patients refused to listen to Wilson and stuck with what he saw as outmoded, unscientific behavior.

Wilson's "foreign" determination to get patients up and out upset the women's sense of how they should act and be cared for in these circumstances. Did he think this was a public clinic? While in the recovery room, women would emphasize their fragile state by asking their husbands or female relatives to help them to the bathroom. The nurses, appalled at Wilson's protocol, brought bedpans to patients while apologizing for his abruptness.

At Dr. Padilla's clinic, following a transfer, IVF patients would lie in the operating room for three hours and then spend a night or two at the clinic. When the patients had been moved to their recovery room, Linda, the embryologist and patient manager, would give a speech they had already heard in the OR, and she would repeat it as they left the clinic the next day: "No physical efforts. That is the most important thing. Be calm. You can move slowly and change position so you don't get sore. You can bathe after two days, but you must be careful not to slip. Everything depends on your body. Make no exertions. And when you leave tomorrow, lie in the back seat. *Susto* [fright] can make you lose the pregnancy. . . . Don't do anything strong or heavy. Nothing but repose. Repose! Repose! Repose!"

The patients who could afford to take time off work were quite receptive to Linda's speeches. Her instructions to rest acknowledged the momentousness of the process, the effort exerted, and the enormous amount of money spent to try to make a child. They reinforced the idea that a patient deserved special care from her husband, family, *empleadas,* and doctors. Her reproductive efforts were of crucial importance. If a patient had to continue working and did not get pregnant, or had a miscarriage, Linda would use her as an example of the perils of overactivity. Physicians rarely acknowledged that patients might need to continue working in order to pay the bills.

Fertility problems are very much linked in doctors' minds to women's work outside the home: they are a modern affliction. As with Tatiana, when patients reported feeling moody or nervous to IVF practitioners, they were counseled to stop work, which was seen as a physical and emotional stressor for women.[12] Patients were often counseled to take a vacation, another sign of privilege. Dr. Leon told me about Lydia, age forty-three, who didn't get pregnant after her IVF cycle "because she had been too busy running a large day care center." She was "overly focused" on her work. When I met Lydia a few weeks later, she was filled with regret that she hadn't been able to take to her bed as she had been told to do, because she had to work.

Patients with means took their mandate for repose seriously. Although their doctors and God played a big part in making an IVF baby, women also saw it as their duty to rest in order to cultivate their bodies. An upper-class IVF patient, Victoria, explained to me that once God and her doctors had played their parts, she had an important obligation: "It is my responsibility to be calm." Like many patients, she imagined her body as having a role to play in this drama, one of calm nurturance, while she endured the fourteen days' wait after the transfer, which for many women is the most agonizing aspect of IVF. While she took to her bed after the embryo transfer and was waited on by her husband and servants, Victoria actively managed her follicles.

> First you have to think, "I am going to produce eggs," because you can produce a follicle, but it must have an egg. You can produce the grape, but without the seed it does not serve you at all. After the transfer is when things really go internal. This is when the bed rest starts, the ten to twelve days of waiting. And you have to be skilled to cultivate the right stance physically, mentally. You have to manage the stress, the anxiety. You have to dominate it. All the expectation. All the money. You could lose it all. . . . This part is the most complicated. It's the hardest part, because you have to be in repose. You have to do things. You have to read, watch television. You can't wander. You can't move much, because suddenly there could be a failure. Until they call you and say positive or negative, you have to be still.

In fact, the bodily discipline of female infertility patients in Ecuador reflects an idealized Catholic femininity, akin to the problematic but evocative concept of *marianismo*, which suggests that Latin American women become feminine through physical suffering, self-sacrifice, and passivity. One of the main criticisms of *marianismo* has been its overly broad application: this class-specific valorization of feminine invalidism (Montoya, Frazier, and Hurtig 2002) ignores the lives of poor and working-class women, who relish their strength and negotiating skills (Cadena 2000). Indeed, the claims of female suffering I witnessed came primarily from middle- and upper-class women patients. Others couldn't afford the time to lie in bed, although they wished they could.

The construct of feminine passivity among well-off IVF patients is complicated, however, by women like Victoria, who saw their suffering as active. They suffer even while they are being cared for in a collective reproductive project. Their efforts have a model in the seventeenth-century figure of Mariana de Jesús Parredes, Ecuador's only canonized saint. Mariana, patron saint of illness, vigorously practiced the greatest of austerities: she ate hardly anything and slept for only three hours a night. When an earthquake shook Quito in 1645 and was followed by epidemics, she offered herself publicly as a sacrificial victim for the sins of the people. As the epidemic began to abate, she was stricken with disease and died. She became known as the Lily of Quito, surely the whitest of all flowers.

REPRODUCTIVE BINGO

When Consuelo and Jorge sought assistance for their reproductive endeavors, they kept their participation in IVF and gamete donation a secret because they used gamete donors, but they did involve their friends and family in paying for medical care for Consuelo and their premature babies. This became the quintessential collective effort. She and Jorge raised money through games of luck. In an atmosphere of chronic uncertainty, it is common for people to participate in games of chance to raise funds for their friends, relatives and coworkers. What better cause to gamble for than a cycle of IVF, an expensive endeavor with slim odds and an uncertain outcome?

Sometimes IVF was not the object of the fundraising but the prize itself. Across the city from Consuelo and Jorge, Eliana and her husband were heavily in debt for their house and for years of infertility treatments that had resulted in three miscarriages. They were about to give up trying to have a baby when they won a free IVF cycle in a raffle held at Dr. Vroit's clinic in 2002. Eliana got pregnant with triplets, making up for her three miscarriages in one fell swoop.

Ximena and her husband had gone through nine artificial inseminations at another clinic before coming to the same clinic as Eliana, where they completed four IVF cycles. The first failed. On the second try, Ximena got pregnant with triplets, all of whom died at twenty-eight weeks. The third attempt also failed. On the fourth cycle, Ximena got pregnant again, and her daughter, born on Valentine's Day, was named Valentina. Ximena and her husband were wealthier than most Ecuadorian IVF patients, making $3,000 a month instead of Consuelo and Jorge's $100, but they had still accrued heavy debts on their way to having Valentina. Like Consuelo and Jorge, they organized a bingo night to pay the bills for Ximena's hospitalization, as well as the hospital bills for the triplets. Ximena thought of herself as a winner: "People say if God doesn't want you to have children, then you won't have them. But I think it's more like a test that he gives us. Like the matter of money. Sometimes we didn't have any for treatment. And then somehow the money always came."[13]

The logic of raffles and bingo relies on a nineteenth-century liberal template of private charity that in Ecuador has never been supplanted by a welfare state. The national lottery was founded in 1894 by the Junta de Beneficencia de Guayaquil (Guayaquil Charity Board), which began as a municipal charitable association. Soon it dissociated itself from the municipality and was no longer accountable to state institutions. To this day, the Junta de Beneficencia promotes social welfare, ministering to "the poorest of the poor." It is supported by volunteer work, private donations, and state lottery proceeds. Infertility services are prominently mentioned on its website.

For many Ecuadorians, calls for charitable solidarity—such as calls to participate in privately organized gambling events to benefit specific causes or individuals—are much more persuasive than the civic-solidarity campaigns promoted constantly through TV, the radio, and newspapers. The latter run up against the substantial obstacle of distrust of state institutions. As chapter 1 shows, Ecuadorians themselves say that Ecuador lacks national solidarity. Private fundraisers like bingo nights provide a smaller-scale solidarity, based on shared uncertainty, within families and sometimes neighborhoods. The experience of uncertainty is surely more pronounced among those with less, but the well-off, like Ximena, also understand its role in their lives: after all, Ximena won the reproductive lottery.

Communities of chance, like those created through fundraising bingo games, stand in mute rebuke to the specter of the always-failing state, whose shoddy resources no one wants to use. Amid shared uncertainty, people organize not politically, by making demands on state institutions, but privately, by attempting to counter the chronic indeterminacy of life and its reproduction (ironically, by exploiting the uncertain odds of games of chance). The neoliberal rhetoric of taking care of yourself and your family has a long history in Ecuador, where different marginalized groups, such as freed slaves, claimed legitimacy as free subjects by arguing that they took care of themselves (Bryant 2008).

What's new about Consuelo's experience is that twenty years earlier, she might have been willing to use the public maternity hospital, even though the care there was not necessarily better then than it is today. Assisted reproduction and the new multitude of private clinics were not yet available. However, in 2003, Consuelo was not a consumer subject. She knew little about IVF before she began the process. She didn't shop around for a doctor with the best success rates. Instead she found a doctor and patron, underwent several invasive and possibly unnecessary surgeries and procedures, and took to her bed. Bingo, bed rest, hormonal regimes, C-sections, and IVF are all care practices that assisted her uncertain reproduction.

Consuelo, Eliana, and Ximena viewed the uncertain outcomes of IVF as ultimately determined by God. In their work on "casino capitalism," Jean and John Comaroff describe contemporary efforts to enlist the divine in gambling for material reward as "locally nuanced fantasies of abundance without effort" (Comaroff and Comaroff 2000, 179). I would agree that they're locally nuanced, but these entreaties are by no means fantasies or lacking in effort. At least among Catholic Ecuadorian IVF patients, the games of chance that alleviate uncertainty, pay off debts, and produce children are no fantasy, and their logic is part of the same hard-working reciprocity that cultivates material, intimate relationships with the divine, as well as with family members.

Miracles are the palpable results of expected divine intervention in return for services. Such services are rendered to God and Jesús Cristo, the Divino Niño, as well as at shrines to the Virgin throughout Ecuador, like Agua Santa, El Cisne, and El Quinche, whose statues are cared for within families through schedules that rotate annually. They are the serious cargo of a family. And it's not only working-class patients who envision these relationships with divine and saintly beings. IVF biologists also enlist divine assistance to tame uncertainty in their laboratories. The God whose help they invoke is not an impersonal, transcendent Protestant God, removed from the daily workings of the world, but a materially present God, surrounded by a pantheon of saints who share in daily life and whose blessing can pay big dividends. God's intervention can generate money, miracles, and offspring.

Along with offering the hope of a child, assisted reproduction allows patients to distinguish themselves from others who cannot afford such services. To partici-pate in the diagnosis and treatment of reproductive pathology is to set oneself apart from poorer, browner women whose robust bodies are supposedly made for hard manual labor and easy reproductive labor. Significantly, the patients at IVF clinics whom I thought of as suffering from poverty-based infertility (such as the second-ary effects of poor nutrition, work-related reproductive injuries, and most common of all, botched abortions like Sandra's), didn't link their problems to the effects of economic inequality. That would have made little sense, given that it's wealthier, whiter women who are seen as reproductively troubled. Although Consuelo had nearly the lowest income of any patient I met, she never attributed her infertility to poverty. By participating in the IVF treatment process, she became worthy of the kind of care that whiter, wealthier women need. Her whiteness was produced in a context in which race can be cultivated, as I explore in chapter 3.

It mattered little to the patients or clinicians that Catholicism unequivocally condemns the use of IVF. God's involvement in the community of chance, his role in mitigating uncertainty in return for acts of devotion, partially accounts for why so many Ecuadorian IVF patients were not particularly concerned about the suc-cess statistics for their treatment. After all, they had God on their side. The mother of an IVF baby has gambled on her reproductive fate and won. She might tell her children, We prayed for you. We paid for you. We played for you. And you came. You cost $9,384, and you were worth every cent.

Consuelo was able to pay for her children through selling land and playing bingo. We commonly understand land as indicative of long-lasting and stable bonds, whereas the realm of bingo involves risk, fleeting pleasure, and impersonal relations. But the stability of land meant nothing to Consuelo: its only benefit to her was its cash value. Bingo meant more. To pay for her IVF treatment, she harnessed the power of bingo reproductively, reemphasizing her participation in a community of care with family, friends, and God. Her community of care endowed her with a sense that she could play reproductive bingo like a whiter woman, and that she could win.

Yo Soy Teresa La Fea/*Ugly Teresa*

Teresa epitomized what most middle-class Quiteños call *humilde* (humility). She was tiny and fine-boned and spoke very quietly, with a birdlike, nervous voice and manner. In Dr. Hidalgo's clinic, where she was an IVF patient and donor-egg recipient, Teresa was deferential, addressing everyone, including the receptionist and nurse, with the formal *usted,* instead of *tu.*

Quiteños of any means would call Teresa an Indian. She was a dark-skinned seamstress from Zambiza, one of the several historically Indian pueblos on the rim of northern Quito. But Teresa didn't call herself an Indian, even though she said her grandparents were Indian: instead, like most Quiteños, she identified herself as mestiza. Teresa was very concerned about skin color. At first she didn't want her egg donor to be light-skinned, because it would increase the likelihood that her child would be lighter than she and her husband were. But as it turned out, she was ultimately glad to have a whiter child.

In 2002, when Dr. Hidalgo diagnosed Teresa with ovarian failure from advanced age (forty-two), he persuaded her to use an anonymous egg donor in order to conceive. His clinic manager, Dr. Castro, selected Irene to be Teresa's donor. Irene seemed to me like most of the egg donors I met in Ecuador: she was light-skinned, in her early twenties, and worked in marketing, a job that probably did not pay all that well but had professional status. Dr. Castro was nervous about Irene, despite her professional presentation. The doctor's task was to synchronize the maturing of Irene's eggs with the growth of Teresa's endometrium through the administration of timed hormone shots, blood tests, and ultrasound scans. Irene was jeopardizing the cycle by arriving hours late for appointments, with no explanation, or forgetting them altogether.

By contrast, Teresa was always on time and eager. The first time I met her, she was already up on an exam table, craning her neck around to give me a big smile as I came in. We all turned to the business at hand—examining the ghostly image of Teresa's uterus on the screen, projected through the vaginal ultrasound probe. Dr. Castro was pleased. Teresa's endometrium had grown well, thickening from 7 millimeters at her previous visit to 11 mm (10–15 mm is the ideal thickness for embryo transfer). When Teresa emerged after the exam, she produced a balled-up wad of cash from her pants pocket and paid the receptionist. She and I went out into the hospital lobby to talk. We kept our voices low because people were walking by, but that didn't prevent Teresa from weeping as she told me how she had ended up in the clinic.

Teresa's first husband, Rodrigo, had left her when she was three months pregnant with her daughter, Adriana, now eighteen years old. He returned when Adriana was about a year and a half old, and they lived together for a time. Teresa got pregnant again, but Rodrigo did not want another baby and convinced her to get an abortion. He left her again soon after, this time for good. This was a terrible time for Teresa. She regretted having the abortion, especially now that Adriana was older and Teresa had no child left in the house. Teresa raised Adriana mostly alone, supplemented by checks from an international charity that sponsored children. The checks stopped coming after September 11, 2001. Teresa assumed that the Dutch woman sponsoring Adriana had been affected by the attacks.

Teresa had met Manuel two and a half years before her IVF cycle. They immediately tried to have a baby, but nothing happened. Manuel worried that someone had bewitched them and wanted to go to the Oriente (the Amazon) to see a shaman. Teresa worried that she was being punished for the abortion. She had never told Manuel about it. On the advice of a neighbor, Teresa ate a fox (because they "have eight classes of vitamins"). She cooked and ate the meat, including the hide, which she found disgusting.[1] When a gynecologist told her she had myomas— uterine fibroid tumors that are usually benign but could prevent pregnancy— Teresa cried for days. She sought out a Belgian woman married to a man in town to explain the diagnosis. Teresa was adept at seeking help from people with greater resources, particularly European and North American women. The woman told her to find a particular doctor in the public hospital in Quito, reassuring her that treatment wouldn't cost much. That doctor, however, explained that public hospitals couldn't offer any treatment and sent her on to Dr. Hidalgo, a private infertility specialist. Though the public doctor said it would cost her money, he told her not to cry anymore, "because now everything is possible."

Dr. Hidalgo recommended to Teresa that she undergo surgery to remove the myomas. Paying for treatment meant Teresa and Manuel couldn't invest in a house. Both had left school when they were twelve years old, and between the two of them they made less than $200 a month. Manuel was a carpenter and a musician. Through his band he had obtained visas to enter other countries, and most of his income came from construction work he found in Spain and the United States, for which he was paid under the table. Teresa eventually got a bank loan for the surgery and two inseminations, which cost $300 each. After the second insemination failed, Dr. Hidalgo advised her "to stop wasting money" and to attempt an IVF cycle with an egg donor. The cost of this procedure was $5,000. Teresa estimated that by the time she had completed one IVF attempt, she would have spent $10,000 on diagnostic tests, surgeries, donor fees, and treatments. Most of this expense was financed by Manuel's work abroad: much came from a single three-month stint in New Jersey.

When Dr. Hidalgo told Teresa she needed an egg donor, she first thought of her daughter, Adriana, who agreed immediately. But Adriana did not meet Dr. Hidalgo's criteria for donors known to the recipient: at least twenty-five years old, with two children.[2] Teresa couldn't think of anyone else in her family to ask, so she reluctantly agreed to use an anonymous donor selected by Dr. Hidalgo and Dr. Castro. Anonymous donors were more expensive than familial donors: and, more problematic, anonymous donation raised the possibility of a child who would look very different from Teresa and Manuel. Specifically, Teresa was worried that if the donor was lighter-skinned, the baby wouldn't resemble her or Manuel. She told me, "I only want the baby to look like its father. It's that we are very *moreno* [dark]. My husband is more *moreno* than I. And if the baby is born *blanquísimo* [very white], then it's not ours." But she was too afraid to ask about the donor's skin color.

The day after this interview, I went to the clinic to observe the ultrasound check of Irene's egg follicles. She was late, as usual. While we waited, Dr. Castro made the usual complaint: "It's almost impossible to find good donors these days." According to her, all the eligible young women had gone to Spain in search of work.[3] I asked Dr. Castro why she picked Irene as a donor for Teresa. The doctor laughed: "I knew you would ask about this." She explained that Irene had been selected as a donor for another, lighter-skinned, patient, but that patient had decided to take a break after her first, unsuccessful IVF cycle. Because Irene had already started taking hormones to stimulate follicular growth, they decided she would be Teresa's donor. "Teresa has already waited eight months. We decided to go ahead because we don't have any other donors right now." Dr. Castro got out a folder of information that they would have shown Teresa if she had ever asked about the donor. The donor information sheet had boxes for five different categories of skin color, ranging from "very white" to "very dark." Looking at the sheet, I noted how many different terms Ecuadorians have to describe skin color. Dr. Castro laughed again, and said, "Well, we are all mestizos, but we are terrible racists. Everyone says, *No soy racista pero . . .*" (I am not a racist, but . . .). Most urban Ecuadorians I encountered were preoccupied with distinguishing themselves from people darker than themselves: "I am white, not mestizo"; "I am mestizo, not Indian."

A few days after Irene's ultrasound, Dr. Castro called me, extremely upset. Irene's follicles hadn't grown at all, though she claimed to have taken all her medications. "But it can't be true, since she is so young. Her follicles should have grown. She must have stopped taking her medication." But Irene had seemed eager to participate in the process of egg donation. Dr. Castro couldn't believe it either. "We have never had a case like this before. Ever!"

Dr. Castro didn't look forward to informing Dr. Hidalgo about this failure. And then there was the problem of money. "Teresa won't have to pay for everything. But someone has to pay for the medications." Calling this episode a "dark chapter" in the clinic's history, Dr. Castro said, "You really don't know people. You think you know who they are, standing right here, but not always."

Five months later, however, Dr. Castro told me excitedly that Teresa was pregnant. Another patient had brought in a friend to serve as her egg donor. Dr. Hidalgo harvested fourteen of her eggs, seven more than they needed. Antonia, the laboratory biologist, inseminated these extra seven with Teresa's husband sperm, and Dr. Hidalgo transferred three of the resulting embryos into Teresa. These embryos stuck. I called Teresa to congratulate her. She seemed very happy to hear from me and invited me to her next sonogram appointment.

Teresa was tired and unable to work much. She kept repeating that her HCG levels at the first pregnancy test were 330, a high number, which meant she might be pregnant with twins or triplets. She repeated this number like a mantra: "¡Trescientos treinta! ¡Trescientos treinta! ¡Trescientos treinta!" Teresa hoped out loud for twins or triplets but admitted that her husband was "very worried about all the clothes we would have to buy." She told me what had happened after the failure with Irene. Dr. Castro told her to continue with the medication so that she would be ready if they found another donor. A few months later, Dr. Castro offered her some extra embryos (not eggs) left over after another patient's cycle. Teresa and Manuel decided against taking these embryos, because a baby might "come out a different color" from them. With egg donation, at least Manuel would be the father. Teresa explained that the parents "could have been *blanquísimo* (very white), and we're not white."

A month later the clinic called Teresa with an offer of extra eggs. Teresa said yes, and Dr. Castro had her come in right away for blood tests. The process went quickly. Dr. Hidalgo did the transfer a few days later. When Teresa asked about the donor, Dr. Castro told her that the donor was pretty, and a little whiter than Teresa. In the clinic one day, she saw a young woman leaving and wondered if she was her donor. She was tall but not that white, although lighter than Teresa, and she had black hair. Teresa asked if I knew who the donor was. At that time I did not, though Dr. Castro and Antonia told me a bit about her later. Although she had never mentioned the issue directly, they knew Teresa was worried about the donor's skin color. Antonia said the donor looked like me, "green eyes and blond hair." She was obviously amused by the difference between the donor and Teresa. Dr. Castro thought it was strange that Teresa was worried. When I asked why, she explained to me, "Dr. Hidalgo thinks that all couples want babies with Anglo-Saxon tendencies."

With a keen sense of the absurd, Teresa narrated the events that transpired after the embryo transfer. Manuel's old car had broken down, so they took a taxi home. At one point the driver hit the brakes, throwing Teresa to the floor and making her think the embryos might have fallen out. To protect the embryos, she stayed in bed for twelve days instead of the three that Dr. Hidalgo had prescribed. Two weeks later, Teresa had her first pregnancy test: it came back positive. She took the bus with Manuel to the shrine at El Quinche, arriving for that night's mass. There she gave thanks and prayed to the Virgin, who, among other things, assists barren women and women in labor.

At thirty-five weeks of pregnancy, Teresa was diagnosed with pre-eclampsia and had an emergency C-section. When I saw her in 2004, she seemed over-joyed about her son, Andrés, who was eight months old. He was named after Dr. Hidalgo, who performed the C-section that she said had saved her life. Teresa's fears about the color of the baby's skin had been partially allayed: "He looks just like his papa, except he is white. His father is *morenito* [dark], but the baby looks just like him."

Teresa invited me to come to her house the following week. My two young daughters and I met Manuel in northern Quito. The four of us took a taxi to Zambiza on roads of pure dust, through the municipal garbage dump, over a hill, and then onto a plateau above the valley of Cumbaya. Zambiza was a sleepy little pueblo that felt far away from Quito, though it was just beyond the edge of the city. Teresa's house was right on the town plaza, opposite the church. Manuel ushered us through a small sweatshop. The staircase to the upper story was lined with old *ollas* (ceramic jars) and stone cooking pots that Teresa told me were from her grandparents. The room was crammed with sewing machines and enormous piles of neon orange and yellow material. Four young women, including Teresa's daughter, Adriana, were transforming the fabric into knock-off Tommy Hilfiger sweat suits. Teresa had a take-out lunch of roast chicken, French fries, and cola waiting for us. I took several pictures of the family posing happily with Andrés, obviously the joy of the household. Passed among the three, cooed over with kisses, he was bundled in a polyester fleece sleeper, as highland children usually are, to keep out the cold. His skin did look lighter than theirs. I couldn't tell if he looked like Manuel.

Teresa breastfed Andrés as she told me about his traumatic birth, for which they were still in debt, though a spiritual debt had been paid off. In her entreaties to Our Lady of El Quinche, she had promised to make fifty shirts for needy infants if she gave birth to a child. Andrés was born on November 21. By Christmas, Teresa had completed sewing one hundred baby shirts. Manuel tearfully described his amazement at Andrés's arrival. He couldn't believe his good fortune and wished he could share it with other people who had undergone IVF. But Manuel was acutely aware of their differences from the other patients at the clinic. He wanted to talk about doing IVF with "a person of our class." At the clinic, it seemed like everyone had money, "people who can pay with their checks or their MasterCard, and us, nothing." The other clients didn't talk to him. "They came to the clinic too elegant in their suits." He pointed to his work clothes and shrugged, saying that his family possessed "nothing but faith in God."

Manuel told me that he had heard their donor was "bigger and fatter than Teresa." He said the doctor had looked for a donor whose skin color matched Teresa's and his: "They did the analysis of us, and I believe they looked for a *parentesco* [kinship] to Teresa."[4] (Here *kinship* referred to skin color.) Manuel wanted to know more about the donor, but he thought that the doctors would not share information about their physical characteristics or background. He was content that he had a child, telling me how intelligent Andrés was and how proud he was to show him off to everyone. In Zambiza, no one commented on Andrés's skin color. They remarked that he looked just like his father. Only one man from outside the pueblo had asked Andrés, "Why is he white, and you are *moreno?*" Manuel began to answer when the man cut him off, telling Manuel that in his own family, "We are all white, but there is one *moreno* child, a very *moreno* child." The man shrugged. "Ah, the life of the family. This is how it is." In commenting on the darker-skinned child in his own family, he evoked Ecuador's racial history of sexual domination of darker women by lighter men, as well as the cuckolding of darker men by lighter men.

When I saw Teresa again in 2007, her perception of her child's skin color had shifted. The ride to Teresa's house was smoother this time, thanks to the newly paved road past the garbage dump. Teresa came to the door with short hair, looking a little older. She was holding Andrés, who was now four. Maybe his skin was a little darker, and to me he looked like Teresa, with fine features. We stumbled through the workshop, which was now dark and idle. I could make out a small pile of half-assembled black T-shirts on a table. This was nothing like the humming room of three years earlier, filled with young, industrious women at their sewing machines. The stairs were lined with an even more pottery and artifacts pulled from the ground. Waiting at the top was Manuel, looking shockingly old, his face haggard and thin.

Teresa brought us plates of potatoes, little bits of meat, and salad. Serving homemade food instead of take-out was a sign of hard times. Looking at photos from our last visit, Manuel commented that Andrés looked a little darker now than he had three years before. "We kept him out of the sun then. Now he's *mas normal.* But his skin is still so much lighter than anyone else here."

Teresa and Manuel were both looking for work, driven by their need to pay for Andrés's education. Manuel had left his band because he didn't want to travel away from Andrés and Teresa anymore, and visas were now impossible to obtain anyway, so his income from construction work abroad was gone. Teresa's sewing business had almost completely dried up. The market for cheap clothing was saturated with textiles from China, Peru, and Colombia. Manuel would help out with whatever small sewing jobs Teresa could find. When I saw her three years earlier, Teresa had had high hopes for Adriana's professional cooking program, but things weren't going well for her either. Reminding me of Adriana's dark skin, Teresa explained that the best job Adriana had found was a low-paying graveyard shift at the airport, cooking meals for airlines. Teresa and Manuel still owned a bit of land. To enter the house I had stepped over drying corn, harvested from their fields. But no one had brought in much income in the last few years. Teresa wanted my help to find an international sponsor for Andrés, like the Dutch woman who had sponsored Adriana.

Amid the couple's palpable despair, it became obvious that Andrés was now the great hope of their household. The future of his darker elders, Teresa, Manuel and Adriana, depended on their ability to cultivate his lightness. Andre's whiteness might allow him entry into an economic world off-limits to the three of them, mired in what Teresa termed their "darkness and ugliness." Teresa had mentioned Andrés's good looks before, but now her constant evocations of his beauty were contrasted with her own ugly darkness. Teresa's worries about Andrés's skin color were completely gone. "People look at Andrés all the time and say '¡Ay, que blanquito!' They ask me if I'm his grandmother, and I tell them no. This always confuses them, and they repeat the compliment, this time more of a question: '¿Que blanquito?'" And then Teresa tells them, "When I was young, I was *guapa* [good-looking/whiter]."

At a family baptism, Teresa saw a cousin for the first time since Andrés's birth. The cousin was shocked at Andrés appearance and asked if he was *rubio* (blond). I noted that Andrés's hair was just as dark as Teresa's, but she disagreed with me: "No, there is red in it." But the real difference, she explained, was in how they dress Andrés: *muy clara* (very light/white), differently from the way they were dressed as children. "It's good to dress him well. Manuel brought him clothes in Europe, which are more elegant. And everyone says how beautiful he is. Not like us, *mas feos* [more ugly.]"

I asked why whiteness is considered more beautiful, and Manuel explained that one sign of being whiter is " having better teeth. We are taking care of Andrés's teeth. When we were young, our teeth were never clean. We never had potable water to brush them." Manuel opened his mouth and showed me his irregular teeth (though, unlike many Ecuadorians, he had a full set). "We take him to the dentist and to a pediatrician, something our parents never did." Teresa added, "Our parents had us drink from the river, not *agua potable*. And we were without shoes. My sister now doesn't raise her children like we raise Andrés. Her kids have cavities."

I asked again why whiteness is considered more beautiful, and Teresa told me, "We have big noses."

"But white people have large noses too," I said.

Manuel mentioned that Andrés is left-handed, a unique trait among his family members. "Does that make him white?" I asked.

"No, just different," Manuel said.

Teresa added, "He's distinct. He's more rebellious than Adriana was. He doesn't sleep, and he runs all over the house. And he's so beautiful."

Manuel continued with the theme of difference.

He's distinct because of his *guardaria* [day care center]. He learns so much there. At the day care, they teach Andrés not to throw garbage in the street. They teach him to be clean. In New Jersey, where there are a lot of Latinos, there's a lot of garbage, since they throw the garbage in the street. The environment is getting worse there because of the Latinos. In Europe if you throw trash on the street, you get fined. But you couldn't do that here, because people are too poor to pay a fine. So people just throw trash on the street.

Teresa and Manuel's efforts at whitening Andrés are similar to the process that their grandparents underwent, transforming from Indians into mestizos by putting on long pants and speaking Spanish. Manuel made the comparison, repeating several times, "This is evolution from indigenous to mestizo." Part of the process of changing races involved changing professions and clothing. "There are mestizos here in Quito and Zambiza. Indians live out in the country, where food used to be healthy and organic. They ate what the earth gave. Indians don't live in the city because no one will give them work—because of racism. So they change their clothes so people will hire them."

Teresa brought the discussion back to beauty: "In offices these days, they don't want *chicas feas* [ugly girls]; they want *chicas claras*, with combed hair."

"And painted fingernails," Manuel added.

Teresa noted that whereas today whiteness and beauty are consistent with thinness, when she was young, her mestizo father, whose parents had been Indians, had spoken constantly of beautiful, fat white women. "Now you have to have a figure. You can't be a big square, like when my parents were young."

Although Teresa's grandparents were able to change some of their attributes to become more white, Andrés's whiteness, the result of a stranger's donated egg, seemed to jump-start the process, making new aspirations possible. Manuel had told me earlier that he wanted to adopt a black child, so I asked them both whether a black person could change to a different race. Teresa said, "No, their skin is too dark."

At first Manuel disagreed. He argued that a black person could change by marrying a mestizo and having children. The lighter children would affect the way the parents were treated. But then he reconsidered: "In reality, their skin is so dark."

I had always believed that Teresa had not expressed her anxieties about an egg donor's skin color to Dr. Hidalgo and Dr. Castro because she was in essence a charity case: because she couldn't afford to pay the full fee for an egg donor, she was in no position to make demands. During lunch I learned that Dr. Hidalgo had sponsored her IVF cycle in more ways than I knew. He gave her other patients' leftover medicine, he charged her less per visit, and he charged her less for her C-section. Teresa didn't know why he had helped in all these ways. "Maybe because I am *humilde*. I never asked for anything." And now that Teresa was happy about Andrés's skin color, she realized that Dr. Hidalgo had given her the biggest gift of all, a whiter son. "I always tell Andrés, 'After God, there is Dr. Hidalgo.'"

Teresa had always seemed unusual in her antipathy to the idea of a white child, so different from the attitude of other egg recipients and doctors. But now, more than any other IVF patient I encountered in Ecuador, Teresa viewed having a beautiful white son as offering a chance at economic salvation in increasingly difficult times. Perhaps Teresa and Manuel will be able to benefit from Andrés's lightness when he is older and looking for work. Teresa knows how to make use of everything. She always astounded me with her ability to find resources, connect with foreigners—especially women—and take advantage of technologies that she couldn't afford. She used her humility to find a patron for her IVF cycle, Dr. Hidalgo. She ran her own sewing business and cultivated her own land. But Manuel looked awful. The travails of the last hard years were written on his browner body, while Andrés's whiteness continues to be written on his.

THREE

· White Beauty: Gamete Donation
in a Mestizo Nation

A SCANDAL OF WHITENING

In 1995 a scandal erupted at the fertility clinic at the University of California, Irvine, when reports emerged that the clinic directors, Ricardo Asch (from Chile) and Jose Balmaceda (from Mexico), had surreptitiously taken eggs and embryos from patients and transferred them to other patients in the hope of achieving pregnancy. The story became front-page news across the United States (New York Times 1995; Dalton 1996). In the media reports, the quest for medical profits was pitted against the sanctity of genetic ties that most North Americans experience as the very grounds of relatedness. Among other malpractices, Asch and Balmaceda were accused of transferring eggs and embryos of blond, blue-eyed North American women to patients who had traveled to the Irvine clinic from Central or South America for treatment. This story of Latin American doctors helping Latin American women in their quest for lighter offspring made sense to the North American press: of course darker-skinned couples wanted lighter-skinned babies.[1] Years later, when I began research in IVF clinics in urban Ecuador, I found that clinicians often endeavored to make whiter children through egg and sperm donation. Sometimes they distributed eggs to patients without telling all of the parties involved. For most patients, using an unknown donor provided an opportunity to fantasize about what their children might look like. Dark-haired, brown-eyed, middle-class mestizo patients rhapsodized to me about the prospect of blond, curly-haired, blue-eyed babies.

The racist longings of both the Irvine doctors and the Ecuadorian patients were different, however, from the racist narratives underpinning U.S. press stories, which assumed that darker women wanted lighter children and that only genetic ties produce kinship. Even while denying that he redistributed "blond eggs" to Latin American recipients, Ricardo Asch declared his own mystification with the North American emphasis on the primacy of genetic connection. "Genes are, at least in my opinion, not that important. I know that they are not important for love, and I know they are not important even for IQ or athletic ability" (Dalton 1996, 330). Asch's refusal to allow genetics to determine his understanding of kinship was similar to the ideas about kinship that I found in Ecuadorian IVF clinics. Egg switching might not have been perceived as scandalous in these clinics because patients, physicians, and gamete donors did not consider the genetic or racial characteristics of the donor as determinative of a child's race or relational status. Genetic material passed on through eggs and sperm were seen as only one material factor among many others that influenced a child's race.

A NEW RACE PRACTICE

In chapter 2, I argue that the specialized care given to patients in private IVF clinics made them into whiter women. In this chapter I trace how the kin-making practice of anonymous egg donation in Ecuador's infertility clinics makes whiter children in the context of nation building. In the new practice of anonymous egg donation, both race and kinship are enacted within the specific political and economic history of malleable bodies in the Andes. This history involves the sexual domination of darker women by lighter men, producing lighter illegitimate children. Because of this charged legacy, anonymous gamete donation can be a particularly fraught experience for browner women like Teresa. The history of sexual dominance and lightening persists in the practices of IVF physicians and sperm donors. Female egg donors have become new actors in this ongoing project, participating in whitening the nation through the bodies of other women.

Although IVF practitioners and sperm and egg donors use genetic material to create children, they don't view that material as producing the only claim to kinship. Rather, in Latin America, with its history of mass illegitimacy, the care and cultivation of children is an extremely important marker of connection. Gamete donors possess the valuable ability to transmit beauty, a trait seen as inseparable from whiteness, but beauty is also considered cultivable through the kinds of care that families invest in their children.

In Ecuador people can change their race (Cadena 1995; Leinaweaver 2008; Orlove 1998; Pitt-Rivers 1973; Poole 1997; C. Smith 1996; Stutzman 1981; Wade 1993; Weismantel 1997). For many people in the United States, this proposition is nonsensical, a conflation of separate domains, nature and culture. For others, the idea might be understood as simply an academic argument about the social construction of race. In this chapter, I take Andean racial malleability seriously. Informed by the science and technology studies that assert the multiplicity and plasticity of the ontological world, as well as race scholarship on the Andes and Latin America, my argument is premised simultaneously on the assertion that race is a material fact in Ecuador (as it is in the United States) and on the notion that facts are "fabricated" and thus can be altered (Landecker 2007; Lock and Nguyen 2010; Mol 2002; Latour 2010). Andean race scholarship and my own work in IVF clinics demonstrate that the fabrication of race is not merely theoretical: race is enacted and can be reenacted through a wider range of characteristics than physical appearance as transmuted through genes.[2]

Scholars in the United States have shown that the configuration of race and racial categorizations are malleable. Changing census categories and the differential treatment of racial groups attest to this (Rodriguez 2000). At the same time, race in the United States has derived much of its power through its deployment as a deterministic feature, based on Enlightenment distinctions between the stasis of biological facts and the malleability of culture (Baker and Patterson 1994). In the United States individuals are not seen as capable of changing races, even though groups may do so over time (as the Jews and the Irish became white during the twentieth century) (El-Haj 2007; Ignatiev 1995).[3] Race, especially with regard to blackness, has been considered an "essential biological category" (Baker and Patterson 1994), which is why it has been so important for scholars in the social sciences to argue that race is a social construction, with little basis in ontological reality. In the U.S. context, arguing for the social construction of race reduces the determinative power of racism.

Recent medical anthropology and STS scholarship takes a different view of the question of biological difference, arguing for an approach "to the human body in which the reality of the material is not denied for one moment but, equally, the biological body is not simply accepted as a universal entity" (Lock and Nguyen 2010). With this framework I configure race not as socially constructed, which presumes a separation between the natural and the social, but as constructed through a multiplicity of forces (Latour 2005). Biology itself is shaped by historical and material processes. Instead of positing a universal biology, we can delineate "local biologies," which take account of "the way in which biological and social processes are inseparably entangled over time, resulting in human biological difference," such as varying disease susceptibility (Fullwiley 2008, 2011), and different endocrine processes (Lock 1993, xxi). Local biologies consider a wide spectrum of material characteristics, as well as political economic histories, in understanding how people are grouped in the contemporary world. This scholarly delineation of the historically contingent formation of biology, which embeds an antiracist politics, is similar to the everyday sense of race I found in Ecuadorian IVF clinics, which serves to maintain racial hierarchies. Both discount the primacy of nature and give material weight to political and economic processes.

As we saw in the last few chapters, IVF participants who wanted children whiter than themselves are part of the long-standing project of whitening, based on the premise that race can be changed at both the group and the individual level. Whitening is a project of domination and inequality that resulted in *mestizaje*, the mixing of races, one of the cornerstones of Ecuadorian national ideology. *Mestizaje* is embedded in practices of race, gender, and kinship that began during the Spanish conquest and were furthered during the Inquisition, reinforced through the battle for nationhood, and promulgated in the labor relations of the hacienda. The project continues today. *Mestizaje* is one of the most powerful templates by which most Ecuadorians understand their race and kin connections. It is constantly reinscribed and celebrated through school textbooks, speeches by national politicians, and explicit state policies (Stutzman 1981). Its goal has nearly always been to whiten the nation.

In the past fifteen years, tumultuous struggles have challenged Ecuador's whitening project. The mass political mobilization of indigenous groups in the sierra and the Oriente and the organization of black Ecuadorians signal new racial and political forces to be reckoned with (Clark and Becker 2007; Torre 2006).[4] Although many people, like Teresa, still say that their grandparents were Indians, though they themselves are not, others now declare (at least in certain contexts) that if their grandparents were Indians, they are, too (Torre 2006).

These trends were not, however, very evident in private IVF clinics. The Ecuadorian IVF patients who participated in anonymous gamete donation shared similar goals for producing whiter children by manipulating the genetic material of gametes and through childrearing practices that focus on cultivation. Their relations of paternalistic trust with IVF doctors persuaded them to agree to anonymous egg and sperm donation despite the fear of using the gametes of strangers who might be "drug addicts," "criminals," or "blacks."

This whitening project made egg donation anxious terrain for darker-skinned IVF patients like Teresa. Although she did not say this directly, Teresa's concerns about the potential difference in skin color between her and her child recall the conquest and the sexual domination of Indian women by white men. These practices, outside the scope of state governance and surveillance, historically served the national project of whitening through the racial mixture of offspring. In Ecuador, IVF practitioners and sperm donors, key male players in assisted reproduction, were engaged in a project similar to that of *hacendados* and the purported project of Asch and Balmaceda—making whiter children.

Lightening the nation is thus still enacted through extramarital reproduction. Male IVF practitioners, perceiving their actions as noble and altruistic, select egg and sperm donors for their lightness. The anonymous egg donors are new players in this whitening project. They are whiter women, historically the most sexually policed group in Ecuador. With the circulation of their eggs, these young white women are now in one sense acting like whiter men. They contribute their "beautiful" whiteness to the national project of whitening through illegitimate means, severing their connection to any children born through the donation. The collective desire for white beauty is evident in the way that practitioners recruit and select donors and patients, in donor-egg recipients' fantasies about future children, and in the ways IVF patients cultivate their children's whiteness.

LA RAZA

When I began my research in Ecuador, I asked patients and gamete donors about their "ethnicity." Using the term *ethnicity*, as social scientists do to view difference through a cultural lens (whether religion, language, or tradition), seemed a way to avoid imposing the determinative biological criterion of race (Ratcliffe 2001). But no one knew what I meant. When I asked instead about *raza* (race), patients and other informants nodded and immediately identified themselves as mestiza or mestizo. Sometimes they said, "We are all mestizos here."[5] This answer exemplifies the continued force of one of the most successful nineteenth-century Andean biopolitical projects, whereby Ecuadorians became members of the distinct *raza* of mixture—walking embodiments of the domination imposed by Christians, then Spaniards, then Creoles, on Indians.

Mestizos are the mixture of two totemic originary groups, the Spaniards and the natives, whose often-violent combination formed many Latin American nations (Pitt-Rivers 1973). The concept of nation itself arose from the colonial processes of domination that produced these originary groups. The conquistadors were not Spanish. They saw themselves as Christians conquering and converting heathens. Spain itself came into being through this colonization process and the simultaneous recapture of the Iberian Peninsula from the Moors. Through these conquests, new kinds of humans were made "for the modern world"—*español, indio, negro, mestizo, mulato, sambo*—born out of the same upheaval that made "nations, bureaucrats, slavers, global merchants and colonies" (Silverblatt 2004, 5). *Casta* (caste) became the means of designating different groups through their relationship to labor and land (Pitt-Rivers 1973). Marking the true Christian in opposition to the heathen Moor and Jew through *casta* became the work of the Inquisition—a means to delineate purity of blood. This was a religious designation based on lineage but was not biological, as biological principles had not yet been developed.[6]

During the sixteenth and seventeenth centuries, *casta* was a legal, economic and religious, as opposed to biological, designation, even though it signified blood purity (Pitt-Rivers 1973). *Casta* helped counter arguments like those made by the sixteenth-century priest Bartolomé de las Casas for Indian rationality and humanity. Casas wanted to prevent the ongoing exploitation of Indians within the *encomienda* system (literally "commission"), the colonial system under which soldiers, colonists, or the nobility were granted a certain number of Indians to protect in return for tribute (Castro 2007). Such enlightenment arguments about the humanity of Indians posed a problem for Christian administrators, as well as for landed elites in the Americas seeking an exploitable labor pool. Purity of blood laws provided one of the solutions: it was "deployed as a means of tracking non-Christian backgrounds over several generations," thus maintaining caste hierarchies that provided the justification for hierarchical legal, economic and labor divisions, especially in the sierra (Harris 2008, 278). The *casta* categories of Indian, Negro, Español, and Jew eventually became the basis for "biological races" that kept Christianity embedded in Andean practices of nationality and race (Silverblatt 2004).[7]

Colonial elites also used *casta* to prevent rampant sexual mixture from dispersing wealth and property too broadly. In the seventeenth century, inquisitors and other colonial, secular, and ecclesiastical authorities, alarmed at how easily local peoples, especially Indians, "were able to change caste as easily as they changed clothes," attempted to establish a hierarchical order (Silverblatt 2004, 127; see also Nelson 1999). Mestizos came to be equated with mongrels, half-breeds, caste traitors, and bastards (Harris 2008; Mallon 1996; Pitt-Rivers 1973).

In the seventeenth-century Andes, *mestizaje* was also associated with the rise of international mercantilism, a newly robust form of trade in which monetary transactions were ostensibly separate from social relations. The promiscuity of trade relations mirrored the promiscuity of caste relations. When Creole women (of pure Spanish blood, but born in the colonies) began to marry wealthy mestizo merchants, mestizos lost some of their taint (Silverblatt 2004). Suspicions about their promiscuous trade practices remained stronger in the sierra, while coastal liberal elites began to champion free markets (Cadena 2000).

Eventually in the nineteenth century, *casta* became *raza*—part of the emerging biological understanding of human difference, separated from the social and political regimes that produced the concepts. In urban Ecuador the materiality of *raza* is embodied in stories of a mestizo nation, a story told at times more negatively (as one of "racial degeneration") and more positively (as one of "racial vigor") by elite groups. Elites struggled to make singular nations out of a plurality of peoples, with the vast majority of residents speaking disparate indigenous languages, participating in communal claims to land, and possessing little inclination to make themselves into citizens. Creole elites labeled these impediments to national unity and a free labor market the "Indian problem," the roadblocks to their civilizing, modernizing, and "whitening" project (Larson 2004). Extermination or isolation of the population on reservations was not the answer, as elsewhere in the Americas, because rural and urban "Indians" (the majority of people in Ecuador) supplied the labor force that sustained the colonial administration, and later the agrarian system, that underwrote the formation of the liberal state. The discourse of *mestizaje* provided a solution for the "trials of nation making" for Creole elites (Larson 2004). Elites, of course, had the most to lose with mixture. They could only "darken," and so they continued to patrol the boundaries of their families by policing their women. At the same time, they hoped that reproductive mixture between lighter and darker would create a new hybrid race that would unify the nation.[8]

The "racial optimism" that championed hybridity was different from French, English and German biopolitical campaigns of betterment through racial purity, in which mixture meant only degeneration, and race came to signify intrinsic biological attributes (Cadena 2000; Horn 1994).[9] For Andean elites, biology and race could not serve the same purifying functions as they did in Europe, because they would exclude the majority of the Indian populace, who had little claim to pure white blood, and elites who had little claim to the soil.[10] While "miscegenation was the road to racial perdition in Europe, . . . it was the way of redemption in Latin America, a way of annihilating difference and constructing a deeply horizontal, fraternal dream of national identity" (Sommers 2002, 110). Unlike many Western European states that supervised sexual practices to prevent degeneracy through racial mixing, the sexual supervisions of liberal reformers in many new Andean nations involved assimilating Indians through the often forced sexual congress of Indian women with Creole or mestizo men, producing mestizo bastards. These were hegemonic "ideas in practice": marriage helped elites preserve whiteness within the family, while producing bastard children helped to achieve whiteness for the nation (Lyons 2006; Sommers 2002, 105).

Mestizaje, as part of a national whitening project, structured the lives of women and men differently. The term implies a history of unequal sexual relations between two people of different races and sexes, the conqueror and the conquered. In the mythic "act that creates the mestizo . . . [t]he man is white and the woman is not, or one could say, the white is male and the non-white is not" (Weismantel 2001, 155). In the early colonial period, women from the Iberian Peninsula were brought to the colonies to keep bloodlines pure. These women were tightly controlled to produce legitimate, pure-blood Christian children. The policing of their reproductive capacities resonates today in the guarding of the virginity of elite Andean women. Historically, the mestiza was a sexually suspect mongrel: her promiscuity was connected to that of the mixture of market relations (Cadena 1995, 2000; Mallon 1996; C. Smith 1996), while mestizos like Spanish and criollo men came to be seen as active, predatory and virile (Cadena 1995). For some Andean elites, *mestizaje* never lost its sense of "race pessimism," seen in one narrative of the mestizos as degenerated Indians (Cadena 2000). Even for "race optimists" who celebrated *mestizaje*, the idea was, and is, that an ideal whiteness would progressively replace blackness and Indian-ness (Radcliffe and Westwood 1996).

Racial optimism was evident in twentieth-century Latin American eugenics movements, in which neo-Lamarckian thought—emphasizing "slow, purposeful adaptation to changes in the environment"—prevailed over Darwinian and Mendelian ideas about inheritance. In most Latin American contexts, Darwin's ideas were less appealing, as they emphasized random variation, individual fixity, and brute struggle for survival. These models of change "seemed to take all design out of the universe" in theories of racial betterment (Stepan 1991, 68). Instead, elite reformers promoted a "soft" eugenics that took into consideration the demographic and biological realties of the Indian majority. For this "softer" approach, which included puericulture, or cultivation of children after birth, they were dismissed by North American and European eugenicists, who saw a child's biology as his or her destiny. These differing ideologies meant that in forums and meetings, Latin American eugenicists voted several times to ignore North American and European eugenic mandates because the latter's approach to race enhancement was so much more deterministic (Stepan 1991). Latin American eugenicists favored a more "constructivist miscegenation" that rejected the "totalitarian [biological] determinism" of the north in favor of "optimistic ideas" like encouraging racial improvement through education (Cadena 2000, 18).[11] This more constructivist history of race formation is essential to understanding what my informants meant when they described themselves as mestizo.

Raza differs from the North American conception of race. Both race and *raza* are configured by "contrasting racial hierarchies through the lens of descent" (Pitt-Rivers 1973). Race in the United States, however, generally means a biologically embodied identity that is inherent to a person. It's considered interior, eternal, and somewhat determinative, a set of characteristics that cannot be changed by human effort or the environment (Baker and Patterson 1994; Clark 1998; Palmié 2002; Stepan 1991). This determinism contributes to the pernicious justification of discrimination against groups designated as inferior races. *Raza* in the Andes also tends to signify a materially and biologically embodied identity; however, this materiality is not necessarily deterministic. *Raza* is experienced as alterable, through changes in body and comportment. It is not entirely genetically determined.

But while *raza* is more pliant than race, it can be used to justify equally pernicious designations of difference. The notion that "we're all mestizo here" is an "all-inclusive category of exclusion" (Stutzman 1981. 45). *Mestizaje* flattens difference while simultaneously placing people along the continuum between dark and light. As Peter Wade has pointed out, although Latin American *raza* might appear as more culturally and socially based than North American race, both are products of historical, social and material processes, and both make associations and links to explain the configuration of a hierarchal world: "What is at issue here is the reproduction of societies, i.e. the maintenance of categories and inequalities over time and the intergenerational transmission of essences and appearances, and in this sense genotype is not less changeable than phenotype" (Wade 1993, 30; see also Pitt-Rivers 1973; Silverblatt 2004).

Though there is nothing liberatory about it, the malleability of Andean *raza* provides another critical means for understanding human difference. In Ecuador, shifting one's *raza*, or announcing oneself to be mestizo, is harnessed to the ultimate goal of whitening. This goal has found one more site of implementation in Ecuadorian IVF clinics.

The formation of *raza* involves the assertion of relational distinctions among kinds of employment, religious practices, dress, language, education, social and sexual conduct, and diet, as well as distinctions based on skin, hair, and eye color. Through cultivating particular educational pathways, languages spoken, exchange relations, and relations of care, *raza* can change between childhood and adulthood. The nondeterministic distinctions of *raza* are reinforced every day by the race optimism embedded in racist comments like the one made by the son of a plantation owner to the anthropologist Rudi Colloredo-Mansfield: "The Indian who has overcome his origins, besides being educated, is an Indian who bathes" (Colloredo-Mansfeld 1998, 185). This thoroughly racist statement assumes that "Indians" can overcome their origins through behavior.

Hygiene practices such as bathing are forms of *decencia* (decency) that allow for racial mobility, especially if linked to improvement through education. Education is considered part of the "innate difference" between people, part of the equation of *raza* (Cadena 2000). In Ecuador, it has been one of the main strategies for making national citizens out of Indians. "Indeed by definition Indians were seen as ignorant, because it was assumed that Indians who were educated would automatically become mestizos" (Clark 1998, 230). Educating one's children, then (ideally in the private sector), is a parent's duty. Private education whitens (Leinaweaver 2008). Children who misbehave are chastised as both *mal criada* (badly raised) and *mal educada* (badly educated). These insults, used interchangeably, indicate a lack of cultivation for which presumably the parents are to blame.

Commentators on contemporary race practice in the Andes have noted that *raza* can be both temporal and relational: many people migrate within Ecuador as well as to other countries and must live within several racial realities. A woman can be an Indian when in the city trading with urbanites and mestiza in her home village when trading with kin who have never left (Weismantel 2001). Children within the same family can be of different *razas*. Individuals can be more and less favored as children, depending on skin color, and as adults, based on differences in employment and geographic location.

Kinship practices are also linked to race. In the rural Andes, the relation between a parent and child is primarily constituted through care and feeding, not through genetic lineage. Some urban Ecuadorians, like social workers and nurses, who are often sent unwillingly to work in rural areas, insist on a more deterministic sense of race when faced with the "fluidity" of Indian *raza* and relatedness (Weismantel 1995). Where the Quiteños see adopted children, Indians see biological relatives, with the bond established through care and metabolic processes of feeding. For these Quiteños, the Indian "misunderstanding" of modern scientific facts of kinship can be viewed as an impediment to national civic participation and modernity. This attitude underscores how in a heterogeneous, developing nation such as Ecuador, any form of otherness, including kinship practice, can be criticized as that blocking progress toward a whiter nation (Weismantel 1997). Urban mestizos contrast their superior understanding of biological relatedness to that of rural Indians. In Ecuadorian IVF clinics, however, their own sense of relatedness often tends to be more fluid than deterministic: there, genes are often considered of little importance in constituting relations or race.

Education, diet, and language are all attributes that social scientists might classify under the rubric of ethnicity. They represent a set of historical processes distinct from physiology. To understand racial realities in Ecuador, it is essential to analyze physiological attributes such as skin color without separating them from these other attributes and characteristics. In Ecuador, the materiality of skin has a "history, flexibility, [and a] culture" (Latour 1999, 3). As described above, Christianity's call for the transcendent brotherhood of all human beings and the ease of mixture between castes and religious practice threatened the structured hierarchy that fueled the colonial labor economy. One of the responses to the problem of hierarchy, employed both on the Iberian Peninsula and in the New World, was the call for the purity of blood.

This mandate was replicated later in many Northern European nation-states that attempted to police their citizens' deep and essential natures (Foucault 2003). But the campaign for purity of blood was a losing battle in most Latin American nations because it excluded the majority of the populace. In the Andes, where "illegitimacy" was pervasive, skin color did come to matter profoundly, along with all the other materialities that make up *la raza* (Harris 2008).

Black skin is a sign of a different sort of being. As Manuel and Teresa told me, blacks cannot whiten. Historically, this distinction was made on the basis of physiological, religious, legal, and economic factors. During the colonial period, Africans were brought to Latin America as slaves. As non-Christians, slaves were placed "outside the circle of humanity" and thus did not have "destinies, as free persons did" (Brown 1992, 61). Heathen Indians, by contrast, could become Christian. Moreover, in the Andes, African slaves or ex-slaves "could never become full legal persons" because they were not descended from free vassals of the king: they were natives of another place (Harris 2008). This distinction has persisted, so that in the context of twenty-first-century egg donation, Indians, mestizos, and whites can shift race, but blacks cannot.

Some arguments for the social construction of race downplay the tremendous amount of status that light skin confers. Family aspirations and material resources tend to be focused on the lightest child. Darker children are taken out of school earlier and placed in trades or made to do more of the domestic work. Whiter children are allowed to attend school longer, because their families assume that with lighter skin the child will have more opportunities in the world. This assumption is repeatedly confirmed and is self-perpetuating (Buechler and Buechler 1996; Cadena 2000; Lancaster 1992; Weismantel 2001).

Reading the different material codes of *raza* requires some sophistication. When I first moved to Ecuador with my children, my seven-year-old daughter and I watched one morning as a woman combed the hair of a young girl waiting for her private school bus. It was clear to me that the woman was a domestic employee, most likely a live-in maid. She was Indian, probably from Otavalo, to the north of Quito, as she wore the distinctive dress of the area, had darker skin, and wore her straight black hair in braids. The girl was very light-skinned and had light brown, curly hair. After observing them intently, my daughter said, "That girl must be adopted."

"Why?" I asked.

"Because her mother is African American," my daughter replied.

At this point in our stay, all my Northern Californian daughter could see was a difference in skin color and a close relationship between the woman and the girl. She didn't know anything yet about Indians or mestizos or the unequal care relations between masters and servants. She did know about birth parents, adoption, African Americans and whites, and care relations between mothers and daughters. A woman combing a girl's hair signified a mother. My daughter was aware that their different skin colors played a role in the relationship, but she wasn't schooled enough in Ecuadorian reality to get the story right.

THE CULTIVATION OF ANDRÉS

Teresa's trajectory through IVF and her shifting experience of her son's skin color reflects the history of race, *mestizaje*, and gender in Ecuador. Teresa's initial anxieties about egg donation were different from, and more acute than, the feelings of most of the other, lighter mestiza middle-class egg donation patients I met at the clinics. These women longed for egg donors who were whiter than themselves. Teresa, at least initially, was troubled by the prospect of a lighter donor. Her concerns were not shared by Dr. Hidalgo, who assumed that everyone would prefer a light-skinned child. His attitude reflected that of a history professor I spoke with at an elite Quiteño university. When she heard about my research, she turned the conversation toward adoption, and commented, "It's natural for Indians and poor people to adopt, because they don't have to worry about skin color." But Teresa had been worried.

The history of Indian and mestiza sex, as well as the differing gender and sex templates available to men and women in Ecuador, were apparent in Teresa's focus on establishing Manuel's resemblance to their child. A lighter child could be considered a sign of her sexual coercion by a whiter man or of her unfaithfulness in taking a whiter lover—not an uncommon strategy, given the "thinly veiled coercion of racial prejudice" that "motivates women to choose the whitest possible of men as sexual partners, hoping to brighten their children's futures by whitening their skin" (Weismantel 2001, 156; C. Smith 1996, quoted in Weismantel 2001, 157; see also Cadena 2000). This is why Teresa was concerned that Andrés reflect his father's race rather than her own.

Teresa knew that surface things, like skin color, mattered profoundly. In and around Quito, people constantly compare their whiteness. Knowing that the mismatch between a darker mother and a lighter child could cause trouble, Teresa and Manuel rejected the first embryos that were offered to them because both gametes would come from parents with unknown skin color. With egg donation, Manuel's sperm contributed to Andre's genetic makeup. Teresa's initial fears about Andrés's skin color were overcome when she concluded he looked like Manuel, providing proof of Manuel's paternity and Teresa's fidelity. His parents' reputations remained intact, and their cultivation of Andrés's whiteness could begin.

Skin color mattered tremendously in determining Andrés's kinship, but it receded in importance as Teresa and Manuel attended to other important components of his *raza* and his beauty: his teeth, clothing, habits, and education. I asked Teresa and Manuel repeatedly why darkness is considered ugly and whiteness beautiful. Their responses were always about education, dental hygiene, drinking water, clothing—all answers that might seem as though they were changing the subject. But they weren't. Andrés's potential for whiteness began with the lightness of his skin, but his whiteness and his beauty were brought out through material practices and behaviors, such as dress and education. Manuel's emphasis on his son's education furthered the longstanding liberal Andean notion that education is the key to nation building and race improvement.[12] The couple's concern with Andrés's hygienic education—teaching him proper trash disposal and attending to his dental care—speaks to the discourse of race improvement in the Andes, where dirt is associated with Indians, as in the epithet *longos sucios* (dirty Indians, with *longo* the equivalent of *nigger*) (Zulawski 2007). Andrés's egg donor gave him a chance to be whiter than his parents, but Teresa and Manuel still had to work hard to cultivate his whiteness through other material means.

These aspects of whiteness are mutually reinforcing. If Andrés had been too white, or if he had looked nothing like Manuel, his skin color might have made it harder for Manuel to claim his son as his own, which would in turn have made it harder to raise him in a way that cultivated his whiteness.

TO "BETTER THE RACE"

If male *hacendados* and other Creoles were encouraged to advance the national whitening project by having extramarital sex with darker women, the same mandate was apparent in the management of gamete donations by Ecuadorian male IVF doctors, as well as in the attitudes of gamete donors. Patients referred to their doctor as the baby's "spiritual papa," and these physicians served as godfathers for countless IVF babies. In this role, they deliberately selected whiter anonymous egg and sperm donors, thereby "whitening" the offspring of their darker patients. Sperm donors' narratives were also replete with the knowledge that they had been selected to donate based on their lighter characteristics. Whiter female egg donors have become part of this whitening project, spreading their reproductive potential in a manner historically reserved for whiter men.

PHYSICIANS

In general, doctors tried to match egg and sperm donors to the patient as closely as possible. This process involved a variety of factors, including but not restricted to skin color. Frequently, though, it was hard to find a close match, and then practitioners would pick a lighter donor. Clinic personnel recruited sperm donors from "good" and "decent" families, meaning whiter donors, where whiteness means more than skin color. One biologist called them the "better social class." When I asked what that meant, she seemed to have a hard time answering. She didn't want to come right out and say it. Finally she blurted out that the clinic director didn't want Indians as donors. He wanted to *mejorar la raza*. I asked if he had actually used those words, and the biologist said yes, but he was joking. For her, social class was a characteristic of *raza*.

It became evident that at least some practitioners who were willing to take Indians as patients, as this doctor did, envisioned themselves as part of a national project to whiten their darker patients' offspring. In the print advertisements to recruit egg donors, their emphasis on whiteness was evident. These advertisements featured lily-white women as donors and blond, curly-haired, well dressed and groomed children. The advertisements seemed crafted to attract patients as well as donors, suggesting that potential clients would receive the ingredients necessary to cultivate a beautiful, light-skinned baby (figure 4).

When Wilson returned from Spain to work in his father's clinic, he instituted a more systematic means of matching donors. Before this, Dr. Molina's clinic had filed egg donor information in three-ring binders, just as the other clinics did. With a limited number of donors, it was easy enough to look through the binder to search for a match. Wilson had ambitious plans to find more donors, and a larger donor pool required a more efficient matching system. He proudly showed me his new spreadsheet, with columns for blood type, *raza*, skin color, and hair type. The *raza* column included the categories *mestiza claro* and *mestizo oscuro,* and I asked him what the difference was. He pointed to me, declaring that I was *blanca* (white). People who looked like him were *mestizo claro* (light mixed), and then there was *mestiza oscuro (*dark mixed). We moved on to the next column, skin color, where the categories included *claro* (light or white), *trigueño claro* (light brown, olive-complexioned), *trigueño oscuro* (medium brown), and then *negro* and *oriental.* The last term sounded to me more like a race category than a skin color, but I did not yet understand that skin color was defined through historical labor categories.

Wilson griped about the difficulty of selecting a donor by skin color and *raza.*[13] Then he lowered his voice and told me that *trigueño* is actually his secret to linking a donor with a recipient when it's hard to find a match for the recipient's skin color. He confided that *trigueño claro* is code for "people from our social class." The word *trigueño* comes from *trigo,* the Spanish word for wheat. Marisol de la Cadena observes that it signifies whiteness but born in the colonies: Creole men "who are immediately descended from the European raza have a *trigueño* color, which is pale and yellowed" (Cadena 2000, 17). *Trigueño,* then, is the color of criollos, people of European stock born in the Americas and slightly baked by the surrounding environment.

While Wilson was explaining the significance of *trigueño* in his typology, another clinic doctor, Milena, walked by. He pointed to her and said, "Milena is *blanca* like you." Milena's sister, an egg donor at the clinic, is a little darker. She was considered *mestiza clara* with *trigueña clara* skin. These sisters, then, were considered to be of two different *razas.* Milena overheard this comment and laughed, retorting that what matters more than *claro* (lightness) is *bello* (beauty).

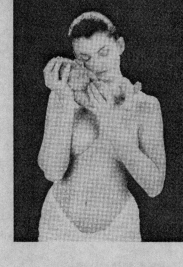

Egg-donor recruitment flyer. The flyer reads:

AYUDE A UNA PAREJA INFÉRTIL A CUMPLIR EL SUEÑO DE SER PADRES

¡¡¡¡DONE SUS ÓVULOS!!!!!

Donación completamente anónima y reciba una gratificación de 500 dólares

Las receptoras de sus óvulos serán una de las siguientes mujeres:

Mujeres jóvenes que les han quitado sus ovarios por enfermedad o tumores.

Mujeres mayores de 38 años que por su edad producen óvulos de mala calidad.

Mujeres que han perdido un hijo y por su edad no pueden usar sus óvulos

Mujeres con enfermedad hereditaria que no desean transmitirla a sus hijos.

PARA MAYORES INFORMES CONTÁCTENOS:

FIGURE 4.

Egg-donor recruitment flyer from Quito, 2003. The text reads: "Help an infertile couple complete their dream to be parents. Donate your eggs!!! Donation is completely anonymous and you will receive $500 recompense. The women who will receive your eggs are: Young women whose ovaries have failed due to sickness or tumors. Women older than 38 who, because of their age, produce bad-quality eggs. Women with a hereditary disease that they don't want to pass on to their children."

I didn't think much of it at the time, but I realized later that Milena's explicit separation of beauty and *raza* was rare. On occasion I heard people comment with surprise that someone was beautiful "even though" they had darker skin. Such comments indicated surprise because beauty is almost always equated with whiteness. Perhaps Milena's observation came from her privileged position as a young, professional woman, confident in her light skin and conventional prettiness. By distinguishing two characteristics that are almost always fused, she could lay claim to two distinctly desirable traits instead of just one.

When Milena left, Wilson continued his exposition on *raza*. "People who are *trigueño oscuro* are more Indian," he told me. His voice got lower still, and then he switched to English. "I observe patients carefully, and people who act more Indian I call *trigueño oscuro*." Thus, for Wilson, behavior informed skin color. It was difficult, he explained, to find similar donors for *trigueño oscuro* patients. This made sense, because practitioners tended to select donors on the basis of their whiteness. Patients who acted more Indian, even if they were the same *trigueño* color, were hard to match, as in Teresa's case. Ultimately, however, Wilson didn't see this as a big problem, since he, like all practitioners, assumed that these patients would be happy with a whiter donor.

Wilson used markers of behavior to determine skin color. In Ecuador, where one's *raza* is understood to be changeable, even if it is physically based, Wilson's approach provided him with a means to differentiate between people who might look the same. Skin color, class, custom, education, tradition, gender, and clothing all constitute *raza*.[14] Wilson's spreadsheet demonstrates how skin color and behavior work together to make *raza*, as well as how physicians in IVF clinics further the project of whitening in Ecuador.[15]

DONORS

The sperm and egg donors I met in Ecuador were well aware of the racial characteristics that made them desirable participants in the IVF process. The context of our interactions also emphasized their privilege. Both male and female donors usually suggested we meet in upscale malls. In these anonymous market spaces, they could tell me their stories away from their families, which was especially important for the young women donating their eggs. In Quito, as in many Latin American cities, malls are places where *gente de decencia* (decent, lighter people) can congregate, a refuge from the racial mixtures of open-air markets. Security guards are posted at every entrance, keeping an eye on who enters. The lighter-skinned donors I interviewed never had any problem gaining admission to the mall.[16]

The sperm donors I met also tended to be taller than average and were either professionals or studying to be professionals: doctors, scientists, and engineers. Their professional aspirations were distinct from those of female egg donors, who tended to study marketing or administration. Sperm donors were always unmarried, although most had girlfriends. Sperm donation was less of a clandestine act than egg donation, as women's reproductive capacities are more rigidly policed (see chapter 4): male donors mentioned that sometimes even their family members encouraged them to donate.

Almost all the sperm donors told me they weren't doing it for the money. They did in fact make much less than the egg donors—$35 per donation, rather than the $500 typical for egg donation—although many donated regularly, making much more over the long run. Most sperm donors perceived the experience as an altruistic and humanitarian act. Like the IVF practitioners, they were involved in the process of spreading a whiter seed through the nation. The young women who worked as egg donors didn't talk about their donation in this way, partly because the credit for their eggs was taken by the doctors who distributed the gametes, not the young women themselves.

The sperm donors were also more boisterous, usually joking about the process. They had more to joke about. Egg donors never tried to make egg donation funny. Donating eggs isn't associated with sexual pleasure. It involves injections and anesthesia, abdominal swelling, and sometimes bleeding. Vaginal penetration by the ultrasound probe threatened loss of reputation because of its association with sex. Sperm donation, on the other hand, involved male sexual pleasure, which was celebrated, especially in the context of inseminating the nation. Most of the young men I met donated once a month. A few donated once a week. This routinized bodily practice involved some sacrifice. Sperm donors weren't supposed to ejaculate for two or three days before their donation. Some reported that their girlfriends found this annoying but still supported their activities. Most of the sperm donors I met had also donated blood in the past, an unusual activity in Ecuador, where blood donation rates are low. Both sperm and blood donation were perceived as contributions to the *patria*, the nation.

Three Friends   One of the liveliest of my ethnographic encounters was an interview with three young sperm donors at an IVF clinic in the summer of 2002. Ricardo, Luis, and Carlos donated together once a month. They had been friends for years: they told me they were friends "to the death." All three attended a private university near the clinic. They all had relatively light skin, though I don't know how Wilson would have characterized them in his spreadsheet. I talked with them in a clinic recovery room, Ricardo and Luis lounging on the bed, both in suits, and Carlos perched on a chair in his cowboy boots, legs dangling over the edge. All three were full of energy and bravado and loved to talk. They told me they were "embarrassed" the first time they donated, but now they "loved it." They got along well with the laboratory biologist, the woman who took their samples and coordinated their donations. They joked about overfilling the collection jar and having to ask for another, and about not needing the pornographic magazines provided in the collection room. All they needed was to close their eyes and use their imaginations. They also joked about how great it was to be paid to masturbate. Luis bragged that if he'd made $35 each time he'd masturbated since he was ten, he would be a millionaire. Carlos pointed out they were all millionaires—in terms of sperm, that is. They all wanted to make it clear they weren't doing this for the money. Because "children are the route to happiness," their donations made people happy. Assisting people in need had never been so enjoyable. Sperm donation and Catholicism weren't contradictory practices, because they were helping families have children.

Ricardo, Luis and Carlos were all from middle-class families. They imagined that couples who used sperm donors would have the resources to raise their children well. Ricardo explained, "These are good people. We are helping the good people that want a child. There are many people in this country that throw out children, and other people that can pay money for them." Ricardo and Luis didn't want to know specifically what happened to children conceived from their sperm, but they were invested in the idea that these children would be "well educated" by "good people," both considered characteristics of whiteness. Luis had a special hope that a child from his donation would have his own room, because he'd had to share a room with his brother his whole life.

Carlos wished he could have information about any child born through his donation. He would wonder about the child's future: "If he looks like me? If he works? What he studies? Is he married? Does he have kids or friends? Is he happy? I would like to know this, and everything about how he looks physically." Yet all three young men seemed otherwise unconcerned about their relationship to any child born through IVF with their genetic material. They clearly felt that relations of care are much more important than genes in forming kinship relationships.

Ricardo said, "It won't be my child, but it will have my genes. It's part of my physical being, but not my being. It will be a child of another person that has another last name. It will spend nine months in another family. It's not my child, since I would want to care for my child from the beginning." His remark articulates a particular set of practices involving the establishment of kinship through care and cultivation in a nation with a prevalent history of mass illegitimacy. Though the donors were involved in producing some physical characteristics, they believed that the parents provided other, more important, material means to make a child.

Ángel   When I met up with Ángel on a street corner, I was surprised. He wasn't like the other sperm donors I had met, all paragons of virility. He was pudgy, short, and disheveled, with a distracted air. But he did have very pale skin and, most unusual, blue eyes. Ángel had been in the country for about six years. He was from Chile and was living in Quito to attend medical school. He had accompanied a female classmate to an infertility clinic to see about becoming an egg donor. The doctor rejected her immediately when she told him she had never been sexually active, which was the usual (though not universal) requirement; then he turned to Ángel and asked if he would like to donate sperm.

Unlike the other donors I met, who were all Ecuadorian, Ángel didn't see his donation as being helpful to an infertile couple or part of a nation-building project. Like many people from the Southern Cone countries, Ángel was disdainful of Ecuador. Of course his sperm was desirable here, he noted with nonchalant superiority. "They are paying for the quality of the sperm. . . . Do you understand they selected me because my eyes are blue? I am the only donor with blue eyes." Ángel told me when he called home to tell his mother and sisters that he was a donor, they all nearly died of laughter. I imagined them finding it hilarious that their baby brother, the foreigner, was spreading blue eyes among the brown-eyed Ecuadorians. Ángel was the only sperm donor who told me he did it for the money. Though he said he didn't really need it, the weekly payment was helpful for paying cell phone, transportation, and cable bills.

Ángel imagined that a child born from his sperm would resemble him. He had already had a child with another medical student from Colombia. Despite the fact that she was darker, their child looked like him. "The mother of my child is *trigueña*, super *trigueña*. Dark hair. Darker skin. And my son is white with blue eyes. So I have dominant genes. Those future children could be the same." In the Andes, *trigueña* signifies light brown skin, closer to white, whereas for Ángel, the Chilean visitor, *trigueña* signified someone darker than himself. Along with whiter skin, Ángel thought that donors, both male and female, needed whiter clothes. He had seen some young women in the clinic who wanted to be egg donors, but they wore "indecent clothing." "Of course they were rejected," he commented. "The doctors and the patients—they want someone better. This is not to be racist or anything. But I believe that the people who pay for this, they want a good product." In Ángel's estimation, skin color, eye color, and clothing all work together to pass on the desirable traits of whiteness. A "good product"—donated egg or sperm—transmits both physiological and behavioral attributes.

Marco Marco had a master's degree in biology and worked at the most elite private university in Ecuador, teaching science and running scientific programs. He was tall and commanding. At twenty-eight, he was older than the other sperm donors I met, and he had been donating sperm for three years. Marco was well spoken and outlined for me his sperm-donating mission. Unlike almost all Ecuadorian men I met, including donors, he didn't want children of his own, but he felt it was his duty to help others who did. He talked quietly, while emphasizing his altruism and the very high quality of his sperm. He called his sperm donation "a noble cause above money" and reported that his whole family was very proud of his donations. "I completed my biological mission that God gave me. My genes will continue. Not many people have the same idea. They put their genes and their ideas in their children. I want to leave my genes in the children [of others] and my ideas in my students." In effect, both of Marco's projects—donating sperm to pass on his genes and inseminating his students with his ideas—worked to whiten the nation.

Marco was also proud of donating blood, which he linked to sperm donation: "I donated blood in the past. I am advanced physically. My size and my physical capacity are bigger than my friends, who are small. I can help more people than them. To donate blood and to donate sperm—they are the same. My blood goes to people with physical complications; my sperm will help a family with emotional complications."

Marco saw his mission as extending beyond the nation to all of humanity: "Jesus has a huge love of humanity, and [my donations] help me love all humanity even more." Unlike the three friends who imagined the specific families they might help, Marco, rather unusually, was invested in the idea of contributing to a collective beyond Ecuador. Like the others, he didn't see his donation as establishing kinship between himself and children born from his sperm.

The experience of egg donation was very different from that of sperm donation. For women with the capacity to produce whiteness, their reproductive abilities have tended to be confined within the bounds of a family. In consequence, egg donation was regarded with less approval.

The link between egg donation and illicit sex was especially pronounced. The public ideal of female virginity until marriage is fairly strong in Ecuador, though nearly all the egg donors I met had been sexually active at some point. Very few unmarried young women in Ecuador have regular vaginal exams: because of the penetration involved, they're considered appropriate only for married women. Several donors were concerned because donation involved multiple insertions of a vaginal ultrasound probe and removal of the eggs through the vagina. One donor I met who had never had intercourse thought this penetration might put her claim to virginity in question. In one case, where a niece was donating to an aunt, she and the aunt lied to her parents, telling them her eggs would be surgically, not vaginally, removed (see the story of Miriam and Doris in chapter 4). The young women who were willing to undergo these procedures to become anonymous egg donors were making money from their ability to instill whiteness.

Ana   Ana was a donor from Colombia, and like Ángel, she was explicit about her racial contribution to children born of her eggs. She was especially disdainful of Ecuadorian women her age, who she said seemed scared of everything, acting like "wet cats." She didn't think many would be brave enough to donate. According to Ana, genes are transmitted in egg donation, "but nothing more." She had a dream about a baby born from her donation that looked just like her: "Very white, very white. It had my eyes, or little darker, with very long eyelashes. It was a very beautiful baby. It was a boy. In all of Latin America we are mestizos, and we are a mix of Indians with Spanish—each time improving the race a little [*mejorando un poco la raza*]."

Beatriz   Beatriz had three children to support by the time she began the donation process. She and her husband ran a child-enrichment center in Northern Quito, where middle- and upper-class children could be tutored for various scholastic tests. The business was struggling but holding on. Beatriz saw herself as an excellent potential donor because, as she explained to me, she was "white"; she was one of only two IVF participants I encountered who thus identified their *raza*. Beatriz was the most explicitly racist donor I met. She was sure the doctors were looking for donors with a white complexion and light eyes. She explained that egg donation was superior to adoption because of the high risk of getting an Indian child with adoption. Beatriz used the derogatory term *longos* for Indians, commenting, "There are little children of scarce resources who are physically ugly, the indigenous *raza*." Beatriz's cousin had adopted a child, and according to Beatriz,

"Everyone knows she is adopted because she looks like the indigenous *raza*. From the beginning, this child has other customs that are totally distinct. While all the other kids are calm, she hits and bothers everyone." As Beatriz saw it, poverty, ugliness, and misbehavior were racial characteristics of Indian children. She was more of a race pessimist than other IVF participants. In her view, cultivation could do little to combat the bad behavior and ugliness of a darker child.

ON BEAUTY [17]

The valorized whiteness of beauty permeates the Andes. A few cases in point:

- While riding the bus through the sierra, you might stare for a long time at the back of another bus from the Trans Andina Fleet, whose icon is a pure white Inca princess. She travels around the countryside, simultaneously evoking the glorious Inca past and hopes for a whiter future. Her opposite, a monkey-faced black savage, is put to work as the icon of the successful, low-priced sierran restaurant chain Menestras del Negro. A *menestra* is a mixture of brown lentils and white rice from the northern coast, where the majority of residents are Afro-Ecuadorians. Sierrans call them *monos,* or monkeys.

- On the Colombian *telenovela Yo Soy Betty la Fea,* wildly popular throughout Latin America in the early 2000s, Ugly Betty had four friends, a Greek chorus called *la quatrel de las feas* (the four uglies). Three of the women were heavy, dowdy, older mestizas. The fourth was young and slender: the only reason to designate her as ugly was that she was black (Rivero 2003, 4).[18]

- Zumbaguan Indians in rural Cotopaxi Province call themselves *runa,* which means both "the people" and "ugly." *Suca* (beauty) also refers to whiteness. The oppositional pairs *runa/suca,* ugly/beautiful, and worthless/valuable are internalized from a young age (Radcliffe and Westwood 1996); Teresa had internalized a sense of herself as ugly.

- On the few occasions that a sierran told me about a successful adoption, the success lay in the child's surprising beauty. The adoptive parents "spoiled" these children for their beauty, and they were allowed to get away with behavior that would never be tolerated from a darker child.

The liberal, multicultural celebration of mixed beauty in North America in some circles doesn't apply in Ecuador, where mixture is reality and whiter racial purity the ideal.[19] Teresa's cultivation of Andrés's beauty might seem to exemplify what Charis Thompson (with reference to North American IVF clinics) has called "strategic naturalizing," with biological kinship configured in a remarkable number of ways" (Thompson cited in Carsten 2001, 113). Thompson demonstrates that relatedness in U.S.-based assisted reproduction is produced by emphasizing and downplaying certain parts of "ancestry and descent, blood and genes, nation and ethnicity" (178). Teresa shifted from worrying whether Andrés's facial features would look like Manuel's to asserting Andrés's white beauty. This could be read as strategic naturalization. But using the term *naturalizing* in this instance is misleading. Strategic naturalizing might help us think about relatedness in North American IVF clinics, precisely because nature, in the form of biology and genes, is such a powerful tool to convey concrete reality. In Ecuador, the "natural," the biological, and the genetic all shape people's thinking about relatedness, but they don't have the deterministic power that they do in North America.

Teresa and Manuel's cultivation of Andrés's beauty might also sound similar to narratives of "passing" (as white) from the American South. Certainly, there are many similarities at work: mestizos are born into a world of mixture, just as mulattos, quadroons, and octoroons were. And beauty and skin color in both Ecuador and the U.S. South are inextricably enmeshed with economic potential. But there is a huge distinction between blacks passing for white in the United States and the idea of people from darker-skinned families becoming beautifully white in Ecuador. *Passing* implies an immutable biological reality, so that those who pass as white on the surface are still considered black. But to Teresa and Manuel, whose grandparents went from being Indian to being mestizo, Andrés will never have to "pass" for something he is not. His elegant clothing is not a disguise or a pretension but evidence of who he is. Acting white is the same as being white. White beauty is a "political economy of the body" that involves practices, behavior and appearance (Lancaster 1992 223). It does not entail notions of deep, unchanging interiority.

Raza, then, does not indicate fixity or depth. It's pointless to make a distinction between exterior or interior, whiteness or beauty. Cultivating beauty and whiteness is part of the care of the self and especially the care of others, a project of ethical management for economic gain. Beauty in the Andes is more than a frivolous (feminine) concern with appearances: it has a long history, going back to the colonial period, where the blood of different *razas* was rated along a scale of stain (Silverblatt 2004). As with other racialized technologies, such as plastic surgery, in gamete donation, the recipients hope that donated eggs and sperm will confer all sorts of possibilities and privileges. The skin color Andrés inherited from the egg donor gave him the chance to become beautiful; Teresa and Manuel are cultivating that potential beauty, tending to his teeth, hair, clothing, and behavior to help him make his way in the world and perhaps thereby bettering their own situation. The family's investment in Andrés's lightening is not only for his benefit but also a cultivation of their collective economic future.

THE REALITY OF *RAZA*

Teresa and Manuel's experience of IVF, along with my accounts of gamete donors and recipients, attests to the difficult question of the reality of race. To what degree, if any, does physiology determine identity? For Andeans, the color of their skin plays a large part in determining their economic destiny, but it's not the only factor in play. Donated eggs and sperm convey important material characteristics, but these must be cultivated. They transmit skin color, eye color, beauty, hair color and texture, but they cannot, by themselves, convey *raza*. Other forms of biological and physical connection also come into play. A woman's placenta transfers blood to a gestating baby, also transmitting emotion over the course of a pregnancy. After birth, a mother might transmit breast milk, and parents also transmit other kinds of nourishment, clothing, and care. Mothers can massage infants to make them grow straight, "like a lump of clay, molding and shaping its body before it hardened." The baby's physiology isn't entirely determined genetically before birth but is "eminently malleable through human interaction" (Morgan 1998, 23).

North American critics of egg donation and surrogate motherhood have long warned that such practices reinforce racial hierarchy and domination, allowing white couples to exploit the bodies of brown women in their quest to reproduce (Corea 1988; Arditti, Minden, and Klein 1984). These early fears were not initially realized, as most American couples who employed surrogate mothers stayed within "the race." They wanted a surrogate to look like them, even if the surrogate made no genetic contribution to the child (Roberts 1998b). This implies that race in North America isn't experienced as strictly genetic: there is an idea that race is catching.[20]

Race and racial hierarchies also play a complicated role in gamete donation in Ecuador. As Teresa's story demonstrates, racial divisions were indeed important in egg donation in Ecuador, but not always in the ways predicted by North American scholars It's difficult for darker women to get anonymous donors who look like them (as Teresa initially wanted to) when practitioners, as well as sperm and egg donors, are committed to contributing to the national project of *blancamiento*.

The UC Irvine fertility clinic scandal demonstrated how Latin American constructivist and optimistic national projects of whitening do not translate well to the United States, where biological essentialism is more powerful. Although the alleged scheme to procure North American eggs for Latin American women implies a strong belief in the materiality of traits conferred by gametes, one of the doctors involved, Ricardo Asch, downplayed the ability of genes to determine relations. Given the history of soft eugenics and race optimism in Latin America and the practice of gamete donation in Ecuador, we might say that genes participate in the formation of kinship and race, but they do not solely determine these traits. Kinship and race are significantly developed through cultivation and care.

In Dr. Hidalgo's clinic, it was left to Teresa and Manuel, two twenty-first-century mestizo Indians, to work through the problems of skin color and connection, race and relatedness, in their encounter with the tensions and pleasures of technoscientific procreation with donor eggs. Teresa's willingness to partake of these technologies to produce a whiter child in turn made her lighter. She took great pleasure in many aspects of IVF, including ultrasound and blood tests, which were all new experiences expressive of private care. Her anxiety about undergoing IVF involved not the technology or the idea of procuring eggs from a genetic stranger but only uncertainty about the skin color of her child. Teresa knew why most patients wanted whiter donors for their gametes, but it took her longer than most mestizo Ecuadorian IVF patients to want the same, because of her own position in this racially optimistic terrain. To understand Teresa's trajectory through IVF, it is essential to remember that in the Andes, what might seem like immutable conditions like racial identity can be changed through cultivation.

When Blood Calls: Frida and Anabela

In the summer of 2003, Frida, a clothing importer living in Queens, New York, returned to Ecuador, the country of her birth. Frida often imported inexpensive clothing from Quito, but this particular trip included a transaction of another sort. Frida and her husband, Arturo, a limousine driver and her business administrator, had wanted to have a child together since their marriage ten years earlier. After two years of trying, they consulted with Dr. Molina's infertility clinic in Quito, where they were living at the time. He diagnosed Frida with blocked fallopian tubes and recommended IVF treatment. Frida didn't have enough money to undergo the treatment, so she decided to dedicate herself to working in order to save enough money for the procedure. In 1996 she moved to the United States, where she could make more money. Frida planned to receive treatment at Dr. Molina's clinic, which was much cheaper than attempting a cycle in the United States.

Less expensive treatment wasn't the only thing that drew Frida back to Ecuador for IVF. At forty-six, Frida was deemed too old to attempt IVF with her own eggs, so she wanted to make use of eggs from Anabela, her nephew's wife, who was twenty-five. Frida and Anabela were close. When Frida left for the States four years earlier, she had given her nephew Javier and his wife $10,000 in merchandise and a year's free rent at her clothing stall in one of Quito's open-air markets. With Frida's continued support and advice, the couple's business had done very well. Anabela had expanded to two stalls, which in turn allowed her to expand her family to two children. Anabela saw egg donation as a way to repay Frida. She told me, "I have so much gratitude for her, and I already have two children. So it's no problem. It makes me feel good. My aunt is like my mother. I have nothing without her."

In fact, Anabela had been willing to do more. When she first learned about Frida's problem, she had assumed that she would need to act as her surrogate mother, because she had seen this arrangement on a *telenovela*. When Frida explained that she only needed to donate eggs, Anabela was happy that Frida would know what it was like to be pregnant. And if Frida carried the pregnancy instead of Anabela, then Frida's maternity was less in question.

After the egg transfer, Anabela was worried she'd gotten something out of the exchange that she hadn't anticipated. She and Javier had unprotected intercourse while she was in the ovarian stimulation phase of the cycle. The clinic doctors had warned her to abstain from sexual relations during this time, but she had an IUD and decided it would be fine. At her postdonation checkup, the ultrasound clinician had seen what might have been a gestational sac. Anabela thought she might want a third child eventually, but her youngest child was only nine months old, and she was too busy with her clothing business to be pregnant again.

The day of the embryo transfer, Anabela and I sat by Frida's bed and talked. I barely got a glance at Javier. He stood outside the room in the hallway the whole time, holding his baby. I wondered if Javier saw the egg donation a way of paying off his debt to Frida. In addition to supporting the couple, Frida had taken care of Javier when he was young. But it seemed that the primary relationship being cultivated with the exchange of eggs and market stalls was between Anabela and Frida.

Throughout her treatment Frida was in constant negotiation with God. Early on she reminded him that he gave Isaac to Sarah when she was ninety, and John the Baptist to Elizabeth when she was fifty. Frida did become pregnant with twins. Just beforehand, when she was worried the IVF treatment wouldn't work, she chastised God for not giving her children. Frida told Dr. Molina about how she scolded God, and he laughed and told her that her strong faith would get her pregnant. Neither knew at that point that she already was. After the positive pregnancy test, Dr. Molina reminded her to give thanks to God. He told her, "God is on top. I only apply my technology, but what he does is above everything."

When I heard of Frida's pregnancy after she returned to New York, I imagined that her transnational alliance with Anabela was flourishing. They were two maternal figures making babies together, just as they'd done business together. As with most of the familial donor exchanges I had observed so far, it seemed that the transaction would have a happy ending.

In 2007 Frida was again living in Quito, now with her three-year-old twins, Natalie and Carlos. Although she was busy managing her children and her new business importing men's clothes from Peru, and looking after her aged mother, she proposed a time when we could meet for twenty minutes at a coffee shop in an expensive hotel near the U.S. embassy.

Frida walked into the coffee shop looking marvelous: well groomed, with glossy skin and hair, and glowing in a pink jacket and matching pink glasses. She had seen Anabela the day before. I asked her if she saw Anabela regularly, and she said, "Of course! She's family." As we got to talking, Frida's twenty minutes turned into two and a half hours. She had so much to tell me that I ran out of tape. When we said goodbye, she told me how good it was to talk to someone so completely unconnected to her family.

Frida and Arturo's relationship had become increasingly rocky in the years before she did IVF, a problem she hadn't mentioned when we first met. She was nine years older than Arturo, and she suspected he was looking for a younger woman to have a child with. When she was five months pregnant, Arturo left her for another woman in Quito whom he'd been seeing for a while and who was pregnant with his child. Frida had known about the other woman because she'd hired a private investigator to track Arturo's movements. But she hadn't expected Arturo to leave her and seek divorce. She had been in the process of applying for United States residency for him; when he left, she withdrew the application. She was nevertheless surprised that he went back to Quito because, as she put it, he "fit so well in the U.S. He is so tall and light that sometimes people thought he was American." Frida wasn't angry at the new woman, explaining, "She didn't do anything, and the only thing I wanted was to have my children."

Arturo's departure was heartbreaking for another reason, however. When Frida and Arturo had married fourteen years earlier, Arturo had brought his four-year-old daughter from a previous relationship to live with them. Frida had come to think of Pamela as her own. The girl even took Frida's last name.[1] They had attended her high school graduation the month before Arturo left, taking photos together, "like a family." Then Arturo took Pamela with him when he moved out, leaving Frida alone. Though Pamela still visited, spending whole days with Frida, it wasn't the same. Frida questioned everything about her life. Why had she worked so much to have a house and a car for Arturo and Pamela, only to end up alone?

Frida gave birth to the twins alone in New York. When they were six months old, she decided to return to Quito, where her mother could help her. The move back had been good, Frida noted. "My children have everything. And I'm happier. There you can't have *empleadas,* and here I can have two. Here I can have [the kids] in Gymboree. There I couldn't pay for it. The stimulation for kids is better here." She was able to renew all her business ties in Quito, and she made around $5,000 a month, more than ever before.

Frida credited God with how well everything had worked out. "God is grand! I have a boy!" I thought Frida was going to finish the sentence with "and a girl," but she stopped there. Arturo had always wanted a boy, but his new girlfriend had given birth to a girl, so Frida's boy, Carlos, was the prize. To involve Arturo a bit more with her children, Frida offered to let him name the boy, but Arturo said he didn't care. Despondently, she picked out the name Carlos. Arturo's girlfriend got pregnant again, this time with twins. Frida suspected they had used some medical intervention. The twins were both girls, and one was born dead. Frida expressed sadness about the death, but she couldn't contain her pleasure in the fact that "my son is the only *varon!*"[2]

Frida had never told Arturo that she used an egg donor when she did IVF, because at that time she was worried that he was about to leave her for a younger woman. It had been easy to keep the information from him. Besides flying to Quito to supply sperm, he was uninvolved with the process. By the time Arturo finally saw the twins, they were several months old. He was surprised at how good-looking they were: big, full of energy, dressed well in imported clothing, and beautiful. Frida gave Anabela and Arturo all the credit for the children's appearance: "Anabela's beautiful. And Arturo isn't ugly either. He's *simpatico.* He's so tall, 183 centimeters [six feet], and white. And the children, it's the same. They are so beautiful. If it had been [my eggs], they would have come out ugly and *morenito* [little and dark]."

Arturo seemed to recognize himself in these beautiful, light children and for a time was drawn back to Frida, who had finally provided him with what had eluded him so far—a son whom he could lay claim to. He started coming to the house again. But his renewed interest didn't last long. He wanted contact with the children, but they weren't enough to keep him with Frida. She was planning to tell him to stop coming at all because she thought his visits were too unsettling for the children, especially Carlos. Still, Frida said, "Children always need the love of a papa. I wanted my children to have a home with a papa and a mama."

Frida missed her own father, who had left when she was seven. She hadn't wanted her mother, who had also been a textile merchant, to work and travel so much. Now she was worried that she was doing the same thing with her own children. When she had been in Lima the week before, Natalie told her on the phone one night, "You work a lot, and you don't come to see us." This remark was like a knife in Frida's heart, and she confessed, "Inside, I'm always crying." But although she was concerned about how her children perceived her work, she was appreciative of her own mother's decisions. "She is a very strong woman, and she gave us everything."

Frida wanted to find someone new but didn't think it was possible in Ecuador, unlike the United States, where there were more divorced men. Frida's mother warned her that a new man in the house would never love her children. He might hit them or molest Natalie. She also believed that in the eyes of God there is no divorce, so any new relationship would be adulterous. Frida sighed but seemed not to dispute her mother's view. "I'm going to be a mother alone and a grandmother alone. What would a man want from me anyway? Only my economic stability."

For now, all Frida's resources were going to the twins. She wasn't interested in helping out other family members as she used to, especially as no one had supported her when Arturo left. "When I didn't have children, I helped everyone in the world," Frida said, tallying up the assistance she'd provided. She had helped Arturo's daughter, treating Pamela like her own child. She had helped her sister's daughter and her brother's children (including Javier). She had brought many of them to the United States, helping them obtain visas and paying for their tickets. But none of them had helped or comforted her when Arturo left her, and these days she only wanted to work for her children. "Now I am happy, because now I work for something that is mine: my children. My world now is my children. Maybe I'm selfish. It's not a sacrifice, what I do for my children."

Frida's relationship with Anabela had also changed dramatically. Right after Frida's pregnancy was confirmed, when things got really bad with Arturo, Anabela and Frida became even closer. Javier and Anabela gave her refuge. They were the only family members who supported her emotionally. But as her pregnancy progressed and she was about to return to New York, relations deteriorated. Before the egg donation, Frida had given Anabela and Javier the market stall and merchandise, but when she was four months pregnant, she asked them to pay her for half the merchandise because she needed the money to fund her prenatal medical visits in New York. Anabela and Javier insisted on giving her the merchandise back instead: piles of out-of-date, worthless clothing. Sitting with me in the coffee shop almost four years later, Frida chalked their behavior up to their youth and their drive to succeed. I got the sense that at the time she hadn't been so forgiving.

The couple now operated six stores, and Frida got along with them much better, but she didn't think she could ever forget what had happened. One of the biggest blows in their conflict came when Javier told Frida that she had never done anything for him. To refute these painful words, Frida made a calculation. An anonymous egg donor would have cost her $500, and that was about how much Anabela and Javier still owed her for the merchandise. To Frida, they were now even. One day she hoped to clarify this with Anabela: "You owed me some money, and I figured you paid it with your eggs."

Frida and Anabela didn't talk about the egg donation. Frida observed, "Anabela respects that they are my children." A little while after Frida's return to Quito, she overheard some of the women at the market where Anabela still had stalls saying that Natalie looked like Anabela. Frida found a way to change the subject. To me, she explained, "I consider my children my children, and nothing more. . . . They get along well with Anabela, but it's just like the rest of the family. It's not like blood calls [*la sangre llama*]." Frida hadn't wanted to use an anonymous donor because she wanted to know "what class of person" the donor was. As far as she was concerned, Anabela's contribution was similar to a blood donation, nothing more. "I won't tell the children in the future," Frida told me. "I don't see it as important that my children know, because what's important is that I had them in my womb."

Anabela was hardly ever at home because she was so busy managing all the stores that she owned with Javier. After leaving several messages, I finally reached her one day when she was sick. She said we could meet later that week at one of her shops in a mall in the south of Quito. I had always imagined Anabela at an open-air market stall, so when I saw her mall store, it made her seem especially successful and established. The store was well arranged, with artistic lighting, and was filled with expensive skater clothing for teenage boys: hoodie sweatshirts with surf logos and obscene captions, cargo pants, and sunglasses. Seeing Anabela, I was reminded why Frida had wanted her as a donor. She was like an Italian Madonna, with a generous mouth and a sorrowful face. Her skin was light.

While we walked over to the food court, she told me about moving up from the market stall, reeling off prices and marketing strategies. She told me that Javier planned to set their oldest daughter up with her own clothing business when she turned fifteen. As we got in line to buy whipped iced coffees, Anabela abruptly changed the topic. She asked if there was any way to select the sex of a child. After two girls, she and her husband wanted a boy. Javier was angry that Frida had had a boy with his wife's eggs, while he had only girls. I explained two different methods for sex selection: sperm spinning and preimplantation genetic diagnosis

(PGD). She asked lots of questions about the costs of PGD and the likelihood of actually getting a boy. She didn't seem fazed by the expense, by the idea of going through another IVF cycle, or by the fact that the procedure was available only in Colombia or Peru. She traveled to Peru several times a year for business anyway.

When we sat down, she showed me pictures of her two daughters. She was obviously proud of their pale skin color and especially the older daughter, Natalie, with her light brown, curly hair. I realized then that Frida had given her daughter the same name as Anabela's daughter. The doctor had told Frida to look for a donor with her own characteristics, but according to Anabela, Frida wanted her daughter to look like Natalie, with her light hair and "precious eyelashes, everything so beautiful. For this reason she wanted me as the donor."

Like Frida, Anabela had a lot to tell and a lot to cry about. It was as if she and Frida were talking through me, both telling me their story of the difficulties and intensities of intimacies built, lost, and partially rebuilt again. When I asked her to tell me what had happened since the egg transfer, Anabela paused and said slowly, "I would never do it again." Then she told me all that had gone wrong. She had become intensely involved with Frida's life during her pregnancy, and when Frida left to go back to New York, it was "super hard." Anabela didn't think the doctors had explained the consequences of donating eggs well enough.

In her litany of complaints, she didn't distinguish between physical and emotional consequences. "Afterwards I had a lot of problems. My gynecologist told me it was from the treatment from the excess of hormones and all that they put inside me. I ended up with cysts." The cysts were probably what Dr. Molina had seen on the ultrasound after the egg aspiration when he suspected a pregnancy. Anabela did in fact become pregnant soon after the cycle, but she had a miscarriage, which she blamed on the cysts. Since then, Anabela had hemorrhaged when she got her period and had to use huge menstrual pads to soak up the blood. She had become anemic and was worried that she wouldn't be able to have more children. She had gained weight and couldn't lose it, and she'd been depressed ever since Frida's twins were born. Anabela's gynecologist counseled her to focus on her own two children, sternly telling her, "You have no others." She felt depleted by everything. "They took sixteen eggs from me, and I don't know if it was sixteen years of my life. Now I have problems with my kidneys. I am twenty-nine, young. But I don't feel it. I don't have the same vitality."

Throughout the cycle, Frida and Anabela had been inseparable. The hormone injections were painful for Anabela, and Frida helped her through them. She came to the egg aspiration, and Anabela was with Frida when they transferred "the babies." Anabela noted, "We both saw it as 'She for me, and I for her.'" When Frida first got pregnant with the twins, their relationship deepened because Anabela supported a distraught and angry Frida when Arturo left. Anabela claimed that Frida was so angry that she sent Pamela, Arturo's daughter, away, which differed from Frida's account of the story. Frida stayed with Anabela until she was six months pregnant, and Anabela felt as though they suffered through the experience of the break-up and the pregnancy together. She encouraged Frida to stay in bed and took care of everything for her. They decided they would raise the children together.

Then, when Frida asked Javier and Anabela to repay the cost of the merchandise she had given them, everything soured. "Everything went in the garbage," Anabela told me. "It was nothing like we had thought or planned. She wounded me, and I believe I wounded her. She told me it had been bad to involve me. . . . I felt so used."

When Frida left for New York, Anabela was bereft. "It was as if she was never going to return. It was very tense. I knew the twins were my children. They are my children. They are my children." Frida didn't introduce Anabela to the twins until their second birthday party, even though she had been back in Quito for a year and a half. Other members of the family showed Anabela photos, which was almost worse than not meeting them. Things got even tenser when rumors began to circulate at the market that Frida's Natalie was in fact Anabela's daughter. Frida insisted that Anabela get rid of her stall. To prove the rumors wrong, Frida brought photos of herself pregnant to the market so that the other market vendors could see her pregnant belly. Anabela was sure that Frida thought she had started the rumor.

It was painful for Anabela to see the twins, especially the girl, Frida's Natalie. "I know the girl is *pegado* [stuck] to me." Denying everything Frida had to say about her connection to the twins, Anabela argued, "Yo se que madre es la que da, sino la que cría" (I know the mother is the one who gives [the eggs], not the one who cares [for the children])." When she saw the twins for the first time at their birthday party, her eyes filled with tears, partly because Frida's Natalie looked so much like her own Natalie. Anabela's mother also said that Natalie looked just like Anabela when she was a girl. Anabela had decided that anonymous egg donation was better because you never see the children again. Time passes and you forget. Each time she saw the twins, the pain started again for her.

Javier, too, was bitter about Frida's twins. Although Anabela was most distraught about the second Natalie, Javier was fixated on Carlos. He was now saying he'd never agreed that Anabela should donate eggs to Frida. Recently he yelled at her: "You never gave me a son. And you gave Arturo a son." It was nearly an accusation of infidelity. Anabela fought back. She told him, "I was never with this man [sexually], ever!"

Now Anabela thought they should have another child, but Javier wanted to be 100 percent sure it would be a boy. He didn't want another girl. They had learned that he had a low sperm count, and the doctor told them that was why they had had only girls. This diagnosis, however, hadn't seemed to diminish Javier's anger at Anabela and Frida. Anabela told me she also longed for a boy, as *varoncitos* attach more to their mothers. She'd been so sure she would have a boy when she was pregnant with Natalie that she went out and bought all blue clothes, which she had to give away.

Her own daughters loved to play with Frida's Natalie. They clamored to visit her all the time, but this made Javier even angrier with Frida. Anabela would try to reason with him, pointing out that Frida was family, although she no longer thought of Frida as her aunt, the way she had four years earlier.

Anabela's father had also disapproved of her donation. Although he had administered the hormone injections during the stimulation phase of the cycle, he had said as he did it, "You're giving away your own children." Anabela argued that Frida had helped her start the business, and so she owed her something in return. "Frida did not oblige me to do it," Anabela said. "I thought I knew what it would be like. But at this stage of the game, I would never do it again." Anabela slammed the table with her palm. "I say to you now, ten thousand times no. Never! Never! Never! With no one. Not even for my own sister."

Anabela still felt grateful to Frida. She listed all the ways that Frida had helped her and Javier succeed. She gave them a grand opportunity, which they knew how to exploit, because Frida had given Javier such a head for business. "She changed our lives," Anabela acknowledged.

After their relationship started to improve again, Anabela once more brought up the donation with Frida. She told Frida, "I didn't do you any damage. I gave you the best that I had. I haven't won anything. I lost more than you did." They had a good business relationship. When Anabela couldn't travel, Frida would buy merchandise for her. She had given Frida money just the previous day for a buying trip to Peru. She had helped Anabela open the mall store I had just seen, and it was prospering. Anabela was increasingly sure that her own children's future was secure, and her resentments were fading. She didn't think about the twins as much when she didn't see them. But when she went to Frida's house, it was obvious that

Frida didn't want Anabela to help with the children. Anabela sighed and looked pained, telling me: "Frida knows she is not the mother of those children. She knows that genes and blood matter. The blood brings something from the other person." Then, directly contradicting what Frida had told me a few days earlier, Anabela added: "As they say, *la sangre llama*."

FOUR

· Egg Economies and the Traffic
between Women

"Cuando la sangre lama, la sangre mata" (When blood calls, blood kills), insisted the author of an editorial in a Quito newspaper in 1994. The article criticized the indigenous political organization CONAIE (Confederation of Indigenous Nationalities of Ecuador) for rejecting a proposed agrarian development law. The law would end agrarian reform, liberalize the land market, privatize water rights, and intensify export production.[1] In her analysis of the article, the anthropologist Suzana Sawyer argued that the author, Enrique Valle Andrade, framed the controversy as a trial of nationhood, with Indians on trial. She quoted Andrade's words: "The nation is not conceived through a genetic complicity that emanates from the past, but rather as a life project moving forward, toward the future, among people whose tie of union is not blood but rather the free will to associate.... The ideologues of this ethnic organization [CONAIE] forget that the nation is a political concept that transcends the ties of blood" (Andrade 1994).

In Andrade's terms, Indians are driven by "blood impulse," "primitive instincts," and irrational zeal" (Sawyer 2004, 15). They reject the transcendent call of nationhood to further their own primordial claims to landed identity, defined through blood.

A contestation over land, nation, and economy might seem far afield from Anabela's and Frida's claims to Natalie and Carlos (see "When Blood Calls"). But both conflicts reveal a fascination with the power of blood ties. Frida dismissed it: "It's not like blood calls." Anabela harnessed it: "They say blood calls."

Like Andrade's Indians, Anabela contested Frida's connection to the twins by emphasizing blood connection. In doing so, she positioned herself as traditional. Nevertheless, in this instance, Anabela was trafficking in a modern distinction, just as Andrade was.

Andrade's opposition between tradition-bound determinations of blood and the progressive transcendence of free association is shaped by the Enlightenment distinction between matter and spirit. Anabela used blood to stake her claim to the twins. However, like Frida and most of the other people I met in Ecuadorian IVF and egg donation, Anabela more often than not participated in modes of relatedness that did not require firm distinctions between matter and spirit. Relatedness, like race, can be shaped through the material relations of care, while genes may be less important than either blood or care (as shown in chapter 3).

Frida downplayed the power of blood ties, making her sound like Andrade. However, the forces that Andrade argued can overcome blood—a transcendent sense of nationhood, life, duty, and *patria*—were not especially meaningful to Frida. By rejecting a blood imperative, Frida was not making a universalist and liberal call for free association and nationhood. Her kinship claims lie in the materiality of care. Carrying her children in utero was one of many material care processes that connected Frida to other people: another was helping her niece and nephew financially. Frida's vision of relatedness focused on the exchange of material forms of care.

Olivia Harris has argued that the Euro-American saying "Blood is thicker than water" does not apply to much of Latin America, given the continent's history of mass illegitimacy (Harris 2008). She claims that care is the more important idiom for understanding connection in the Andes. But for Frida, Anabela, Andrade, and a host of others in this chapter, blood is preeminent in determining relatedness. Among Ecuadorians involved with egg donation, blood tends to be more important than genes in making connections between adults and children.

Andrade separated the materiality of blood kinship from the transcendent spirit of nation, which embedded another implicit division: between blood and economy. In his account, Indians mired in blood relations prevent the economic progress that the agrarian development law would allow. Here, Frida's and Annabel's thoughts on relatedness differ from Andrade's. Both women saw blood and economic resources as part of the same materiality. They exchanged eggs, blood, and money. Their conflict lay in ontological disputes about the characteristics of these three entities.

Frida's was one of the several egg-donation cases I followed in Ecuador in which the donor and recipient were known to one another. Egg donations between sisters, between nieces and aunts, and between mothers and daughters not only served to make new children but were also economic transactions: they provided occasions to reflect on and maintain pathways of inheritance and property transfer. Most of these relationships were much less vexed than Frida and Anabela's. I also followed anonymous egg donations brokered by IVF practitioners, like Teresa's case (see *"Yo Soy Teresa la Fea"*). Recipients of eggs from both known and anonymous donors sometimes characterized these as transfers of blood and sometimes as transfers of genes.

Most Ecuadorian IVF physicians advocated using eggs from an anonymous donor rather than a family member. They sought to delineate the bounds of the private, heterosexual, and heterosocial nuclear family to forestall conflict within the extended family, such as that exemplified by Frida and Anabela's fraught relationship. For these physicians, blood or genes were connective substances whose power could be diminished by money. In some nations, this effect of money is not considered distasteful; in others, it is seen as so disturbing that egg donation has been made illegal.

Many patients did not share their practitioners' qualms about familial donation. Their first concern was to avoid an exchange with strangers. Crucially, egg donation between kinswomen tended to be understood as strengthening existing familial connections through the exchange of material resources, and because of this there was little secrecy about the process. In general, these patients' antipathy to paid anonymous donation was not the fact that money changed hands between family members but the fact that anonymity did not foster continued material alliance and care relations. These alliances were not taken into account by practitioners because they represented forms of female transactionality that stood outside their ideals of a heterosocial family. While Ecuadorian IVF practitioners were often invested in making IVF into a sperm-meets-egg heterosexual romance (Martin 1992), for most of the families I encountered, IVF fostered a larger network of relationships.

In Ecuador, egg donation between kinswomen differs from the "elementary structures of kinship" proposed by Claude Lévi-Strauss (1969), which always entail the exchange of women between men. It is true that the sociotechnical "assemblages"(Ong and Collier 2005) that constitute the expanding assisted-conception industry represent a traffic in women, primarily between men. Yet even though these technologies are not inherently liberatory (to say the least), they are being used by some Ecuadorian women to produce female economic alliances that have dramatic effects on their family's fates. The transfer of eggs and blood between female relatives sustained the relationships between them. The resulting ties of affection and commerce did not reflect Enlightenment distinctions between blood connections and freedom of association, kinship and economy, or between matter and spirit. Thus I argue that in Ecuador, egg donation by known donors is a traffic *between* women.

ORIGIN STORIES OF KINSHIP, SOCIALITY, AND EXCHANGE

Familial egg donation in Ecuador speaks to the mutually constituted anthropological literatures on kinship and exchange (Strathern 1985). Susan McKinnon points out that "the analogy that focuses on the power of paternity (and fraternity) to mobilize more 'natural' female resources through the enterprising spirit of the market is not 'just' a metaphor but an analogy central to anthropological understandings of what kinship and the creation of culture are all about" (McKinnon 2001). McKinnon is referring to Lévi-Strauss's oft-told origin tale of social life, in which kinship, produced through the incest taboo and exogamy, worked to bind different groups together through the exchange of women between men. Women were "the most precious possession" that fathers and brothers "naturally" wanted to keep for themselves. The incest taboo functioned to compel these men to exchange sexual and reproductive access to their women with other groups of men. This act of exchange ultimately turned "fear to friendship," diminishing intergroup hostility, providing the basis for interconnected, ongoing, and cascading reciprocal exchanges, and constituting social life—always between men (Lévi-Strauss 1969, 62, 68).[2]

This "traffic in women" and its analysis was revisited and revitalized by Gayle Rubin in her now-classic critique and expansion of Lévi-Strauss's argument, in which she grappled with the implications of productive and reproductive economic kinship systems in which women's labor is always converted into male wealth (Rubin 1975). She argued that "the traffic in women" is shorthand for expressing the social relations of a kinship system where men have certain rights over their female kin. Because women are the basis for all exchange, they are not in the position to give themselves away, and they are always less able to engage in exchange relationships: thus they are excluded from much of social life. This "asymmetry of gender equals the difference between exchanger and exchanged—and entails the constraint of female sexuality" (183). In Marxist language, Rubin called for a "revolution in kinship" (199) made possible by Lévi-Strauss's "profound perception of a system in which women do not have full rights to themselves," where sexuality and marriage must be incorporated in the analysis of sex oppression, and where "obligatory sexualities and sex roles" are eliminated (199, 204).

Although my analysis here is inspired by Rubin's reading of Lévi-Strauss, egg donation between kinswomen in Ecuador should not be understood as emancipatory or revolutionary in Rubin's sense. These women are not trying to overcome the obligatory nature of sex roles. My argument intersects with those of Rubin and other feminist anthropologists by noting how the material and gendered basis of political power and social adulthood is linked to the ability to exchange. In another provocation of structuralism, Luce Irigaray asked what happens "when the goods get together" (Irigaray 1980, 107). For Irigaray, "getting together" was a sexual challenge to the elementary structures of kinship. What if the goods (women) have sex with each other? Less excitingly, but more generally, we can ask what happens to the traffic in women when we explore the exchanges between them. How does it affect our understanding of social life when for example, the Ghanaian food distribution system is organized through the efforts of the market women who make up more than 70 percent of the vendors (G. Clark 1994)?

Feminist anthropologists have also noted that the structures of gender can turn exchanging women into structural men in at least some aspects of their lives. Lovedu women in southern Africa who give and receive cattle can marry women and become husbands (Sacks 1975), and *devadasi*s in southern India, who never marry mortal men, often perform the financial and kinship duties of sons in their natal families (Ramberg 2009). These are certainly not revolutions in kinship: they might be better read as signs of just how entrenched the traffic in women is when a woman can obtain rights to exchange only by becoming a man and by avoiding the role of wife. But these ethnographic examples do guide us toward the variety of ways that women have structured their productive and reproductive lives to exercise rights over themselves and others.

Another of Lévi-Strauss's interlocutors, Pierre Bourdieu, provides an alternative, complicating frame for Lévi-Strauss's origin tale of social life. In his examination of practices in Kabylia, Algeria, Bourdieu used the negotiations and exchanges involved in marriage arrangements to distinguish his "theory of practice" from structuralist accounts of kinship. Marriage provides a good opportunity for observing what separates official kinship—single and immutable, defined by the norms of genealogical protocol—from practical kinship, whose boundaries and definitions are many and varied. It is practical kin who make marriages; it is official kin who celebrate them (Bourdieu 1977).

In Bourdieu's account women, who are constantly making exchanges between themselves, are the practical kin who make marriages, precisely because women, at least in Kabylia, are "the persons least qualified to represent the group and to speak for it" (Bourdieu 1977, 34). In other words, Kabyle women initiate most marriage negotiations because their actions and intentions are easily disowned if things go awry. Bourdieu's argument with Lévi-Strauss is not so much that he was wrong about the exchange of women between men but that in delineating the overarching structures of kinship, he left out the myriad daily practices that shape these structures, making official kinship appear seamless to the ethnographer.

Practice is crucial to my understanding of the traffic in eggs between kinswomen in Ecuador. But, unlike the practices of women who negotiate marriage in Kabylia, the practices of these Ecuadorian women were not hidden to make way for the overarching structure of official kinship: instead these arrangements were presented as crucial to the official production and continuity of familial, economic, and social life.

Lévi-Strauss drew heavily on the work of Marcel Mauss for his theory of kinship and exchange in "archaic" societies where economy and kinship (and everything else) had not been divided into separate domains (Mauss 1990). Mauss argued that gift exchange remains a part of our own economic life; but like the social theorists who came before him, he lamented that buying and selling in a money economy contributed to the deadening of social relations, extinguished reciprocal responsibility between employer and employee, and hid the labor of workers embedded within commodities (Durkheim 1995; Marx 1976; Mauss 1990). Other social scientists have demonstrated that gift and money economies are intertwined and that the exchanges of money can be productive of sociality and intimate association as well (Simmel 1990; Zelizer 1994b). Ara Wilson calls these associations "intimate economies," which require the historical division of the economic and the intimate and then their reunification with the relations of transnational capitalism, often with attendant anxieties (Wilson 2004). This divide between the economic and the intimate remains a powerful rhetorical tool for some moderns (Latour 1993). Yet in egg donation between kinswomen in Ecuador, love and money were enmeshed with little anxiety on the part of participants.

The intersection of economy and kinship was problematic to the North American and Western European middle classes of the nineteenth and twentieth centuries. Ideally, marriage was a "haven in a heartless world" where family affairs were never mingled with the corrupting power of money, commerce, and the market (Lasch 1974). Capitalist economic relations were built up through a division of intimate affect and unpaid domestic labor separate from the market. Much of the philosophic rationale for the separation of the realms of love and money was articulated by Immanuel Kant in his discussion of value and dignity. "Whatever has value can be replaced by something else which is equivalent; whatever on the other hand is above value and therefore admits of no equivalent, has a dignity" (quoted in Rabinow 1999, 102). As economic production moved from the house to the factory, reproduction and women's labor became increasingly domesticated and privatized, removed from the taint of money; and love came to be seen as a feeling that should exist separately from economic concerns. Home and family became the repositories of dignity, while the market became the maker of value.

This separation between realms of home and market, public and private value and dignity, has gone global: it is now heard in universalistic human rights discourses against human trafficking, often painfully knocking up against more site-specific understandings of dowry, bride wealth, and death payments (Adams and Pigg 2005; Keane 2002; Strathern 2005).[3] These divides currently fuel some of the preeminent anxieties about the arrangements entailed in new reproductive technologies. The possibility that a person, especially a woman, could employ her private reproductive potential in the business of egg selling or surrogate motherhood collapses the two realms of kinship and economy (Blakely 1983; Gimenez 1991; Ragoné 1994; Roberts 1998a). It is no surprise, then, that paid egg donation has been banned in many countries and is debated in others (Steinbrook 2006). In Ecuador, however, entanglements of family and finance, and reliance on assistance for reproduction, are less problematic.

Indeed, in Ecuador, most of the IVF patients I met looked forward to telling their children that they were test-tube babies *that they had paid for.* Although pricing children according to the costs of IVF procedures might disturb sensibilities in places like Australia, Norway, Germany, and to a degree the United States (Zelizer 1994a), in Ecuador the cost of IVF children and the amount of debt accrued in their production are matters to be documented, discussed, and displayed. The expenditure of money was equated with love, sacrifice, and parental devotion and care. IVF children paid back this effort by providing companionship, effecting an exchange of intimacies and care. The expense of IVF was of great consequence for the majority of IVF patients. But spending money to generate children was seen to have inherent value. Patients' willingness to take on great debt and burdens to alleviate their childlessness signified how much they wanted their children.

Working-class and poorer patients *con bajos recursos* scraped together the money needed for IVF from their families, community bingo games, moneylenders, and small capital-improvement loans they received for their businesses. The expense of IVF made for many conversations about finance, which often led to discussions of the value (not the dignity) of children. Children were never positioned as beyond price, as they have been in North America since the late nineteenth century (Anagnost 1995; Ariès 1962; Layne 1999; Pribilsky 2007; Taylor 1997; Zelizer 1994a). The IVF patients I encountered regarded children sentimentally, but they were also regarded has having a price. Love and money were not necessarily distinct.

In 2003 Laura, an IVF patient with Dr. Padilla, sat with me at her dining-room table and took from a box all the medical receipts for her failed IVF cycle. "We have never done the accounts to see what we spent. The day that I have my child, I will figure out how much it has all cost me, and tell him." Another IVF patient, Dora, used her Diners Club card to pay for IVF. Dora and her husband owned a hardware store and also got a bank loan for new merchandise, which they used to finance their IVF cycle. When I asked her how she would feel about a baby if it was born from IVF, she replied: "I will feel normal. Well, no. I believe that I will care for it so much more because this has cost me, it cost us terribly. Everything costs. That is what they have given me, this privilege, a gift from God." Carlos, a father of IVF twins, explained: "It cost us a lot. We will tell them that they cost us a lot." His wife, Marisol, agreed. "Yes they were very expensive. We had to work very hard to have them come."

Many patients talked about doing IVF as an investment made instead of buying a better house or making some other big purchase, like a car or a television. This comparison, invoking "moralized ideals of consumption" (Pinto 2004, 9; see also Pinto 2008), was echoed by IVF doctors. They told me how impressed they were with the economic sacrifices patients made in order to undergo IVF. They lauded patients for spending their money on the generation of children instead of on large material objects like TVs. When less wealthy patients were willing to make this sacrifice, practitioners were likely to want to assist them by discounting their services.

In Ecuador children (however they are conceived) cost a lot. They are consumers with material needs and desires. What parents were prepared to give them was explicitly tied to what the children could give back in love and companionship, as well as (for some parents) how they could help the families' future economic prospects. Workers' pensions in Ecuador, where they exist at all, are often small and unreliable, and state institutions do not provide much of a safety net. Children would become members of a community of care and would give economic security in their parents' old age.

The working-class patients I met spoke more frequently about what children give in return for their care. Women in their forties, on their second marriage and with grown children, expressed the need for a child's companionship most acutely, telling me, "My child is big, and I lack a baby in the house." The companionship of children was important to women whose husbands were away for long periods working in other countries. Children were a more valuable and trustworthy source of companionship and support than a husband (Leinaweaver 2008). Thus, even for those with few resources, IVF is a productive use of money.

Many Andean ethnographers have demonstrated that kin and exchange relationships, especially among rural indigenous and working-class women and men, do not observe bourgeois distinctions between value and dignity or public and private. One of the central figures in this literature is the Andean market woman, a troubling and sexualized creature for the bourgeois order, where women ideally stay in the domestic realm (Allen 1988; Buechler and Buechler 1996; Cadena 2000; Weismantel 2001). There is no need for a term to denote merchants as market men, because in Euro-American contexts the market *is* male. Market women commit a variety of category mistakes. Their relationships with other women, children, and men are not solely defined by private nurturance but instead involve commodity and gift exchanges. Their lives cannot be easily separated into domains of private consumption and public transaction. In the Andes, interaction between siblings, spouses, parents, and children tends to revolve around more formalized exchange relations. Female nurturance is not experienced as "an obstacle to economic participation" (Wilson 2004, 15). In fact, economic participation is productive of the care relations that make up that nurturance.

The transfer of eggs between kinswomen as part of ongoing reciprocal exchanges also finds templates in *compadrazgo* (godparenthood) and child circulation, long-standing Latin American methods of enhancing and formalizing familial relationships. Although the relationships between godparents and godchildren are important, of equal importance are the exchanges that solidify the relationship between the godparents and the parents of the godchildren, *comadres* and *compadres* (Allen 1988; Bastien 1979; Davila 1971; Foster 1953; Hubbell 1971; Mintz and Wolf 1950; Poole 1991). Egg donation in Ecuador creates similar relationships.

Child circulation in the Andes, which involves informal arrangements in which indigenous Andean children are sent by their parents to live in other households, often those of relatives, works similarly to *compadrazgo* (Leifsen 2008;

Leinaweaver 2008; Weismantel 1995). The movements of children between households for labor and different kinds of economic support and care strengthen connections between adults as well as between children and the adults with whom they live. These children are not only beings that require nurturance but also economic actors in their own right. As with Anabela and Frida, ideal relationships for Andean market women consist of exchanges of gifts that are often unequal, although that inequality may diminish with time. If children are circulated into the households of market women, these market mothers expect their charges to contribute to household wealth rather than only consume it. Children in this world are wanted as much for their labor as for their love; the two are not separable.

Mary Weismantel argues that Euro-American family life is governed by generalized reciprocity, an ideology of "boundless love, . . . which creates ill defined exchanges filled with unresolved guilt and resentment. The movement of material goods within indigenous families in contrast was marked by a mannered courtesy at once more distant and more generous than the casual intimacies of middle-class life in North America" (Weismantel 2001, 140). We can see this mannered courtesy in the relationship between Frida and Anabela, which consisted of ties of both affection and money as well as carefully tallied betrayals. Anabela's donation of eggs to Frida was not part of a generalized reciprocity, or what David Schneider calls "diffuse enduring solidarity" (Schneider 1980), but rather a specific act of reciprocation for past economic assistance.

Initially, the egg donation enabled Anabela to repay her aunt for an initial gift that expanded her business and her family. As Bourdieu pointed out, ideal gift relationships are ongoing: debt keeps relations alive (Bourdieu 1977; see also Taylor 1992). The canceling of debts can be interpreted as a hostile act. When Frida decided that Anabela had paid off her clothing debt through her eggs, and Anabela decided that her eggs had paid off the debt and years of financial advice, neither woman owed a debt to the other; but Anabela lost a share in the care of two much-valued children. By systematically canceling their debts, Frida and Anabela inched closer to the perceived impersonality of the market.

EGG EXTRACTION AND EGG CIRCULATION

The use of donor eggs has been one of the most contentious issues in the development of assisted reproduction around the world. Much of the anxiety over gamete donation centers on issues of money and recompense (Ahuja, Simons, and Edwards 1999; Robertson 2006). Anxieties about the practice are manifest in the use of the term *donation* itself, when in several countries young women are in fact paid to "donate."[4] In many nations with a ban on remuneration, including most of Europe, Israel, and India, the infertility industry, along with many infertile couples, the popular media, and the medical press, has fostered a sense of a "worldwide shortage of donor eggs."[5] Explaining how this shortage came to be, when donated eggs did not exist twenty years ago, entails examining changing modes of production and reproduction that involve a vast array of new technologies and worldwide demographic and economic shifts (Cooper 2008; Waldby and Mitchell 2006).

Although paid donation is legal in the United States, there are considerable tensions around issues of payment as well as anonymity and disclosure (Mamo 2007). Nevertheless, the use of paid, anonymous egg donors for women over the age of forty has become standard in many large IVF clinics around the United States because of the higher pregnancy rates that the younger eggs of donors provide. Accurate statistics are difficult to gather in the United States because the assisted reproduction industry is not regulated, but it is estimated that 11.4 percent of all IVF cycles involved donor eggs (Steinbrook 2006).

Throughout Latin America, IVF clinics commonly offer egg donation, though arrangements vary (Borrero 2002). For instance, in some Argentine and Brazilian clinics, patients who are diagnosed as needing egg donation must provide a donor. The eggs from this donor are given to another patient anonymously, and the first patient receives eggs from another unknown donor brought by another patient. These are unremunerated exchanges with strangers. In other nations, paid anonymous donation is common. In Ecuador, practitioners coordinate both anonymous paid donation and known donation. Known donation usually involves a female relative, sometimes a friend. These transactions are not considered paid, but for the female family members, the transactions are nearly always economic.

Ecuadorian practitioners generally recommended egg donation to older patients, near or over forty, and to patients who had been diagnosed with ovarian dysfunction, (those with no ovaries, no eggs, or hormonal imbalances). I was privy to twenty-eight cases of egg donation in Ecuador, of which eleven involved known donors and seventeen involved anonymous paid donors. In Guayaquil, the practitioners counseled patients to use anonymous donors selected by the clinic. Dr. Jaramillo advertised for donors, and whenever he appeared on television, he invited potential egg donors to contact him. The practitioners in Dr. Molina's and Dr. Hidalgo's clinics in Quito preferred anonymous egg donation but would often arrange known-donor cycles as well, if the patient brought a suitable donor. Dr. Padilla, in Quito, did not arrange anonymous egg donation, so all of his patients needed to find their own egg donors. This requirement added to the number of people involved in the collective project. The presence of mothers, friends, and husbands of donors enhanced the informality and familiarity of Dr. Padilla's clinic.

In anonymous donations, I frequently met both the patient and the donor and observed their parallel cycles, though they were kept strictly separated from one another. When a patient or egg donor asked me if I knew anything about the other party, I wondered if I should follow the rules that all participants seemed generally to agree with or divulge the information. I usually said I did not know. Even those patients who wanted a few small details about the donors (or vice versa) did not fundamentally challenge the necessity of anonymity: I never got the sense that the patients or donors actually wanted me to tell them anything.

In 2000 the clinics with anonymous egg-donor programs were finding egg donors only through word of mouth. That changed in Dr. Molina's clinic when Wilson arrived home from Spain in 2003. Wilson began a concentrated effort to find egg donors, through advertising mostly at local universities, though the clinic continued to recruit by word of mouth as well. Wilson wanted to use donor eggs in more cycles because they were commonly used in IVF clinics in Spain and provided good results. Whenever I was with him outside the clinic, on the street or giving presentations at universities, and he saw groups of young women, he would joke about recruiting them for egg donation. Wilson's jokes had a sexual overtone, as they came from an elite man commenting on availability of younger, usually less elite women in public spaces. Historically, only sexually suspect market women took part in street life or in trades (Cadena 2000). Wilson's aggressive recruiting methods were successful, and the number of procedures using donor eggs quickly climbed after he arrived. The numbers dropped again when he left the clinic in 2006 and his brother Diego was in charge of finding donors, which he did mostly by word of mouth.

Church views on gamete donation seemed to have little effect on the recruitment of egg donors or patient participation. While patients, donors and practitioners usually were aware of the Catholic Church's negative views about IVF, few of them knew anything about its condemnation of gamete donation. The practitioners who did know found it perplexing, given the Church's support for organ donation. In their minds and in the minds of many patients, organ donation and egg donation were similar kinds of exchanges. As one biologist said, "It's like giving a very small organ."[6] In consequence, eggs were not necessarily conceptualized as genetic material, and even when they were, genetic identity was not seen as providing the "whole truth" of relatedness.

All the paid egg donors I met worked in some capacity, most at low-paying white-collar jobs, often part-time if they were students. They were mostly lower-middle- to middle-class in their aspirations and comportment. They were between the ages of nineteen and twenty-six, and all of them had at least finished high school.[7] Most important, all were relatively light-skinned. Several of the donors I met were Colombian, living in Quito to avoid the violence back home. Colombians are thought to be better educated, wealthier, lighter, and more cosmopolitan than Ecuadorians. Several of the paid donors were mothers: some were married, others raising children without a male partner. Some were living with their parents. Some of the donors without children had boyfriends. The married donors all had children. Doctors did not see childless married women as appropriate donors because their reproductive potential had not yet been fully harnessed for their own families. Practitioners often complained to me that finding paid egg donors in Ecuador was exceedingly difficult because young Ecuadorian women were "too conservative, closed, and religious" or (echoing a common lament about the availability of labor) had migrated to Spain in search of work.

Except for the involvement of the male clinicians who arranged their cycles, egg donation was very much a feminine activity. Most of the paid egg donors were friends or relatives of women who worked at IVF clinics. Although married donors told their husbands about the process, in general I found that egg donation was something to discuss only with other women, like the number of one's lovers or having had an (illegal) abortion, all realms of female social experience rife with the potential for male attempts at control. The female secret of egg donation contrasted sharply with male openness about sperm donation. This contrast is rooted in stark differences in men and women's ability to engage in sexual exchanges, which has much to do with the history of race and nation building in the Andes.

Most paid donors never told their fathers or brothers of their activities. These young women believed that their fathers would act to stop them from selling their eggs or at least strongly disapprove. Indeed, when egg donors did tell family members, it was usually the fathers who were the most disapproving. One young woman become a paid egg donor after her father had forbidden her from donating eggs to her half-sister a few years earlier. At that time she made a promise to God to donate eggs when she got older, a promise she kept when she moved out of her father's house. Other male figures tried to prevent egg donation as well. One young woman who wanted to donate eggs was warned by her male gynecologist, "This is your child you are giving away." She didn't agree, telling me: "It's not my child, because my child is someone that I grow inside of me that I care for. This is a part of my body that in reality I throw out each month. With this part of my body I can make a person happy. It is the same if I die and I wanted to donate my organs, and I could help." This sort of circumvention of male wishes also sometimes played a part in known donor situations like with Juliet, Consuelo's donor (see "Crazy for Bingo"), who donated her eggs even when it involved subterfuge—including avoiding sexual intercourse with her husband for several weeks.

Dramas like these exemplified one of the intangible benefits that paid egg donors seemed to derive from donation. They commonly used the term *experimenter* [to experiment] when they described how it felt to circulate their eggs out into the world. Egg donation offered them a particular means to experiment with the outer limits of behavior. It allowed them to test themselves. Could they do this? Would they be chosen? Could they evade attempts by their fathers, boyfriends, and brothers to control their reproductive and sexual potential?

In distributing their reproductive material, these young women were also assuming a historically male role, which in Ecuador has an explicitly racial valence as well. As Lévi-Strauss and Rubin argue, men tend to have certain rights over their female kin. Women are less able to engage in exchange relationships. By trafficking in their own eggs, these young women found a way to subvert their roles, to become the exchangers rather than the exchanged.

Experimentation also played out in the way that these young women took up the discourse of rights as a justification. Although I never heard women talk about abortion as being connected to a woman's right to choose, several of the egg donors I met portrayed their decision to sell their eggs as exercising their right to choose what they did with their bodies.

One young woman who involved her boyfriend in her decision to donate eggs also talked about her "right to choose" to be an egg donor in the context of her virginity. This was before most of the clinics instituted a "no virgins" rule for known donors, and this young woman had twice donated her eggs anonymously. For her, the most difficult part of her decision to be an egg donor was that although she had never had intercourse, she wasn't sure whether she could call herself a virgin after the donation. This quandary was something that she and her boyfriend discussed for a long time before she donated (she never told her parents about her donation) He eventually gave his support for the procedure. Most egg donors didn't involve their boyfriends to such a degree, but her boyfriend was a sperm donor. They both felt it was better that she help people have children than remain a virgin. And she told me "it was her right to choose" what she did with her body. Egg donation in Ecuador should not be construed as overt resistance to gender or class norms.

Becoming an egg donor involved, among other things, normative understandings about helping other women become mothers and racist views about ideal reproduction. Likewise, these donors did not imagine themselves as radical or empowered in their decision to sell reproductive body parts. The supposed "shortage" of anonymous eggs should, by the rules of supply and demand, have created a seller's market that commanded higher fees, but the donors were sellers of a clandestine sort, like sex workers, who have difficulty making collective demands for better pay and working conditions.

Uniformly, the paid donors told me they were underpaid for their donation, but they never attempted to negotiate for more. They did not complain to the doctors when the egg-extraction process was more painful than they had been led to believe. In general they accepted the terms set by the practitioners. They seemed more interested in eliding the control of male relatives than in making demands on the practitioners. Even with the low fee, most of the donors were happy with their experience. They all said they liked the anonymity of the process. I met only one paid donor who expressed regret about donating her eggs for money. She was a young mother who talked about the eggs as her "own blood."

The logic surrounding payment for egg donation in Ecuador differed from the logic in Western Europe and United States. Egg sales and surrogate motherhood are prohibited in most Western European states (Melhuus 2003; Strathern 2005). In Britain, donors are compensated only for transportation and expenses, making their actions consistent with the ideals of anonymous social altruism valorized by the British social-welfare theorist Richard Titmuss in his classic work on blood donation and the gift relationship (Titmuss 1971). The ban on compensation for eggs in Britain continues to reaffirm the Enlightenment divide between value and dignity and ensures that sentiment and economy remain distinct. In the United States, although egg sales are allowed, the process is choreographed to avoid the appearance of economic exchange. The transaction is referred to as donation. Egg donors are described by themselves and others as altruistic. Wary of charges of exploitation, practitioners in Northern California, as well as those interviewed in popular media accounts, emphasize that donors are paid for the time and effort expended, not for the eggs themselves. Egg-donor contracts stipulate that if the cycle is canceled for any reason, the donor will still be paid a prorated amount.

In Ecuador attitudes toward payment for egg donation were usually neutral to positive.[8] Everyone involved in egg donation was clear that the young women donated eggs primarily "for the money." Although the clinics used the word *donor* (*donante*) to describe women who sold their eggs, I got the sense that they might have been equally comfortable with the term *seller*. One IVF physician told me: "In general they [the donors] are persons of a lower economic level. It is not done with a girl from a moneyed family. They don't need the money. It's rare that donors say, 'I am doing it to help.' They say that when it's for a cousin or a sister. Then they are not interested in the pay. The girls who want pay, they study, they're students."

Donors told me they had used the money for buying new clothes, buying things for their children, or helping out their parents and siblings. One donor was using the money to help pay for her father's back surgery. She had felt terrible that she hadn't been able to donate blood to her grandmother when she needed it because she was too thin. Almost every egg donor told me the money was the best part of the experience, and that was why they did it. (The worst part was invariably the injections.) They told me they liked helping couples have children, but that they would never do it for free.

The structure of payment in Ecuador made clear the underlying philosophical differences between egg-donor programs in the United States and Ecuador. In Ecuador, payments to donors were understood as an exchange for goods received. When something went wrong in an egg-donor cycle and no eggs could be harvested, the donor was not paid. I observed this happening in three cycles in three different clinics. The donor's follicles did not grow as expected, and in all three cases the doctors believed that the donors had not taken their medications properly. I was able to speak with two of these egg donors, who both protested that they had taken the medication as directed. However, they had no recourse for obtaining payment from the clinics. They were upset but not outraged, since they agreed with the assumption that the money was to be paid in exchange for eggs.

RELATED BY BLOOD, GENES, CARE

When Rosa and her husband, José, underwent IVF in Quito, Rosa did not get pregnant on the first attempt, and Rosa's practitioner tried to convince her that she should use an egg donor for the next cycle. Rosa did not like this idea. She didn't have any young female family members she could ask to donate eggs, and she could not imagine using an anonymous donor, which seemed almost as horrifying to her as adoption. José had no such qualms. He was all for using anonymously donated eggs. He also thought he and Rosa should explore adoption.

It was rare to meet a couple so explicitly divided over anonymity and adoption. I believe that these differences stemmed, at least partially, from the fact that Rosa was from Quito and José was from Guayaquil. In both cities, patients and practitioners' attitudes toward egg donation were informed by reckonings of relatedness that involved material expressions of care. But I found pronounced regional differences in the ways people thought about relatedness, blood, and genes; these differences were apparent in patient and practitioner approaches to egg donation. (For work examining regional differences with regard to adoption, see also Verdesoto et al. 1995; R, Smith 1984; McKee 2003, 133; Garcia and Mauro 1992).

Doctors and patients from Guayaquil were generally more comfortable with both anonymous donation and adoption and less likely to see genes as determinative of connection. (The few practitioners in Quito who had always seemed unusual to me in their advocacy of anonymous egg donation were originally from the coast.) Most Quiteños were vocally against adoption. Patients in Quito were much more interested in known donations and more likely to invoke genes in reckonings of relatedness. Practitioners from Quito were slightly more inclined to encourage anonymous donation. Like the coastal doctors, they found it easier to arrange, broker, and manage and saw it as less likely to create family conflict. Their preference was less firm than that of coastal doctors, and it was often overcome by sierran patients, who were much more strongly inclined to select a family member as a donor. Most of the sierran patients who used an anonymous donor did so only reluctantly or after they had exhausted familial possibilities. Known donors were preferred because they reinforced family ties and the boundaries of the extended family.

The majority of Guayaquil patients I met in IVF clinics told me they liked the idea of adoption, and some had even tried to adopt through legal channels but were discouraged by their dealings with state institutions. In fact, Guayaquileño IVF patients usually brought up the topic of adoption before I asked them about it. Most of the practitioners in Guayaquil were also quite positive about the idea of adoption and sometimes counseled patients to try it, though they acknowledged the bureaucratic obstacles to legal adoption. Dr. Vega, the psychiatrist at Dr. Vroit's clinic, had a positive view of adoption, which was linked to his exceedingly explicit understanding of genes as labile and unimportant. This approach facilitated both adoption and anonymous gamete donation. He explained to me that with hundreds of years of experience with adoptions, we know that "genes thanks to God, are moldable, by the environment. They don't determine the future of a child. The child is going to have certain features of the donor, but you have heard of cases where pets look like their owners, very ugly with big cheeks. That is people in an environment that come together, begin to look the same." Vega's view of genes is very different from the popular understanding in the United States, where genes are often represented as determining fixed traits (Keller 2000, 9). For Dr. Vega, as for the Latin American IVF physicians at the UC Irvine clinic (see chapter 3), genes were less powerful: this understanding reflects a view of the material world as malleable.

Part of the reason that Guayaquileño practitioners advocated anonymous donation was to maintain clear family roles once children were born. Dr. Vega was especially firm in guiding patients away from familial donation because of the possibility of confusion and family conflict over a child's parentage. He presented himself as an ethical actor and gatekeeper and was loquacious about his role in guiding potential patients toward the correct path. He also advocated absolute secrecy as to the donor's identity, believing that in a family fight, someone might use the fact of donation against the parents, threatening their *patria protestad* (legal paternal rights). He did not believe that children have a right to know about their IVF origins.

Dr. Vega's firmness persuaded most patients at Dr. Vroit's clinic to opt for an anonymous donor. These patients accepted that the environment of family life was a more powerful influence in shaping a child's identity than its genes. Dr. Vega's antipathy to known donation ignored the ways that female relatives could use the transfer of eggs to cement and further their relationship. His version of the family, which concentrated on relations between a mother, father, and child, posed these female alliances as confusing to the child.

Dr. Leon, who practiced in Quito but was from the coast originally, was willing to use known donors but much preferred anonymous donation. She thought sierrans were predisposed to give things only to their family members and friends: as she told me, "Here, you don't invest in sentiment with strangers." She described a recent troubled case of known donation between friends. The recipient's best friend donated her eggs, but the patient kept the fact of egg donation and the donor's identity a secret from everyone, including her husband. When the two friends were together, people said that the child looked like the donor. This made the recipient unhappy, and she was trying to see less of her friend. In response, the donor had become critical of the recipient's mothering and her plans for the child's education, much as Anabela began to criticize Frida.[9]

Linda, Dr. Padilla's lab biologist in Quito, was from the coast and shared Dr. Vega's view of genetically inherited traits. Her opinions became clear one morning as she administered hormone shots to Maritza, a patient. Maritza's husband, Franklin, lingered for a while after his wife pulled up her pants and left the room. He finally blurted out a question to Linda: "If we used donor eggs, would any of Maritza be in the child?"

His question was hypothetical. Maritza had been diagnosed with blocked tubes and thin endometrial lining but was planning to use her own eggs for IVF. Dr. Padilla might have mentioned egg donation as an option, but as far as I knew that was not the plan for this couple. Linda answered by first explaining that genetically, a child would be the egg donor's and Franklin's. The donor would give the genes, "the [intended] mother transmits nothing." But, she added: "The mother would exchange blood with the baby. If the woman gets pregnant there is an interchange of blood, and the child already looks like the father because it's his sperm. In fact, children always look like the family that raises them. It's like adoption. It's incredible. Everyone thinks they look the same. They have similar characteristics over time." Franklin left seeming satisfied with this answer.

In her response, Linda activated three narratives of relatedness. The first dealt with genetics. A child born from Franklin's sperm and a donor's eggs would not be Maritza's child genetically. For Linda, however, genetics was only one means of understanding relatedness. The second narrative was about blood. Linda constructed blood and genes as countervailing forces of inheritance, arguing that the exchange of characteristics through the continuous exchange of blood in the womb would prevail over the transmission of information through genes, making it more and more Maritza and Franklin's child. Linda also linked blood to care, the third narrative. Linda evoked adoption's powers to cultivate physical similarity and connection over time, through care, as blood does in utero.

Linda's argument invokes care and cultivation as robust markers of connection. In this instance blood and adoption evoke the same material processes. Blood, unlike genes, continues to nourish over time. The genetic contribution to the creation of identity is a one-shot deal, so to speak. Like Frida and Anabela, Linda discounted the notion of an underlying, fixed, or transcendent understanding of relatedness. Her opinions resonated with those of the other practitioners and patients I met in Guayaquil. Patients at Dr. Vroit's clinic shared their practitioners' emphasis on the primacy of environment and education as factors that mold the person. The role of genes for these patients was explicitly downplayed. This view is perhaps linked to the fact that many of these patients were willing to entertain the idea of adoption. These patients gravitated toward anonymous egg donation. The nine months that a baby would spend in their bodies was enough to make it their own.

Even before I began my observations of IVF patients, I had a sense that many Quiteños were opposed to adoption. When I told people outside the clinic about my project, inevitably the conversation turned to adoption, and I usually got an earful about what a bad idea it is to adopt a child, which they saw as a strange

North American custom. I was telling one middle-class Quiteño woman about my research when she interrupted me. IVF made sense to her. "But," she asked, "Why? Why? Why are North Americans so interested in adoption?" She could understand bringing gifts to orphanages, but nothing more. Adoption was so exotic to some middle-class Quiteño friends of mine that they put a huge effort into arranging a meeting for me with the one woman they knew who had adopted a baby. She was full of stories about how awkward the subject of adoption was for her friends and family in Quito.

Quiteños' sense of the North American attitude toward adoption was skewed, of course, because it was based on their knowledge of North Americans who came to Ecuador wanting to adopt a baby. Obviously, this is a small and select group: most North Americans don't adopt. But neither, in my experience, do they exhibit the immediate and viscerally negative reaction that most middle-class Quiteños did toward the practice.

Because of this reaction, I included questions about adoption in my interviews with IVF patients. What did they think of it? Did they know anyone who had ever adopted? If IVF didn't work out, would they consider adoption? In Quito, the overwhelming, immediate response to these questions was almost always no. Besides expressing their antipathy toward and distrust of state bureaucracies, Quiteño patients responded empathically that an adopted child is "not of my own blood. Not of my own body. " Then they would list the myriad problems an adopted baby could have: born of drug addicts, born of criminals, born black.

Among Quiteño infertility patients, adoption was always a third or fourth recourse, if it was considered at all. One IVF patient from the sierra, Delores, mused a bit about adoption when she did not get pregnant with IVF, but she quickly rejected the idea. She told me there were too many "genetic" risks with (legal) adoption: you don't know where the child comes from. After her failed cycle, Delores concocted what seemed to me an extremely complicated and far-fetched plan to have her sister fly home from Spain to act as her surrogate mother. When it was obvious this plan wouldn't work, she began gingerly to consider adoption again, changing her mind several times throughout my stay, always afraid of what she might get. Months after I left Ecuador, I heard from the biologist at the clinic that the director had arranged for Delores to adopt a baby from a patient in the OB-GYN unit of the clinic, a young, unmarried woman. He did this by putting Delores's name on the birth certificate, so that officially no adoption had taken place. Delores's willingness to adopt an unknown child through this arrangement demonstrated the trust she had in her doctor. A few years later I visited Delores and her son in a town a few hours south of Quito. She had not told him he was adopted.

In Quito, although genetic discourses do not predominate in understandings of relatedness as strongly as in North America, IVF patients used genetics to understand relatedness to a much greater degree than in Guayaquil. The concept of genes, along with ideas of blood and custom, was put to flexible use. Many patients invoked genes to maintain family boundaries rather than to determine individual identity. In describing why familial egg donation would be more acceptable than anonymous, a Quiteño IVF patient explained: "I would look for someone in my family, my sister, because it affects all the genetic parts. It would not be my child [if she used an anonymous donor]. I would not know what diseases they would have, the risk of genetic illness."

Another patient, Fernando, cited genes in his explanation of why he and his wife would never consider adoption. "Genes are transmitted through the means of blood, and all the organic liquids. With adoption, it's not 100 percent my child." Genes connote the boundaries of a family grouping. Anonymous donation was a risk because of genetic disease that a stranger could impart.

Even in Quito, however, blood prevails over genes. One Quiteño patient who reluctantly agreed to use an anonymous donor also justified the process this way: "It's my child, because it [the donor egg] is only some gene cells. The whole process that will develop, it's my life, my blood." Genes are only cells, whereas blood gives life. Genes do not have the same charge as blood. No one claims that "genes "call" as blood does.

In most cases of familial egg donation I encountered, the parents planned to tell the child and other family members who the donor was. Frida was an exception. Frida's desire for secrecy grew out of her wish that Arturo would think she could make her own beautiful children and from the fact that she and Anabela were not related by blood. This secrecy contributed to the conflict between Frida and Anabela: it made it impossible for Frida to allow Anabela the role in the children's lives that she had come to expect. By limiting her intimacy with Anabela, Frida moved their relationship more toward business than mutually supportive kinship: she denied the importance of blood.

THE TRAFFIC BETWEEN WOMEN

In cases of familial donation, the decision about whom to ask to be a donor involves rules of relatedness reminiscent of the anthropological literature on marriageability (Barth 1954; Goody 1959; Leach 1951). Instead of determining whom one can marry in order to produce legitimate offspring and create alliances between families, the questions are: Who can give eggs? Who will best share in the experience of having a child? And with whom do I want an enhanced relationship?

The act of sizing up one's kinswomen for this role might seem related to the analytic notions of biovalue (Waldby 2002) and bioavailability (Cohen 2004), terms that speak to the recent technological ability to extract, manipulate, and store bodily tissues for future use. In North America and Western Europe, decisions to do so involve distinctions between value and dignity, biology and sociality. The sale of newly detachable body parts and the novelty of biosociality has created what Paul Rabinow calls a crisis of "bodily dignity" (Rabinow 1999). But what of sites like Ecuador, where categories of value and dignity have never been radically opposed, and where biology and sociality have worked together for a very long time within *nuestra realidad?*[10] Egg donation in Ecuadorian clinics doesn't pose a new or uncomfortable formation of kinship and economy, as the neologisms *biovalue, bioavailability,* and *biosociality* imply: instead the practice is used to reinforce the ongoing cultivation of kin that is simultaneously material and malleable and usually unequal.

Here, to supplement and complicate the story of Frida and Anabela, I describe four cases of egg donation between kinswomen. Two of these involve relationships between women of the same generation: sisters and sisters-in law. Two involve women of different generations: a goddaughter (niece) and godmother (aunt), and a daughter and mother.

In the clinics, in contrast to my observations in North American IVF clinics, the relationship between these female relatives often took precedence over the relationship between the husband and wife. The strengthened connection between these women was seen as one benefit of using a known donor. It involved formalized exchanges in a way unimagined by those who bifurcate kinship and economy. Frida and Anabela exemplified the complexities of this connection.

While my discussion centers on how egg donation maintains or establishes material and immaterial bonds between kinswomen, in these accounts, another crucial matter for all concerned was defining the relationship between a child born through familial egg donation and the adults in its life. In parsing all aspects of these relationships, my thinking is informed by Bourdieu's concept of practice (Bourdieu 1977) as it relates to Charis Thompson's discussion of the "ontological choreography" that takes place in U.S. infertility clinics. Thompson found that those involved with IVF and gamete donation use a "mixed bag of surprisingly everyday strategies for naturalizing and socializing particular everyday traits, substances, precedents and behaviors" in order to align "procreative intent" with "biological kinship" (Thompson 2001, 145). When kinswomen and their whole families were involved, clarifying parenthood was seen as a manageable task, not an impossibility. In fact most often the donor was understood has having an enhanced relationship to any child born through her donation, a relationship that did not threaten the primary parenthood of the egg recipients.

SISTERS

Lucia and Ingrid, sisters from a large, working-class family in southern highland Ecuador, came for IVF at Dr. Padilla's clinic. Ingrid (age thirty-two), who owned a small store, donated her eggs to Lucia, her younger sister (age twenty-five), an English teacher, who had been diagnosed with ovarian function problems. Ingrid had three children and a husband with whom she kept in constant touch during the month she was in Quito. Ingrid clearly saw herself as Lucia's guardian, even though Lucia's husband also came at crucial moments of the process. It was Ingrid, not Lucia's husband, who stood with Lucia during the embryo transfer, and it was Ingrid who kept watch over Lucia as she slept in the clinic the night after the transfer. The next morning, Ingrid told Lucia and me about a dream she had had the night before, demonstrating how seriously she took her role as protector.

> I was frightened, I couldn't get up, couldn't move. I had seen that she [Lucia] left with the nurse to get an injection or to urinate, but she slipped on the stairs, and they fell out—the embryos. She fell, and I ran. And they fell. And there were six that fell. They came out in a little fountain. Like little balls of cotton. Like water. Like gelatin. And I said, "My God!" And the Doctorita Linda came and said, "Fine. We have to try to put them back inside." And I woke up, and Lucia was sleeping very calmly. I went back to sleep, but I couldn't leave the dream because of my nerves.

Ingrid's concern stemmed from her own and her whole family's desire for Lucia to have a child. In one of our formal interviews, I asked the sisters what they thought of anonymous donation. Lucia told me: "Anonymous, I wouldn't like because I don't know who it is. And one day if he [the child] wants to know, I won't be able to give an explanation. But in this situation, I am going to be able to say I took an egg from my sister. To know that it is your family, and I don't know, maybe he will come to have a worry, a doubt, and this is what I don't want. It is preferable that it would be a sister-in-law, even a friend." Ingrid added, "That it is someone that you know. You know who they are."

I asked Ingrid if she would think of a child born from her donated eggs as being different from her other nieces and nephews. Unlike Dr. Vega, who thought that known donors cause familial confusion, Ingrid understood her contribution in a positive light.

> Clearly. Clearly. It will be also part of myself. I believe that I will always be looking to see that Lucia will care for the baby especially well for me. I told her I am going to feel this way. I am going to feel like it is part of me as well. That is because I have wanted to do it for her. And then it will have, a part, I don't know, a part of my heart. My children say, "Mami, what is it that you are going to do?" I say I'm going to take out my love and they will put it in Aunt Lucia, because this is what she lacks, no more. And afterwards she will be able to have a baby.

If Lucia became pregnant, she would in effect repay Ingrid by caring for the child especially well.

Lucia added, "I told her it is going to be like a child for her." Ingrid donated the egg, and it will be a part of her heart. Lucia saw her own physicality contributing to the child: "I think that it will be the same as me, because it will form with my blood that is with all of my body. If I had the egg and I had to give it to someone else to raise in her womb, maybe then no. I will care for it like it was mine, and more than another person's. My husband says [the egg] is just a little piece. It's like a little piece, and so it doesn't mean that the child is not yours."

For both Ingrid and Lucia, the eggs confer some connection but not the only or preeminent tie. Like the Zumbaguan Indians in highland Ecuador described by Weismantel (1995) and the families in Germany constituted through care described by Borneman (2001), Lucia gives priority to the care, feeding, and form-ing of a child. The tie of blood allows her to make relatedness claims because she will feed the baby with her blood all the time it is in her womb. The practice of egg donation compels Lucia to downplay the contribution of eggs, privileging the care and feeding of the child in utero. Gestation in this case is not a passive process but one in which a woman actively engages, an active means of caring for her child.

The question of a potential baby's connection to the larger family emerged in the sisters' discussion of what Lucia owed Ingrid for her egg donation. Lucia and Ingrid made it clear that the child would be Lucia's physically, but at the same time they imagined the entire family as having an interest in the child's existence and growth. While I was with the sisters after Lucia's transfer, Lucia mentioned that she planned to give Ingrid money to compensate her for the time she had missed from work. Ingrid told her no. "I will recuperate to be the same. Afterward, if God blesses us, you don't have to do anything. Your baby will be the best pay. For everyone. For the whole family, that is because for everyone with this uncertainty we need a payment, and the payment will be this [a baby]. We can rest then, everyone complacent and tranquil."

I had witnessed structurally similar exchanges in California, where sisters protested that they did not need recompense for their egg donation; however, in those cases children could only be described as "gifts." In contrast, Ingrid was comfortable talking in the idiom of payments; in this case the baby itself, a new member of the family, would constitute payment.

SISTERS-IN-LAW

When Dr. Padilla told Laura that she needed to use an egg donor, she resisted the idea at first. "Well at first it seemed ugly. I said no, the child would not be totally mine." Laura's family convinced her that it was normal to use a donor as long as it was a family member. They imagined that the corporeality of carrying a child in utero would make the child hers. "They told me if you are going to have it in your womb, with your blood, all of this, then it is your child." Once Laura accepted this idea, the question became who would donate. Her sisters were all too old. Her niece would have been ideal, but she was pregnant. Laura was beginning to feel desperate because she had a date to begin treatment at Dr. Padilla's clinic, but no donor. Her brother stepped forward and said that his wife Nanci would donate. "She can give you what you want, because she is *liga* [has had her tubes tied]."

Laura and Nanci went through the entire cycle together, sometimes accompanied by their husbands. The two women had not been particularly close before, but Laura thought they had become much closer through the donation process. As she said, "It united us." Later I found out that Nanci's donation was paying back a long-standing debt between siblings. Nanci was married to Laura's youngest brother, whom Laura, as the oldest girl, had cared for while their parents worked outside the home. This was a relationship similar to the one that Frida had to Javier, Anabela's husband. An exchange relationship already existed: Laura was godmother to Nanci's and her brother's children. Laura imagined her desire to have a child as involved in another sort of transaction as well. She explained that if she ever did get pregnant through IVF and egg donation she and her husband, who were married civilly, would finally have a church wedding, paying back God for the favor of a child.

Laura's early pregnancy tests came back positive, but she miscarried soon after. She told me Dr. Padilla had said that the miscarriage resulted from the fact that she and Nanci had "some degree of incompatibility between us."

LAURA: Between the egg and my blood. Or also it could be the uterus does not retain well. In the next treatment he [the doctor] is going to try to combat the two [problems]. Then I am going to do it with my niece, and in January we will do a treatment on my uterus.

ER: Why won't you have this incompatibility problem with your niece?

L: Because it will be more—we are family. We are closer. There is a bit more kinship. We are relatives, because with my sister-in-law in reality we are more alien to each other.

ER: But donors are sometimes anonymous.

L: This is what they tell me. But the doctor told me we have to combat the two [family incompatibility and uterine problems]. It's not for sure that there is incompatibility, but because it is not sure, then we have to combat both.

Laura's assertion that the doctor suspected a physical incompatibility between her and Nanci sounded inaccurate to me, as most IVF practitioners are heavily invested in the idea that any reproductively healthy young woman can donate eggs to a stranger. Indeed, Linda and Dr. Padilla confirmed that they thought the real problem was in Laura's uterine lining. But they could understand why Laura was intent on trying again with a closer relative. Like other patients, she wanted a donor as familiar as possible. It made sense to Laura that she didn't get pregnant because Nanci was not a close relative.

NICE AND AUNT

Forty-four-year-old Miriam, a self-employed seamstress, and her forty-six-year-old husband, Hector, a self-employed mechanic, each had children from previous relationships. They had met about a year before showing up at Dr. Molina's clinic in Quito, intent on having more children. Miriam's twenty-four-year-old niece, Doris, had agreed to donate her eggs. When I first met Doris, she was lying in bed after the egg aspiration. Watching cartoons and playing a game with her pink cell phone covered in tiny foil stickers, she seemed impossibly young. Doris had recently finished nursing school and was taking a year off.

When I asked Doris about her siblings, she told me she had two older brothers and a six-month-old sister. Twenty years seemed like an unusually large gap between children. Doris explained that when she was finishing her nursing training, an "illiterate" woman came into the hospital to give birth. She gave the child to Doris and left. Doris took the child home to give to her parents, but she had decided that if her parents didn't want the baby, she would keep her. Doris's parents did take the child, whom they also named Doris, and the adult Doris cared for baby Doris. By the end of the interview, Doris seemed much older to me because she had made such a concerted effort to procure children for her parents' generation. She found a child to fill her parents' "empty" home, and she provided eggs to her beloved aunt.

A few days after the embryo transfer, I interviewed Miriam and Hector for the first time. Doris sat with us. Although she seemed happy to sit back and let us talk, she occasionally jumped in to explain medical terms and procedures to her aunt and uncle, which they appreciated—another service provided to her elders. When I was alone with Doris, she told me how she had decided to donate her eggs to her aunt:

> How it started I don't know. One day Miriam called me and asked if I could do this, a favor to give *unos huevitos* [some little eggs]. But she didn't explain anything. Then later she explained more to me, and I said, "For me there is no problem." I had never imagined that I would get to be a donor! That I was going to be the assistant! Miriam told me that she and Don Hector didn't think of anyone else. The doctors said there are [anonymous donors], but if you have someone it's much better, because they don't know whose eggs they are. They thought of me immediately because of the affection they have for me.

Doris was obviously very happy to provide eggs for her aunt: being selected as a donor was a sign of Miriam's affection for her, a form of privileged attention. Doris was even willing to participate in subterfuge with Miriam by lying to her parents and telling them that her eggs would be removed through a surgical incision rather than vaginally. Miriam and Doris feared Doris's parents would say no to a procedure that involved vaginal penetration.

To facilitate egg donation and IVF, Miriam employed *compadrazgo*—the ties between godparent and child, and more important, godparent and parent—the ubiquitous Latin American strategy for enhancing and reinforcing familial relationships (Allen 1988; Bastien 1979; Davila 1971; Foster 1953; Hubbell 1971; Mintz and Wolf 1950; Poole 1991).

In Quito a year later I saw Miriam and Hector at the clinic, along with their baby. Both Miriam and Hector were generous in giving credit to others for their child. They called Doris the second mama and described how the doctors, and even I, were crucial to their son's creation.

MOTHERS AND DAUGHTERS

One type of familial donation, using an adult daughter's eggs, occurred in cases of a woman's remarriage after divorce or the death of a husband. This strategy was possible only when the woman had a new partner, as daughters could not donate eggs to be mixed with their own father's sperm. The mixture of their eggs with their stepfather's sperm did not appear to provoke concerns about incest or inappropriate sexual relations. One patient, Marlena, used her daughter, Ceci, as her egg donor after her remarriage. Marlena was forty-eight at the time. Her husband was thirty-three. They owned a hardware store together. Ceci, her daughter from her first marriage, was a twenty-year-old college student and a local beauty queen in Ambato.

Like many patients whose daughters or sisters were donors, Marlena expected Ceci to feel an intensified connection to the baby, but Ceci's social life prevented an interest in babies in general and Marlena's gestating baby in particular. Marlena thought Ceci would eventually change. "Today we are talking only words. But the moment she sees the baby, it will have certain features of hers, and then she will have an affinity with the baby."

After the embryo transfer, two leftover embryos left over were cryopreserved, because Marlena wanted to save them for her daughter. "I will guard them for my daughter. Because this is what the doctor told me. Guard them for her. She does not care for children. She doesn't love them because she is still an adolescent. I think that in the future maybe she will have a partner, and if she can't have children they will go [to the clinic]. Now, no, she is not caring. I was like her, the same, and now I have two, but I didn't want children when I was twenty."

By freezing the embryos, Marlena saw herself as presenting her daughter with something of value. She also planned to share the baby with her. "You know that she has given 50 percent of it. And so with my husband, we have talked about how we are going to share. That is to say, if something happens to me, then it is not going to be only inheritance of the home. He [her husband] is going to share and give the child to her as well."

Marlena didn't see Ceci's contribution as just a "little piece," as so many other egg recipients did, perhaps because Ceci was her own daughter. If Marlena died, Ceci would inherit the house, the baby, and the frozen embryos in a narrative of female transmission of property that bypassed her new husband.

Marlena's husband initially wanted to use an anonymous donor, but Marlena convinced him otherwise. Possibly her new husband was hesitant to use his step-daughter as a donor because Marlene's first marriage ended in death, not divorce. In the other situations where daughters were the donors, usually the first marriage had ended in divorce, and the new husbands did not seem to have a problem with egg donation from the daughters. In the event, Marlena claimed that after the transfer and pregnancy, her new husband came to have more affinity for Ceci because they had produced a child together.

In Charis Thompson's investigation in North American IVF clinics, she describes cases of intergenerational egg donation involving a daughter and second husband, and a surrogate pregnancy in which the surrogate carried the genetic child of her brother and sister-in-law (Thompson 2001). These cases had the potential to be called incestuous. Like Thompson, however, I found that any potential anxieties about incest between the daughter and the mother's husband were diminished by emphasizing the relationship between the two female protagonists of the conception drama—egg donor and recipient—and deemphasizing the role of the intended father, until at least after conception.

Marlena's comments about inheritance came when I asked Marlena if she planned to give her daughter a gift for donating her eggs. In my work on surrogacy and egg donation in the United States, I found that it was common for patients to give jewelry or other gifts, rather than money, to their known donors or surrogates. In Ecuador, where the exchange of money for eggs of anonymous donors was less troubling, I knew of no one who gave material goods to known donors (usually family members), although sometimes the patient paid the donor's transportation costs or compensated her for lost work time. Instead, the baby itself was often characterized as a "gift" and even more often as "payment" for the donor. Marlena seemed proud of her daughter's active life but foresaw that Ceci would want an intensified connection with this child, which would constitute a clear and formalized return from Marlena to Ceci for the gift of her eggs. Like skin color, donation provides a material base for the reckoning of race and relatedness, but these relations can be enhanced or mitigated by other material practices involving care and cultivation. In many cases of egg donation between female relatives, these practices include the transmission of property.

THE INEQUALITY OF ALLIANCE

Female ties of kinship, obligation, and commerce were central to most of the known-donor egg donations I encountered in the Quiteño clinics. Marlena and Miriam, like Frida, were successful *comerciantes* (retailers). Frida and Marlena were married to younger men who were not (at least yet) as economically or professionally successful as their wives. Both Frida and Marlena, not their male partners, took on the primary financial responsibility for IVF treatment. Their egg donors were younger women who were connected to them through exchanges of property and other material and immaterial forms of support.

Lucia and Laura, in their twenties and thirties, received eggs from family members closer in age, but these exchanges, too, were mediated through family debts and obligations. Laura created a new, stronger set of ties with her sister-in-law, whose donation worked to pay off some of Laura's brother's obligations, while Ingrid protected Lucia through a perilous time in order to provide her whole family with a new baby. All of these women had relatively stable relationships with men and were not critical of normative kinship institutions like marriage. But as with highland market women absorbed with their female trading partnerships, the importance of their male partners receded during this time of intensified female exchange. Frida's husband, Arturo, for example, flew from New York to Quito to deposit sperm months before Anabela's egg donation. He was completely absent from the egg aspiration and embryo transfer.

Before I learned of Frida and Anabela's conflict, every participant I talked to in these egg-donation relationships presented their experience in a fairly positive light, and I was concerned that I might romanticize interfamilial donation in Ecuador. To counteract this tendency, I would remind myself of the story an IVF patient, Rosario, told me about a kidney donation between her two brothers-in-law that went awry. After recounting the family feud that ensued over the ownership of their parents' house after the "gift" of the kidney, she remarked, "Y como sangre duele" (And how blood hurts).[11]

Rosario told me this story in her apartment, part of a lively compound housing all her in-laws, who walked in and out during our visit. She was undergoing IVF because of her husband's infertility, a rare situation in a place with so little diagnosed male-factor infertility. Unlike her relationship with her natal family, from whom she was estranged, her relationship to her in-laws seemed strong. I wondered afterward if the "pain" of her own blood ties had contributed to the decision to undergo IVF, which she saw as a sacrifice she was making for her husband and his family.

Rosario's story about organ donation gone wrong reminds us that intrafamilial egg donation is open to abuses. More vulnerable family members may be pressured to be egg donors. I was not privy to cases of truly egregious abuse, but when younger women are asked to donate eggs to their husband's relatives, when husbands offer their wives for egg donation, and when daughters donate eggs to mothers, we must be wary of the "gendered moral demands of prestation" involved in making certain women's bodies available for others' use (Cohen 2005, 85). Asking kinswomen to donate often involves calculations of obligation that come from relationships of indebtedness and unequal exchange. For those involved, however, egg donation does not necessarily constitute a wholly different kind of prestation from that of physical labor and financial contributions made as material debt relief to one's kin.

Egg donation between Ecuadorian kinswomen does not usually involve equal trading partners, nor is it meant to. Younger family members incur debts to older generations. These obligations seemed to make egg donation especially appealing to known donors, at least at first, enabling them to make a substantial repayment with relatively little effort, and their donation served to substantiate relationships that they saw as eventually benefiting themselves.

Unlike Engels and Lewis Henry Morgan, who trafficked in narratives of overcoming matriarchal pasts that could be revived (Engels and Untermann 1902; Morgan 1877), Lévi-Strauss never imagined another possibility for the basis of social life besides the exchange of women between men (McKinnon 2001). Attention to the contemporary practices of relatedness and economy involved in Ecuadorian egg donation demonstrates consequential exchanges between women that are directly productive and reproductive of relations between themselves, their male kin, and their children.[12] These transactions give weight to the argument that participation in social life demands exchange. Intrafamilial egg donation in Ecuador involves not the hidden exchanges of unofficial kinship, as Bourdieu would call it, but rather the sureties of women who are full players in an economy of kinship.

One of Gayle Rubin's most devastating criticisms of Lévi-Strauss's account of exchange concerns his blindness to sex oppression, despite the fact that he never assumed an "abstract, genderless human subject" (Rubin 1975, 171). A consequence of this blindness was that resulting psychoanalytic theories of femininity came to be "based largely on pain and humiliation," which required some "fancy footwork to explain why anyone would enjoy being a woman" (Rubin 1975 197). It might have been possible to avoid these rationalizations by paying attention to the richness derived from female exchange, which clearly makes and marks social life. Women like Frida and Anabela, maternal figures standing inside the marketplace making babies together (just as they make business together), represent a model of female exchange rather than an exchange of females.

Rubin argued that "men are in constant need of valuables to disburse, and they are dependent upon input" (Rubin 1975, 206). In Lévi-Strauss's model, women served as both valuables and input. In some ways Anabela and Frida were not so different from these men. When starting out in business, Anabela needed valuables and input, which Frida provided. Eventually, Frida needed valuables and input (eggs), which Anabela provided. Even though the reproductive incorporation of Ana's egg into Frida's reproductive project soured, and Ana and Frida continued to contest the call of blood, they also continued cultivating the entwined fates of their families, enriched through earlier exchanges of eggs and a market stall.

Abandonment: Vanessa

Even in her surgical bouffant cap, Vanessa was beautiful; high cheekbones and luminescent brown eyes. She was followed into the operating room by her husband, Juan Carlos, who looked like a rock star, with his bleached blond, tiger-striped hair, his heavy silver earrings, and chains peeking out of his scrubs. At thirty, Vanessa was on the young side for IVF patients; she had been diagnosed with blocked tubes. A year before, in 1999, she had been to a clinic in Cuenca, in southern Ecuador, for infertility treatment. It had been a disastrous journey. The doctor didn't know what he was doing and filled her ovarian follicles with water. When she arrived back in Quito, a woman at the airport, "her guardian angel," had told her and Juan Carlos about Dr. Molina's clinic. And now here she was, climbing onto the table for her egg retrieval. Dr. Molina harvested nine eggs during Vanessa's aspiration. Seven were fertilized, and two days later, Vanessa and Juan Carlos were back in the OR for the embryo transfer. Dr. Leon, Dr. Molina's lab biologist at the time, recommended that they transfer three embryos and freeze four. But Vanessa insisted they transfer four and freeze three. I heard Dr. Leon mutter under her breath, "Some people are scared to freeze embryos."

Vanessa had hated the aspiration; she was in great pain afterward. But she loved the transfer. The best part was lying on the table, looking through the window into the lab at the video monitor, where she got to see her four embryos on the screen. She murmured, "My babies are so beautiful!" Her father was a twin, and she wanted twins herself. As she watched the embryos, she imagined watching a video of herself giving birth.

I visited Vanessa a week later, while she was waiting for the results of the cycle. She met me at her trolley stop in southern Quito, accompanied by a young man whom she never introduced. We picked our way to her house through empty lots filled with rubble and garbage. She began talking about the IVF cycle right away, so apparently it wasn't a secret from her companion. Vanessa's street was a little more established than the streets we had passed: the houses were surrounded with barbed wire and high-security fences. It took Vanessa a while to unlock all the deadbolts on her gate and usher me into the courtyard. Inside I heard a tremendous racket. The entire concrete yard was filled with kennels of snarling, jumping dogs. There were more dogs gnashing their teeth above our heads on the roof. We had to shout to hear each other until we got into the house and shut the door.

It turned out Juan Carlos wasn't a rock star. He owned two buses with his father and reared and sold dogs, mostly pit bulls. There were a number of young men around the house who helped him. When I left, another young man accompanied Vanessa and me back to the trolley stop.

The house was still under construction, so we sat in Vanessa's bedroom while she told me about coming to Dr. Molina's clinic. She and Juan Carlos had been married for four years. They had used the rhythm method to avoid having children for two years and then started trying to have a baby, but nothing happened. Neither wanted to adopt and care for a child "that wasn't our own." Vanessa started taking herbal remedies and seeing a bioenergetic healer. The healer diagnosed her with a mental block that was preventing her from having children. She took what the healer said seriously and tried to work on her blockage. But after a while she decided she needed biomedical intervention as well, and she found her way to Cuenca to the "awful" doctor who "destroyed" her.

So far, IVF with Dr. Molina had been a very positive process. Vanessa also felt "super" supported by both her and Juan Carlos's family. Everyone knew they were doing IVF. "There is no reason to obscure these things," she said. Vanessa was taking two weeks off from her work as an accountant to rest while she waited for the test result. If she got pregnant, especially with twins, she planned to stop working outside the house altogether. She had dreamed about twins and felt that with them her life would be complete. But she was a bit worried about having more than two babies. The day before, she'd watched a cable movie in which a woman had sextuplets through IVF. Vanessa acted out for me how one baby started to cry, then another, and then another. It looked so difficult. But if she got pregnant with all four embryos, she would "sacrifice everything." She told me, "I world not work anymore. If the four babies came, I would accept them. God is the only person that decides what to do with us. He is the only person that sends babies."

Vanessa agreed with Dr. Molina's view that the remaining embryos should be frozen. She couldn't imagine throwing the other three in the garbage when she and her husband had made them together. "They are my children. I would prefer they have life." But Vanessa worried that if she got pregnant, Dr. Molina would ask her to donate the extra *embrioncitos* to a stranger, and they would "have this other señora, even though I know they are mine." Still, she decided that she would donate them if Dr. Molina asked, because it would "help someone else be happy." A week after our visit, Vanessa had a positive pregnancy test, suggesting that she was probably carrying twins. She sounded thrilled when I called to congratulate her. She joked that I should be their godmother.

When I returned to Quito to start my extended fieldwork in 2002, I asked Dr. Molina about Vanessa right away. He told me she had eight-month-old quadruplets that he claimed were all completely healthy. Vanessa had lost the pregnancy from the IVF cycle that I observed. Then she had the three frozen embryos implanted, but she still didn't get pregnant. A few months later, she underwent another IVF cycle and had four embryos implanted. This time she got pregnant with the quadruplets. She had just been on TV the week before. Dr. Molina seemed happy about the publicity for his clinic. I called Vanessa to ask if I could come see her, and she laughed, remembering me from two years earlier. She asked if I had heard about all her babies.

We met at the trolley stop again. Vanessa looked great, her sleek, short hair dyed a shiny dark brown, with red and black streaks. No young man accompanied her this time, but she was holding a chubby baby in her arms, who I assumed must be one of the quads, though he looked a lot older than eight months. Vanessa introduced me to Chelo, a very jolly baby, and he giggled. I marveled at what a big boy he was for eight months. Vanessa explained that Chelo wasn't one of the quadruplets: he was her husband's one-and-a-half-year-old son. I made a confused face, and Vanessa patiently explained that when she was two months pregnant with the quadruplets, Juan Carlos told her about Chelo, whom he'd had with another woman. She said: "I'll tell you all about it when we get back home."

The streets around the house looked the same as before, uncared for and covered in garbage. This time I held Chelo as Vanessa undid all the locks and chains. Again the ferocious caged dogs were barking and twisting their bodies in a fury. I followed Vanessa into her bedroom, huge after a remodel but crammed with bassinets and other baby paraphernalia. There were two playpens in the middle of the room, with a baby inside each one, and a huge crib next to the wall with another baby inside. A young man stood next to the crib, holding the fourth baby. All the babies looked minuscule for eight months.

The walls were covered with blown-up pictures of the quads. There was also a black-and-white picture of Vanessa with an enormous pregnant belly, lying on the bed with Chelo. Juan Carlos walked in, fresh from a shower and ready to go out. This time his hair was spiky orange and brown. While he fetched me a drink, Vanessa introduced me to Martin, the young man holding one of the babies, a friend of Juan Carlos. He had moved in to help when the babies were born. Vanessa and Juan Carlos paid for Martin's school, clothing, and food. They called him "the other papa." He was great with the babies, holding them, cooing over them, and feeding them. At one point he took Chelo into the kitchen to make him his lunch.

Vanessa told me the story of Chelo. When Juan Carlos told Vanessa about Chelo, she "didn't take in the magnitude of it all. I didn't think it was an impediment to us staying together." She was preoccupied by being pregnant with four kids, and she wanted her kids to have a father. They had a stable relationship, and she was happy with how supportive Juan Carlos had been during the IVF treatment, so she "accepted the baby." Chelo came to live with them soon after, when he was six months old, because his mother was so young, and she thought it would be better for him. Vanessa decided it would be "ignorant" to leave Juan Carlos or to reject his son. "Chelo is a sweet boy. It's not his fault." Now Vanessa thought of herself as Chelo's mother. "The mama is who the child calls 'Mama,'" she said. Juan Carlos's family knew that Chelo was his son, but Vanessa told her own family that he was the child of a distant cousin. When he and the other children got older, she planned to tell them everything.

Then Vanessa told me about the quadruplets. The doctors warned Vanessa it was a high-risk pregnancy, but the first two trimesters were uneventful. At six months, she started feeling awful. The quads were born by C-section at thirty-two weeks. Her doctor said she could wait two more weeks, but she felt so terrible that she wanted them out of her. She had considered giving birth at the state-run social security hospital, where the neonatology unit was supposed to be one of the best in South America, but she was concerned about the cases she'd heard of where something went wrong. "It would have been free, but no thanks," she decided, and gave birth at a private clinic instead.

Each of the quads, three girls and a boy, weighed a little over three pounds at birth. The boy, born last, was the smallest and weakest. All four stayed in the hospital for forty days after they were born. They were doing fairly well at eight months, but they still hadn't reached certain milestones, like learning to roll over, which most babies learn at between four and seven months. Samantha, born first, was the biggest and the most physically adept. When I picked her up, she arched her back and wiggled. The second girl was Jennifer, so named because in American movies, "the girl named Jennifer is always the blondest," and she came out the whitest of the four. Next was Maureen. She was the darkest, so her parents gave her a name common to Afro-Ecuadorians. Sebastian was the smallest and the most flirtatious: while I held him, he cooed and smiled at me. Sebastian and Maureen both had heart murmurs, and Vanessa was terrified that the pediatrician would say they needed surgery. She was afraid of both the risks and the expense. She was thinking of starting a foundation for pediatric congenital heart defects.

Vanessa talked a lot about what her life was like now. She had tried to go back to work, but her boss couldn't understand what it was like to have four babies. All she did was take care of them. She could barely leave the house. Every visit to the pediatrician required one adult to hold each baby, plus a driver. She acted out her typical day: one baby crying, then another, then another, then another. I couldn't tell whether she remembered acting out the same scenario, mimicking the IVF sextuplets, two years before. But Vanessa didn't seem as overwhelmed as she had imagined she might be back then. Her sense of calm might have been due to her feelings about God: "It was divine that he sent the four. They were left with me for something."

While the four small, sickly-looking babies surrounded her on the bed, demanding attention, Vanessa reflected on the three extra embryos she had frozen two years earlier.. When she was pregnant the first time, she had asked herself, "My God! What am I going to do with my other children?" She talked to her mother a lot about the frozen embryos. If the doctors had donated them to someone else, she would have felt that she was abandoning a child. When she had the first miscarriage, her mother told her, "It's for the best. It's from God, I tell you. You were very worried about the babies, the frozen ones." Immediately, Vanessa had Dr. Molina transfer those embryos, but she miscarried again. She was relieved there were no embryos left to worry about. "There won't be other children that are going to be mine, and that someone else could have." Maybe the embryos could have made other people happy, but she couldn't imagine giving them to another family. She believed it was her own emotional state that had caused her to miscarry the frozen embryos, and it was better that they were gone. It was just like her mother said: God made sure her children weren't "abandoned."

In the summer of 2007, I tried again to reach Vanessa, but I couldn't find her. None of the phone numbers I had worked anymore, and I couldn't find her house. I did learn from Dr. Molina that Sebastian had died when the quadruplets were about a year old. He couldn't remember why. As I was taking in that news, he started joking about Juan Carlos, with his dyed hair. "He was a mulatto, no?"

It had never occurred to me that Juan Carlos was anything other than mestizo. But I had met with the couple so early on in my research, and maybe I hadn't been sensitive to the cues. Or maybe this was just Dr. Molina's racist way of diminishing any patient who seemed outlandish. Two weeks later I ran into Dr. Lucero, who had worked in Dr. Molina's clinic when Vanessa was a patient. I asked if he remembered Vanessa. He nodded his head vigorously and confirmed Sebastian's death: "Maybe his heart?" Dr. Lucero gave me more news. Vanessa had gotten pregnant on her own—a complete surprise. Dr. Lucero implied that she hadn't been happy about it. He did her C-section and had been trying to find her ever since. She had never paid the bill.

FIVE · On Ice

Embryo Destinies

On May 25, 2005, the front page of the *New York Times* carried a picture of U.S. President George Bush at a press conference, holding a baby born "as a result of one couple's donation of frozen embryos to another." The donation was arranged by a Christian embryo "adoption" agency.[1] At the conference, surrounded by children born from frozen embryo adoption, Bush stated that "the children here today remind us that there is no such thing as a spare embryo" (quoted in Stolberg 2005, 1). Bush held the press conference as a preemptive strike against Congress's push to expand federal financing of embryonic stem-cell research, which Bush, along with many other conservative Christians, saw as destroying human life. Despite Bush's efforts, the bill passed, although without enough votes to prevent a presidential veto. The reporting on this event represented "life" as contested. The ethical debate about the proper use of embryos boils down to the status of embryos. Are they human life or not?

Initially, Vanessa, in Quito (see "Abandonment"), agreed with George Bush about embryos, believing that they were human life that should not be destroyed. But she was a little hesitant when she said this. Later on, after Vanessa consented to the cryopreservation and donation of her embryos, she reversed her position. The thought of her embryos being born to and living among strangers was too disturbing. The mandate to preserve life was not a good enough reason to agree to what she considered abandonment of her children.

In this respect Vanessa was like many IVF patients and practitioners I met in Quito who found the practice of embryo cryopreservation deeply unsettling. Some, like Vanessa, initially acceded to the process; others rejected embryo cryopreservation from the outset. Either way, they felt it was ultimately preferable to discard embryos rather than allow them to be circulated outside family boundaries.

During the 2005 press conference, Bush declared that "every embryo is *unique* and genetically complete: "These lives are not raw material to be exploited, but gifts" (quoted in Stolberg 2005, 1). But in some respects these embryos are not unique. All of them share the universal quality of life, and frozen embryos are interchangeable between families. In Ecuador, by contrast, IVF practitioners and patients, like Vanessa, who were unsettled by the idea of frozen embryos tended to see them not as potential human life in the abstract but as potential relatives within a very specific framework of family relations.

The various responses to the technological ability to freeze embryos, of which Bush's and Vanessa's views are only two examples, are embedded in their own material histories. In Guayaquil, different material and political conditions have produced more liberal practices of personhood that emphasize individuality, universality, and atemporality, qualities shared by Bush's embryos. These practices stand in contrast to the views I encountered in Quito, which tend to valorize specificity. In Guayaquil, then, patients and practitioners tended to emphasize the value of embryonic life. Embryos were seen as individuals that should be brought into being, regardless of when or within what family they were produced, whereas in Quito, people tended to emphasize the specific temporal and familial relationships in which the embryos were enmeshed. These views were not static: the status of embryos could change, as they did for Vanessa.

The valuation of human life is embedded in discourses of human dignity. For Immanuel Kant individual rational beings have no equivalent thus possess dignity, and exist above value (Rabinow 1999). By this definition, nonrational humans unable to exist autonomously, those who would fit into the current categories of the brain-dead, the mentally ill, or the unborn, lack dignity and therefore, following Kantian logic, could be objects of exchange. The view that dignity belonged only to those capable of reason was radically altered after the atrocities of World War II. In Giorgio Agamben's view, the body, or "bare life," became the locus of human dignity, because to deny the dignity of the "husks of men," left mindless and shattered by the camps, "would be to accept the verdict of the SS and to repeat their gesture" (Agamben 2000, 56).

Now the concept of dignity is again undergoing transformation, as the association of the body with dignity beyond value has become increasingly problematic.

As Paul Rabinow observes: "What had been (relatively) stabilized in the period following World War II in Western countries, as the body, society, and ethics—and their relations—are today, again, being remade, and the assemblages in which they functioned, desegregated" (Rabinow 1999, 12). Technical and medical practices have made new forms of human life possible while also expanding the possibilities of using these new forms for economic gain. Body parts have become newly alienable and valued. Thus battles rage about whether the brain-dead, fetuses, and embryos, although perhaps lacking in subjectivity, should be treated with the dignity accorded to human life (Kaufman 2005; Lock 2002; Scheper-Hughes 2005; Sharp 2006).

The freezing of embryos renders them available not only for IVF (which, despite the potential for destruction of embryos, is a practice accepted by most Christian denominations, with the significant exception of the Catholic Church) but also for other scientific and medical purposes. Cryopreservation allows embryos to be stored, manipulated, and exchanged, thereby forcing the question of whether such uses are ethically consistent with understandings of human dignity. Are embryos human life or not life?[2] Are they "researchable"—suitable for scientific use—or not? These debates concern not only human life and dignity and God's will, but also commerce and research. They have palpable effects on IVF practice as well as on policy and law, such as the regulation of stem-cell research.

Although some institutions, such as the Catholic Church, claim they have resolved the question of the beginnings of life within the human embryo, a long line of comparative anthropological writings has shown that understandings of the beginnings and ends of life are more variable across cultures than the mostly Eurocentric field of bioethics has assumed (Franklin and Lock 2003; Kaufman and Morgan 2005; Morgan 1989; Stevenson 2009). Is the sanctity of life always the preeminent concern? It's striking that the Catholic Church has not won the support of all Catholic Ecuadorians for its position in life debates. Among the patients I spoke with who were hesitant to freeze embryos, establishing kinship boundaries mattered more than preserving life. Life, it seems is a "contingent concept" (Kaufman 2005).

Toward the end of my field research, a story widely reported in the international media prompted me to take a closer look at embryos in Ecuador. A survey conducted by the American Society for Assisted Reproductive Technology found that more than 400,000 frozen embryos were being held in cryopreservation storage tanks in the United States (Wade 2003). In these stories, this number contrasted with the holdings in most countries in Europe, where IVF is regulated by state ministries. For example, Britain's clinics were estimated to have 52,000 and Spain's 40,000.[3]

The news stories implied that the surplus of cryopreserved embryos resulted from the lack of regulation in the United States. The example of Ecuador, however, counters this argument. In Ecuador, the IVF industry is even less regulated than in the United States, but the rate of cryopreservation is a very low, and some practitioners actively avoid it.

One explanation for the low number of cryopreserved embryos in Ecuador might be the cost. But that economic reasoning cannot fully explain the difference. IVF is much less affordable for most Ecuadorian patients than for the majority of middle-class IVF candidates in the United States. (A cycle of IVF in the United States can cost from $10,000 to $15,000; a typical IVF cycle in Ecuador, where incomes are substantially lower, costs between $3,000 and $6,000.) The cost discourages Ecuadorian patients from attempting repeat cycles if IVF does not succeed the first time. Because cryopreservation could reduce the cost of repeat cycles (by obviating the need for ovarian stimulation), one might expect that Ecuadorian IVF doctors would encourage it. More than half the IVF clinics had the necessary equipment. Few, however, actually did so consistently. The pressures against cryopreservation go beyond direct economics or religious ethics.

Before the availability of cryopreservation, the clinicians and patients at the two Guayaquileño clinics were troubled by the destruction of unused embryos. The solution for some Guayaquileños was to donate these live embryos to other patients. When cryopreservation became available in Ecuador in 1998, it ameliorated this life problem because embryonic life could now be saved in perpetuity. By contrast, in Quito, where IVF participants generally seemed less troubled by the destruction of unwanted embryos, the addition of cryopreservation to the IVF apparatus created rather than appeased anxieties: leftover embryos could be used in the anonymous exchange of frozen embryos, and that practice threatened to disrupt family boundaries.

As with egg donation, then, there is a regional story to tell about embryos in *nuestra realidad*. These regional differences were not acknowledged: I noticed them only because of my observations in laboratories and clinics in the two cities.

EMBRYOS

The entity that goes by the name of *embryo* is created with assistance from a diversity of objects and processes, including petri dishes, powerful microscopes, culture mediums, scientific debates, laboratories, state-level regulations, cellular masses of different cell counts, reproductive politics, women's bodies, men's bodies, eggs, sperm, pipettes, and incubators . These objects and processes have differed at different times and in different nations. In the early twentieth century, embryos were created in the context of debates concerning evolutionary approaches to race and the human/nonhuman divide. In the United States today, embryos are produced in the context of the abortion debates of the last forty years and the question of exactly when life can be said to begin (Morgan 2009).

Since the early twentieth century, the term *embryo* has generally referred to the developing entity from fertilization until the eighth week of gestation. However, the American College of Obstetrics and Gynecology (ACOG) uses more specific terms to refer to the early developmental phases. The single-celled entity formed at fertilization is termed a *zygote*. From day 2 to day 15, the mass is called a *pre-embryo*, divided into the stages of blastomere, morula, and blastocyst. After implantation, at day 15 or 16, when differentiation has passed the point of twinning, the cell mass is called an *embryo* (ACOG 2004).

In IVF clinics in Ecuador, practitioners would occasionally call these cell masses *blastomeres* but most commonly referred to them as *embryos*. Thus, cryopreservation, which takes place when the mass has reached four to eight cells, is generally understood as "the freezing of embryos." In Latin American IVF clinics, as well as clinics in nations with a Christian or specifically Catholic history, the distinction between a fertilized egg (a single-celled entity) and an embryo (multicelled) is contested. At a Pan–Latin American conference for reproductive medicine, a Chilean infertility specialist explained to me that in Chilean clinics, fertilized eggs are referred to as *pre-embryos* to circumvent the Catholic Church's strong influence on state policy.[4]

Regardless of the distinctions made by specialists, the embryo (at least in North America and Europe) has become synonymous with early human life: indeed, IVF practitioners and patients envision these externally manipulated cells as "babies." Doubling back to abortion politics, the representation of these cells as babies has made it possible for right-to-life groups in the United States to refer to IVF clinics as "orphanages" and for George Bush to recommend that couples be matched with orphaned embryos.

Scholars Sarah Franklin and Celia Roberts describe British embryos as "work objects," sociomaterial actors that exist in Britain "in the midst of complex legal, technical and temporal requirements" (Franklin and Roberts 2001). Embryos in the United Kingdom are produced and cultivated in the context of debates that involve experts and citizens and legislation. Each embryo is documented and tracked at the state level and produced under laboratory conditions that meet ISO compliance guidelines. These conditions shape embryo ontology and the destinies toward which they circulate (Franklin 2006a).

In Ecuador, embryos are created under different political and legal conditions and outside state oversight. The 2003 Adolescent and Child Civil Code states: "Boys and girls and adolescents have the right to life from their conception. . . . Experiments and medical and genetic manipulations are prohibited from the fertilization of the egg until birth" (Congreso Nacional 2003). Yet no Ecuadorian lawmaker or state institution has ever intervened or tried to regulate IVF clinics or the practices that make embryos (see chapter 1).

Technical and legal definitions of *embryo* also vary from popular understanding. Patients in both Ecuador and North America sometimes call these entities *eggs* instead of *embryos*. I was with many Ecuadorian couples during embryo transfers, when they saw their embryos for the first time. Typically, the woman was lying supine on an operating table waiting to receive the embryos. Her husband, partner, or female relative was at her side, both of them craning their necks to see the video monitor through a small window that opened into the laboratory. The nurses told them how to identify the embryo, often prompting them with the instructions like "Look. It's like a rose in black and white." Practitioners told patients that the embryos they had seen were their potential babies; sometimes they personified them further by calling them *guaguas,* a popular Quichua endearment for children. But although embryos were imagined as babies or children, this naming did not necessarily provoke concerns about their death.

EXTRA EMBRYOS

An understanding of cryopreservation requires a discussion of the term *extra embryos,* what Bush denied were "spare embryos." These are embryos not transferred into a patient's uterus during an IVF cycle. Decisions about the number of embryos transferred back to the patient and what to do with those that are not transferred are determined by national and local laws and practices. To increase the chance of pregnancy, practitioners may decide to transfer several embryos. One of the most prevalent criticisms of assisted reproductive technologies, however, is the number of multiple pregnancies and births that result, which can lead to increased prenatal problems for the mother and health complications for the babies as a result of low birth weight and premature births.

In Ecuador extra embryos caused concern or relief, depending on the region. Technically, IVF practitioners can retrieve anywhere from one to forty eggs in a single cycle. Practitioners usually aspirated three to ten. This number varied for a variety of reasons. For example, the amount of money the patient had to spend could determine the dosage of hormones they were given, thus affecting the number of follicles that produced eggs. The extracted eggs are inseminated in the laboratory and checked after a period for fertilization. These fertilized eggs are embryos (see the introduction for a longer discussion of this process).

Practitioners usually transferred two to four embryos into their patients, although as many as sixteen embryos might be created in a single IVF cycle. The transfer of a limited number of embryos into a woman's body results in extra embryos, wholly new objects brought into existence through assistance of IVF. In about 60 percent of the IVF cycles I witnessed in Ecuador, there was at least one embryo left over after the transfer. These embryos could either be immediately transferred to another patient (if she had received appropriate hormone treatment), frozen for storage, disposed of, or, very rarely in Ecuador, used for study.

Freezing took about three to four hours, after which embryos were stored in pipettes in liquid nitrogen tanks (figure 5). The three Ecuadorians clinics that had cryopreservation facilities charged patients $800 to freeze embryos and about the same to defrost them. They also charged about $200 a year to maintain the embryos, but in the cases in which patients had stopped paying this fee, the practitioners did not defrost embryos to dispose of them.

Some representatives of the Catholic Church have opposed the cryopreservation of embryos as well as IVF. "The horror of spare embryos" has been deemed an affront to human dignity, "an abusive situation against those lives, which can be compared to therapeutic cruelty" (Zenit 2003b). However, neither Pope Benedict nor Pope John Paul II before him made magisterial statements about cryopreservation, and within the Church there are debates about these "unethically" produced humans. In Spain, the local episcopal conference recommended the unfreezing of embryos to let them "die in peace," while other Church theologians have advocated adoption, despite the fact that they were produced a procedure that the Church condemns. For now, the Church continues to call for prohibiting IVF instead of focusing on the consequences of cryopreservation (Zenit 2003a, 2003b, 2005).

The Church's *Instruction on the Respect for Life* has influenced some IVF practitioners and patients in Ecuador, but their approach to saving embryonic life—

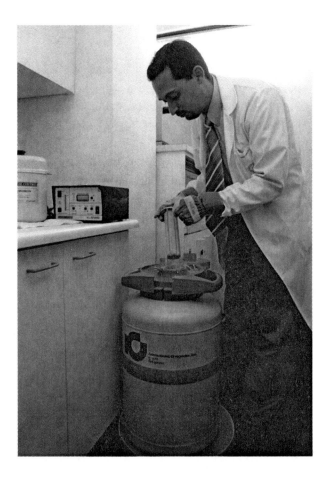

FIGURE 5.
Freezing embryos. This photo accompanied a story about local
IVF clinics in *El Comercio*, one of Quito's daily newspapers, on
June 20, 2004. The headline read: "Muchos padres pagan para
congelar y mantener sus embriones intactos" (Many parents pay
to freeze and maintain their embryos intact). Courtesy Foto:
Archivo / El Comercio (Quito-Ecuador), Eduardo Valenzula.

through cryopreservation—is not fully consistent with Church policy, because
cryopreservation puts the dignity of embryos in peril. And for those who are
hesitant to freeze embryos, as Vanessa came to be, Church arguments about life
mattered little. For these Ecuadorians, anxieties about the cryopreservation of
embryos center on kin relations more than the autonomous dignity of life.

EMBRYONIC LIFE: FROZEN FOR THE FUTURE

The practitioners at Dr. Vroit's large clinic in Guayaquil were proud of their new cryopreservation program, which had started about six months before my observations in 2003. They all independently mentioned how enthusiastic their patients were about the possibility of freezing extra embryos, because embryos "are life." Reducing costs for patients was one benefit of cryopreservation. Dr. Castillo, the biologist at Dr. Vroit's clinic, was frustrated, however, that they had had fewer opportunities to freeze embryos than they had anticipated.

Marisa the coordinator of the IVF program at Dr. Vroit's clinic, explained that they had always used relatively low doses of ovarian stimulation hormones to avoid producing too many extra embryos. Before their cryopreservation program began, she was always "uncomfortable with the elimination of a good embryo, because of my religion." She expressed relief that science now enabled them to freeze embryos. When I asked her why her religion was against the elimination of embryos, she explained:

> Because the embryos are life. We know that. The minute we manipulate [embryos], they think we are playing with life; that we think we are gods, that we can form creatures. But I don't see it like this. It's not like I believe that I am God. I do it because I think I can help someone. I don't do it to destroy life. It's true, as they say, to create a life we needed to destroy the embryos that remained. But I don't only look at the bad part. And if I don't do it, it's not allowing a child to be created.

Nancí, one of the laboratory biologists at Dr. Vroit's clinic, told me that all of their patients had been enthusiastic about the possibility of embryo cryopreservation. Embryos were stored for patients for one year; at that point, the clinic asked patients to decide what to do with their extra embryos, offering the option of donating embryos to other couples. I mentioned that in the Quiteño clinics, I had met patients who were reluctant to freeze embryos. Nancí thought for a moment and told me that it must be because those patients had read about the possibility that freezing damages embryos during the defrosting process. It seemed that Nancí could imagine only technical, not moral, worries about cryopreservation. In her mind, cryopreservation solved the problem of life: it did not create problems.

For these IVF biologists, cryopreservation specifically addressed the Catholic Church's concerns about the preservation of life. In my discussion with Dr. Vega, the psychologist at Dr. Vroit's clinic, he told me: "I understand that [disposing of embryos] is a waste of life. The church experts say it is considered human life, the new cell, and the union of sperm with the egg. To avoid this controversy, you can say to the Church, "Look, we are freezing these embryos," and after ten years you can revive them and they continue being the same being. Nothing is lost. Nothing."

Dr. Vega saw no philosophical or ethical difficulty with the temporal suspension involved in freezing embryos. His concerns with the live embryo as a being were, to him, consistent with the mandate of the Catholic Church to preserve life. Yet although these practitioners saw cryopreservation as offering a solution to the moral quandary about preserving life, they still acted contrary to official Catholic doctrine, which also condemns cryopreservation as an affront to human dignity.

For Eliana and Samuel, a middle-class couple from Guayaquil who became parents of IVF triplets, cryopreservation offered a scientific resolution to the dilemma of life posed by the Church. They agreed with the Church position that embryos are life. Eliana explained: "Because, yes, already it is made. The life. And if it is in the place where it should be, that is inside the uterus, then it begins. It forms to go giving more life." Samuel observed: "The science continues advancing. . . . They, the scientists, can give a future, with freezing, that used to be thrown out." This couple had undergone IVF right before the clinic began its cryopreservation program. Their IVF cycle resulted in six extra embryos, which Eliana wished they had been able to freeze because of her fear that something might happen to the triplets in utero or shortly after birth: "If the pregnancy fails or if they are born but fail, then this is the option of the other embryos that are frozen in the machine. I would have done it at least for a year. I read that they can freeze [the embryos] with contracts for a year. Here they are our children. They are frozen for the future." Eliana and Samuel imagined cryopreservation as providing a form of insurance.

STRATEGIES TO PREVENT DEATH

Although many clinicians adopted cryopreservation in defiance of Church doctrine, Dr. Castillo told me that he and other clinic staff had struggled with the question of the Church's condemnation of IVF. To minimize its effect, Dr. Castillo took to thinking of the fertilized cell masses as pre-embryos and pointed out that many naturally occurring miscarriages also result in the deaths of embryos. But for him, cryopreservation was the best solution to the dilemma of embryo disposal. At one point he said, "No están en el tacho al menos están en el tanque [Better that they are in the tank than the dustbin]." This aphoristic statement demonstrates that to Dr. Castillo, what is at stake is the life of the embryo, not its status as a family member. This was just one of the several strategies used by practitioners and patients to work through their ambivalence about participating in IVF.

Embryos Out of Body   Almost every patient I encountered who was against cryopreservation was also against abortion, but they did not necessarily equate embryo disposal with abortion. Lydia paraphrased the sentiments of many patients with her comment that embryos "are not alive until they are inside my body." Moira made a clear moral distinction: "Abortion is a crime because they are inside. The [IVF] embryos are outside, and I imagine they will have life as well, [after implantation], but now it is not a life." IVF embryos produced in a laboratory were conceptualized as different from embryos produced inside a woman's body through intercourse. When Dora and I discussed the fate of her three extra embryos, she explained why their disposal was not equivalent to abortion: "For me provoked abortion is my will, my desire. That what I have here [patting her abdomen] is not what I want. I go to the doctor and I tell him *sáqueme* (take it out of me), this implanted thing that is part of me. One goes to the doctor [for an abortion] as if he were an assassin. It's a very grave thing, very bad. On the other hand, [with IVF] someone else is going to make an embryo that has not yet implanted. It is still not inside. What's more, it's not the mother. It's science."

For Dora the fact that science assisted in creating these embryos made them something altogether different from embryos produced in the womb. Intentionality was crucial: out-of-body embryos were made in the hopes of assisted life, and their disposal did not constitute an intention to destroy life.

Embryos that began outside the body tended to be understood as more fragile once transferred into the womb. Patients feared that they might fall out. Part of the reason that so many women wanted bed rest, lying immobile, with their legs together, after their transfers was to prevent the embryos from leaving. Several patients recounted dreams they had about the embryos falling out after they fell down flights of stairs. In these accounts, embryos were precious and in need of protection precisely because they had begun outside a woman's body (see the story of Lucia and Ingrid in chapter 4).

The distinction between internal and external embryos carried over into another justification for embryo disposal. When talking about extra embryos, practitioners and patients frequently pointed out that not all embryos stick, and that many pregnancies naturally miscarry. One of the most common ways that patients made sense of the disposal of extra embryos was through the idiom of selection. Selection concerned the ability of IVF doctors to select the best embryos for transfer, which allowed most patients to reason that the leftover embryos would not have stuck (*no se ha pegado*) and become a pregnancy. Again, what was crucial was the general intention to have children, not the decision about the fate of each embryo.

Donating Life   Until cryopreservation became available in Guayaquil, those who wished to prevent embryo death had only one plausible option: the immediate, anonymous donation of embryos to other IVF patients. Both Guayaquileño clinics offered this option to patients who might be willing to pass on their embryos either to save life or to help other infertile couples have children. This was an uncertain undertaking, however, because the embryos had to be transferred rapidly, and the process required a patient on hand who was in the right phase of her reproductive cycle. The recipients of this type of embryo donation were usually patients who had no embryos because of limited egg retrieval or failed fertilization. After the coming of cryopreservation, most Ecuadorian patients wanted to freeze their extras, so the practice of immediate donation fell away, though patients still had the option of donating embryos after cryopreservation.

In the two Guayaquileño clinics, the circulation of extra embryos among patients was an expected and even positive part of the process. Even before they had the means to freeze embryos, Eugenia, the laboratory biologist at Dr. Jaramillo's clinic, claimed: "We have never thrown out embryos. They are life." The extras were all given to other patients. Such transfers were easier at Dr. Jaramillo's clinics because he stimulated patients in groups. One of Dr. Jaramillo's patients, Diana, proudly explained: "Dr. Jaramillo has never thrown out embryos." Diana would willingly have donated any extra embryos because she believed Dr. Jaramillo would make "good use" of them. "Better that he [the doctor] uses them then throws them out. No?"

The anonymous redistribution contributed to the sense that embryos were autonomous rather than linked to a particular family. Their circulation to unknown recipients prevented their death. My discussion with other IVF patients about embryos and IVF, especially in Quito, made it abundantly clear, however, that there is nothing natural about configuring the embryo as an autonomous life. For Ecuadorians like Vanessa, preserving life was not the overriding issue in determining the fate of embryos. Indeed, embryos became troublesome only when it became possible to extend their lives.

Cryopreservation, although generally welcomed, raised new and troubling issues for some Ecuadorian IVF practitioners. Cryopreservation facilitated anonymous embryo donation, exacerbating fears that embryos might end up outside the patient's family, raised and cultivated by strangers. Some people expressed concerns about the temporal discontinuity that could arise between embryos frozen for years and the rest of their family.

These concerns can be understood in the context of Ecuadorian attitudes to abandonment. Abandonment is an accusation of withholding care. It is a racially based accusation, because it is poor or darker people who are typically accused of abandoning their children to the street (Leifsen 2010). With no social safety net except charity and no one to care for them, abandoned children are at risk of meeting horrible fates.

The altruistic aspects of anonymous donation often did not mitigate these concerns. In nations with robust histories of tissue circulation and blood donation, like the United Kingdom, France, and to a degree the United States, the word *donation* can imply a greater good, a transcendent civic relationship, and a sense of shared biological citizenship (Copeman 2009). Those nations have political institutions that produce trust and transparent procedures that document the flow of blood, embryos, eggs, and organs (Franklin 2006b). For many Ecuadorians, by contrast, donation does not convey a sense of a legitimate destination. Releasing one's tissues, to say nothing of one's children, into the unknown can be understood only as abandonment.

Laboratory practitioners in Quito expressed these fears in a highly morally charged language. Practitioners would tell me that patients "abandoned" their frozen embryos, never returning to claim or transfer them. Even in IVF clinics in Quito that had the ability to freeze embryos, cryopreservation for some was the exception, not the norm. In Dr. Molina's clinic one morning, as Diego peeled (cleaned) some newly aspirated eggs in the darkened laboratory, he remarked that when he trained in Brazil, sometimes the clinicians would aspirate thirty-five to forty eggs at a time, whereas Ecuadorian clinics usually harvest four to ten. When I asked about this difference, he explained that Brazilian doctors give patients more fertility stimulation drugs. His clinic did not administer a high dosage because "then you would have all these embryos to freeze, . . . and couples just abandon them." The sentiment of this offhand comment did not match Diego's remarks in more official moments, when he told me that he froze all embryos of good quality and that he froze embryos in 90 percent of the cases. Cryopreservation for Diego, as with most other practitioners, was a sign of technical advancement, and he disparaged clinics without a cryopreservation program, calling them "contra la vida" because extra embryos had to be thrown out. But I had often witnessed Diego dispose of embryos. In fact, by my count Diego froze embryos only 30 percent of the time, and only when there was more than one embryo left over after transfer. On all other occasions he discarded the remainder.

After Wilson's return from Spain, the two brothers, Diego and Wilson, argued about cryopreservation. Wilson's approach was more aggressive: he favored using more drugs, more eggs, more egg donors, more embryos, and more cryopreservation. He was less concerned with saving life than with expanding the volume of procedures at the clinic. When one patient produced a bumper crop of embryos, Wilson directed Diego to freeze five of them on day 2 instead of waiting until the transfer, which was the usual protocol. After the transfer, there were five more embryos left over. Wilson considered these five worthy of cryopreservation as well. But Diego argued that freezing these embryos in addition to the existing five was a waste of time and resources. This was another point of contention between the two brothers, one used to the abundance of Spain and the other to the shortages of *nuestra realidad*.

In Dr. Hidalgo's clinic in Quito, Antonia, the biologist, told me that they had frozen embryos only twenty-three times in the three years since they had obtained the cryopreservation equipment. Like Diego, she advocated *suave* (soft) stimulations, which resulted in fewer embryos to freeze. Her approach stemmed fears about "the future of frozen embryos, because the parents here are frivolous and don't think about them responsibly." I asked her, "Why worry about them at all?" and she replied: "Because the embryos are cells with future potential. They are going to be children. . . . And for this single reason, [the parents] who make the decision to freeze them and leave them have to be responsible about what happens to them."

After an embryo transfer one afternoon, I noticed Antonia at the microscope placing something in a petri dish that she had taken out of the back bottom of the incubator. She told me that this dish was filled with unfertilized eggs and embryos left over after transfers. She kept one of these dishes, containing a preserving fluid, for about a year, depositing the extra embryos from every patient's cycle into it, until it was time to sterilize the lab. Antonia used them to show patients what embryos look like instead of removing their own embryos, slated for transfer, from the optimal conditions of the incubator. In addition, Antonia described herself as incapable of throwing the embryos out. "Are they life? Yes. Like bacteria, and I would be sad throwing out certain bacteria that I worked on. The embryos are special because they are of my patients. I am a biologist, not a doctor. I connect to them because I worked on them, not because they are human." What made these worthy of her time and care was not the fact that they represented human life but the specificity of her material and professional connection to them and their connection to particular patients.

Letting the embryos die in a dish was much less problematic for Antonia than storing them indefinitely in a freezer. As she told me, "Having them and having them be dead is better than freezing. I prefer to have a dead child than a disappeared child, not knowing what happened to it." In other words, she needed to know how an embryo was situated within their relations. Dr. Leon made a similar comment when she explained that biologists and gynecologists care about very different things. "For gynecologists it's patients, for biologists it's entities like embryos." Dr. Leon thought she would have a hard time disposing of frozen embryos, but, again, not because they represented human life per se: "I respect the embryos, because they are a part of me, or that is, they are a part of what I do." These biologists would rather have had fewer eggs to fertilize or have to throw out a few extra embryos than leave an embryo frozen and perhaps unclaimed.

The clinics' official position on embryo storage and disposal was carefully worded. When I interviewed Dr. Castro, the manager at Dr. Hidalgo's clinic, she claimed that their lab (run by Antonia) never threw out fertilized embryos. I immediately thought of the dish of extra embryos sitting in the incubator—not discarded, but not implanted, either. These practitioners' attitudes made it clear to me that regardless of their own concerns about the kinship of embryos, they felt they had to represent themselves and their laboratories as maintaining the life of embryos. Given the Catholic Church's position on embryo death and global debates about the transcendent value of life, this approach is hardly surprising.[5] Even so, these Ecuadorian biologists' avoidance of cryopreservation and their characterization of embryos stood in stark relief to the position of biologists who saw embryos as alive. If Dr. Castillo believed that embryos were "better in the tank than the dustbin," one could imagine Diego and Antonia reversing the sentiment: "Better in the dustbin than the tank."

ANXIOUS PATIENTS

While the lab biologists worried that patients might abandon their embryos, some patients were anxious about the potential for clinic staff to move the embryos outside the bounds of circumscribed kin relations, and about the family dysynchrony that might result from having both live and frozen children. These patients were for the most part unconcerned about the possible disposal of their extra embryos until I pushed them to think about it. When asked directly, many told me that embryos are life, but not necessarily life that must be preserved at all costs. Some patients, in fact, like Julia, one of the few Afro-Ecuadorian IVF patients I encountered, declared that embryos are not life. "Embryos, they are not yet . . . well maybe they are life when they are four months or five. Maybe they could be. But embryos? No." Although life was not a major concern among patients such as Julia, the specter of cryopreservation could provoke strong reaction without much prodding. One patient, Dora, explained her feelings to me:

DORA: Imagine one year, two years that they maintain them, this gives me a bit of fear that they should endure all this time. Or that they would sell them . . . it makes me a little afraid that they are going to confuse them and when they put other embryos in me, like what happened with that English woman that had a black child. Remember that? And they say that the clinic confused the embryos. That makes me scared.

ER: But you could donate the embryos to other couples.

D: Well no, it seems like a noble cause to give a hand, to help, but no.

Dora was especially concerned about the racial mixtures that the movement of embryos might produce. She was also concerned about the temporal dimension of the cryopreservation. This fear surfaced so frequently with Dr. Cruz-Espinel's patients that when she explained embryo cryopreservation to them, she spent extra time going over how two embryos conceived on the same day (out of body) could be born years apart, if one was frozen. Anxieties about frozen embryos involved a very specific temporality. Dr. Vega argued that frozen live embryos remain the same being, even after long-term cryopreservation. In contrast, patients who cared more about embryonic care relations than embryonic life worried about embryonic suspension in time. Circulating an embryo among strangers or freezing it for ten years threatened its status as a family member because it would have moved through time without them.

Some patients, including Lucia and Ingrid, worried (like Diego and Antonia in the clinics) about what would happen to embryos frozen in perpetuity if they could not return and claim them. This was a realistic concern for women who lacked the money to finance additional IVF cycles. Flor, another young woman without much money, had a similar concern: "With freezing, you don't know what destiny they are going to have. What happens to them if you can't come back?"

For patients who were comfortable imagining the circulation of their extra embryos, cryopreservation and routine embryo donation represented a form of insurance. For those who were concerned about containing their embryos within certain social boundaries of care, cryopreservation represented the potential for child abandonment: Vanessa asserted that God would prefer the embryos dead than abandoned to cryopreservation. IVF biologists shared these worries about abandonment when they acknowledged discomfort with the responsibility of tending other people's "children" stored in pipettes and cryopreservation tanks. Cryopreservation represented a failure to fulfill care obligations to one's kind— with attendant racial concerns.

Patient concerns that doctors would circulate embryos without their knowledge were ubiquitous. In patients' narratives, the problems of external circulation over-rode concerns about preserving life and the stance of the Church. In 2002, Tatiana explained: "The manipulation that exists can really affect families. I heard this is why some priests are against it, for this manipulation. There is no care taken here because of the lack of ethics. Maybe in other places there is more professional eth-ics. Here, no. Here still it can be a sale. They might use [my embryos] like this. They would be misused, put in another person."

Tatiana, an upper-middle-class Quiteño woman, could only imagine that the church found IVF objectionable because of the possibility that unethical doctors might transfer her embryos to unknown persons. This fear still preyed on her mind in 2007, when I visited her again (see chapter 3). She never had extra embryos, but she was still concerned about what the doctors might have done with them if she had. She found herself imagining the doctors giving her embryos away or experi-menting on them.

Inez, a middle-class doctor, one of the few patients from Guayaquil who had reservations about cryopreservation, also conceived of kin relations as more important than life: "The embryos that are thrown out, it's like an abortion for them [the Church]. That is, you could think of it as abortion because it's already an embryo, that is, it is already a life. But they should destroy it before another per-son uses it. Freezing doesn't seem good to me. I believe it's better to destroy them. In my case, if I had embryos and we had them to donate to someone. . . . No, it's better to destroy them."

Tamara, a Quiteña IVF patient, expressed the same views, asserting that thawing out embryos is preferable to embryo donation. "Well, maybe I am being very selfish, because this could help for other people, but it would hurt me in the soul, that a part of me is in some faraway place that I cannot ever see. . . . I prefer to decide that this child is mine, that is it is ours. My egg and my sperm, our embryo."

Fernando, a working-class Quiteño patient at Dr. Molina's, who was in the early stages of an IVF cycle with his wife, agreed with the Church that embryos are life, but his concerns about his connection to the embryos overrode his concern for preserving life in deciding the fate of extra embryos: "They are life. Yes, they are human life. And so it would be ugly to put them in the trash. They told us that sometimes there are couples that cannot have children, and they want what is donated. But, in contrast, my wife and I think that if they are your cells and my cells, then maybe they are going to remove some similarity from you or me. And what if after a time we see them in the street?"

Clearly, he felt some ethical obligation toward live embryos, but what concerned him more was the possibility of his embryos circulating outside his family. The fear that he might run into a child produced from his embryos reflected concerns expressed by many people in Ecuador. For instance, Dr. Leon thought that people should not donate embryos in Quito because it is a small city, and the chances of meeting a child "on the street" were high. In both Fernando and Dr. Leon's scenarios, the "street" is represented as a hazardous site, involving the possibility of mixtures with strangers. Catching sight of one's embryo—simultaneously a stranger and one's abandoned child—on the street would be an incomprehensible experience.

As in Vanessa's case, some patients' attitudes toward their own embryos changed as they went through IVF. In 2003, Ximena and Victor from Guayaquil (see chapter 2) donated three extra fresh embryos from their third IVF cycle because embryos "are with life." They did not want to feel responsible for killing them. The staff had asked Ximena if she and Victor would donate the embryos to another patient who couldn't ovulate. Ximena and Victor did not know whether this woman got pregnant and did not want to know. They thought of the woman as part of a couple "just like them." During their fourth cycle, the clinic froze some of their extra embryos, and it was with this cycle that Ximena and Victor finally had a child, Valentina.

Four years later, a lot had changed. Their daughter was now three and a half, and Ximena and Victor were splitting up. Ximena reminded me that she and

Victor had thought they would donate the extra frozen embryos to someone else. "But now, after having a child, . . . there is no way we would donate them. Imagine a brother or sister walking around that she doesn't know. We paid for another year [of cryopreservation]. We don't know what to do with them."

After she had had a child, Ximena thought of her embryos differently. At first, she saw the embryos as imbued with transcendent human life that it was important to preserve, whereas later, she saw them as embryos part of her family, especially her daughter. If they were preserved and circulated, her embryos might be treated as either experimental subjects or children sent to live among strangers.

AND GOD PROVIDED

For many patients, the potential dilemma of what to do with extra embryos was resolved by God. Several patients recounted narratives in which they had not wanted to freeze embryos, and God had "blessed them" with only the number of embryos that could be transferred. During her IVF cycle, Laura, a middle-class Quiteña, had talked with her husband about what they would do about cryopreservation: "I wouldn't have wanted to freeze, and then God gave me only those that I needed. I didn't want more. It gave me peace that they did not have the possibility to continue the process to freeze. Three were good, and the rest were bad. They didn't have to freeze them. Thank God" (see chapter 4).

Berta, an upper-middle-class woman from Ambato in the sierra south of Quito, also attributed the fact that there were no extra embryos at her transfer to God's intervention: "With freezing, I would have been left with my living children [she already had two older children] and my frozen ones there, and in five years the doctor would have discarded them. And I don't want to do this again. And I believe that God facilitated here, because only four formed out of the six [eggs]. Two didn't form, and they put the four inside me." Berta's anxiety about freezing embryos had to do with temporal suspension, not a concern that their lives were at stake.

God also helped Vanessa overcome some of the complications of having to make decisions about frozen embryos. Implanting the extra embryos after her first miscarriage alleviated her dismay that she had abandoned her children to strangers. Additionally, in Vanessa's narrative, God was portrayed as more concerned with the potential of uncared-for, abandoned children than with preserving the life of embryos. Like the majority of Quiteño practitioners and many of the patients, Vanessa saw the most salient characteristic of her embryos as their relatedness, not their life.

The expansion of the IVF industry seems to have fostered similar anxieties about the related status of frozen embryos in other parts of the world as well. Life debates and the presumption of individuality are not always the dominant issue, especially in non-Christian contexts. In some Muslim countries, where the right to life from conception is not an issue, the maintenance of familial boundaries and familial futures are of great concern. Marcia Inhorn has described the reaction of an Egyptian Muslim couple confronted with extra embryos after traveling to undergo IVF in a Los Angeles clinic. The clinic staff gave the couple three options: freezing, destroying, or donation. The wife reported, "We said, 'destroy.' It is our religion." This couple feared that donation would "inevitably lead to an immoral and genealogically bewildering [and possibly incestuous] mixture of relations" (Inhorn 2003).[6]

The ethnographic record is filled with other examples in which forms of relatedness, kin, and religious belief are more important than individual life in determining the uses of assisted reproductive technologies. In Israel, issues of Jewish nationalism and the lives of women who give birth to the nation's children are prominent themes in debates over IVF and gamete donation (Ivry 2009; Kahn 2000; Nahman 2008; Teman 2010; Birenbaum-Carmeli 2009). Anthropologists have also documented that in Vietnam (Pashigian 2009), China (Handwerker 1995), and India (Bharadwaj 2005), IVF participants have concerns about relatedness, lineage, and the nation that loom larger than individual life. A privileging of relatedness over life might be expected in Jewish, Muslim, Hindu, Buddhist and Shinto contexts, but in Ecuador, the prominence of Christianity does not result in the primacy of life debates either.

In Europe, North America, and in other areas that have adopted European liberal traditions (like Latin America), the post–World War II valuing of transcendent life has particular material consequences for IVF. In these regions, it is acceptable for embryos to circulate outside family groupings. There is some pressure for patients to donate live extra embryos to other couples.

A competing view posits embryos as special but not fully human. In this view, embryos can be donated or circulated for scientific uses, usually as sources for embryonic stem cells for medical research.

Disputes between these two positions tend to drown out other possible views of embryos, even in North America. After a slew of articles in the *New York Times* about embryo adoption, advocated by Bush and right-to-life proponents as a solution to the "thorny" problem of what to do with extra embryos, the *Times* ran an article titled "It's Not So Easy to Adopt an Embryo" (Belluck 2005). Despite the ethics of Bush and embryo-adoption agencies, few couples in the United States with frozen embryos actually decide to donate their embryos to other couples, even if they were initially enthusiastic about doing so. In the *Times* article, couples explained that they are uncomfortable with the idea of having their genetic children raised by someone else, or with the possibility that children born from donated embryos might wonder why they were not the embryos chosen to be raised by their "real" parents. These couples, like Vanessa and others in Ecuador, see their embryos as related.

More recently a Duke University survey of 1,020 IVF patients with frozen embryos from around the United States found that 20 percent said they were very likely to want their embryos discarded. These patients did not want their frozen embryos to come to fruition either as individual persons or as stem cells. They wanted them destroyed, although many specified they wanted this done "compassionately" (Lyerly et al. 2008; see also Roberts 2011).[7]

As a long-time observer of IVF in the United Kingdom, Sarah Franklin notes a similar phenomenon among IVF patients in Britain: "The sense that a cryopreserved embryo suspended in a liquid nitrogen tank is a biological relative is a commonplace experience for couples undergoing in vitro fertilization"(Franklin 2001, 313). In the United Kingdom, however, patients may trust their practitioners to leave their embryos frozen in perpetuity and not circulate them surreptitiously. For many Ecuadorian patients, cryopreservation lays bare fears about their doctors' circulating their children without their knowledge or consent.

Other ways to situate embryos are embedded in specific realities that aren't fully global or local. For example, India has positioned itself to become a global player in the stem cell research industry by appeasing moral concerns and regulation emanating from other nations. India was home to ten of the sixty four stem cells lines created before August 2001 that George Bush deemed allowable for federal funding. Additionally India put strictures in place to meet British guidelines for stem cell production, namely that embryos for stem cell research can only have been created for reproductive purposes, in order to prevent the exploitation of potential gamete donors. (Bharadwaj -2009). In India then, where embryos are not located in life debates practices producing and governing embryos are influenced by foreign concerns about the transcendent life and the specific relations of embryonic production.

PERSONHOOD AND DESTINY

The difference between live and related embryos parallels Marilyn Strathern's discussion of the differences between contemporary bourgeois English personhood and personhood for the Hagen in Papua New Guinea. In English kinship, according to Strathern, a baby tends to be a new person that can likewise exist independently of its relations (Strathern 1992b) and can circulate beyond them. Live embryos are interchangeable. They can be saved by circulating them beyond the family or freezing them. These actions do not change their essence. They are not understood as context dependent. They could have a life in any home: their place in a particular lineage is less important than the individual life. At Bush's press conference about embryo adoption, the older children in attendance wore T-shirts with the slogan "Former Embryos." Embryos were presented as dissociable from their genetic families and easily adopted by other couples. Life can trump "genetic truth," or other forms of connection, in determining personhood.

For patients and practitioners who are more concerned with an embryo's place in a family than with its value as transcendent life, cryopreservation presents a problem. This technology brings with it the possibility that the bounds of a particular family may be breached through abandonment. An embryo is not an autonomous individual in the bourgeois sense but one formed by its role and position in a family, as Strathern describes for New Guinea, where "persons embody their relationship with others" (Strathern 1992a). Similarly, in his article "What Kinship Is," Marshall Sahlins describes a mutuality of being, persons who are members of one another (Sahlins 2011). For the Ecuadorian patients I spoke with, cryopreserved embryos represented "unfinished business."[8] These were like the babies of poor, malnourished families in Brazil, who aren't given names until they can establish their hold on life (Scheper-Hughes 1992). The trouble with cryopreservation is not the possible death of the embryo but the risk of neglect and abandonment by the family. Related embryos are similar to the Roman *res mancipi* described by Marcel Mauss, a category of "precious things" that included "immovable goods, even children. No disposal of them could take place" (Mauss 1990). They could not be traded with strangers.

Personhood for patients and practitioners in Quito's IVF clinics is not derived from a concept of transcendent life but is performative: it develops through processes of cultivation, association, and care. These processes preclude circulation of related embryos outside the family. Live embryos, by contrast, can circulate outside a family. They are closer to the Roman *res nec mancipi*, "things that are transitory": food, cattle on the distant pastures, metal, and money (Mauss 1990). Live embryos can be gifted or circulated anonymously through embryo adoption, as Bush advocated, or frozen for use or donation.

In Ecuador the regional distinction between related and live embryos and the cryopreservation practices that surround them might sound like story of social evolution. In traditional Quito, embryos are bound in traditional kin relations, whereas in liberal Guayaquil, individual embryos can circulate among families. But the story is actually much more complex. First, in both locales, there were exceptions to the general trends. In Guayaquil some patients eagerly embraced cryopreservation and then later decided that it posed too many problems, and in Quito some patients wanted their extra embryos preserved. In addition, embryos have different, complex economic and religious histories. In Guayaquil, respect for embryonic life comes from influential contemporary Catholic teachings about the sanctity of human life, and a history of individualized labor. Guayaquileño embryos tend to be seen as alive and almost completely bare, as they do not possess "modern" genetic ties. As we saw in the last chapter, Guayaquileños often dismiss genes as substances or markers of connection. This dismissal made adoption and donation possible, even embraced.

By contrast, "traditionally" religious Quito does not privilege Church arguments about the dignity of embryos, and in fact some Quiteño patients believe that it must be cryopreservation, not IVF, that the Church finds objectionable. However, in Quito, seemingly more modern genetic discourses are a significant factor in understandings of persons constituted by relations. The fact that genetic reasoning makes sense in the context of a "traditional" kinship of alliance reminds us that it can be difficult to untangle modern biological "truths" from long-standing European "folk biologies" (Franklin 1997; Schneider 1980).

Two specific features of both kinds of Ecuadorian embryos become apparent when they are compared to the British embryos characterized by Catherine Waldby. She describes how biovalue is harnessed through the ability to temporally manipulate tissue fragments extricated from the body (Waldby 2002). The fact that embryos can be frozen for indefinite amounts of time allows for their controlled circulation. This is one of the attributes that can make cryopreservation so appealing or so troubling for different Ecuadorian practitioners and patients. Extra embryos had little or no value when they had to be disposed of or immediately transferred to another woman; but for IVF participants with live embryos, extra embryos became more desirable when they could be kept on ice. For Ecuadorian

IVF participants with related embryos, the manipulation of embryos in space and time made cryopreservation disturbing: it endowed embryos with negative value through the threat they posed to family boundaries.

Waldby's insights might have been different if she had compared British embryos with embryos elsewhere. She argues that for those who champion embryonic life and oppose stem-cell research, "the life of the embryo is biographical, the beginning point of a human narrative that should be allowed to run its social course" (Waldby 2002, 313). But the statements made by those with live embryos, such as Ecuadorian IVF patients and practitioners, or George Bush, suggest that the project to save the human lives of embryos stems from the desire not to activate a particular biography but rather to preserve human life in the abstract, interchangeable and bare, unencumbered with specific ties to the living

For Ecuadorian patients and practitioners with related embryos, embryos are indeed connected to biographies, not of individuals but of families. They are embedded in a kin group with its own history and its own race and class status to preserve, and if their individual trajectories threaten this history, they need to be curtailed. Sonia Merlyn Sacoto, the Quiteña lawyer who argued so vehemently against cryopreservation, told me that the problem with embryo cryopreservation is "their destiny. . . . Who knows what will happen to them?" (see chapter 1). This is the problem for so many people involved with extra embryos. A good destiny for a related embryo is either the right womb or the trash. Its biography should not involve strangers. The destiny of live embryos, by contrast, should involve the eventual transfer to a woman's womb, any womb, allowing for circulation with strangers.

EMBRYONIC PATHWAYS

In the United States, embryo value is at least partially produced through the life debates themselves. While the Catholic Church consistently condemns IVF and the cryopreservation of live embryos as violating human dignity, other life proponents, like North American evangelical Christians, accept the existence of frozen embryos, an acceptance well aligned with the interests of private, unregulated industry.

The US federal government has never sponsored a single grant for IVF research. In the early days of IVF, life debates centered on fetuses, terminology that effectively precluded the government's ability to recognize, much less regulate, the industry. The resulting lack of oversight made possible the rapid expansion of the private IVF industry (Marantz Henig 2003). Now, twenty-five years later, extra embryos, new objects or actors created through IVF, have become a symbol for a similar debate about when human life begins. And again the terms of the debate in the United States seem likely to preclude government involvement and to keep the majority of stem-cell research in the private sector, less regulated than research in nations like Britain and France. Now extra American embryos embroiled in life debates can be disconnected from specific families as either live embryos, which can be donated to other families, or researchable embryos, which can be passed on to scientific research, much of it in private sector. In both cases, they can circulate in a "free" market.

In many nations, like the United Kingdom, where life debates are less vociferous, embryos circulate along well-documented legal and ethical pathways that are publicly discussed and regulated. They are harnessed for all sorts of movement; they are frozen for later use, donation, and experimentation. Although they cannot be sold, they generate transcendent value for the nation or for humanity (Franklin 2006b). Embryos are valuable not as things for sale but as objects that promise a better future, through either embryo adoption or stem-cell research (Roberts 2011).

Ecuadorian embryos situate and provincialize other approaches to these practices. The embryo is not everywhere the same: it is an object assembled within specific material and political realities through which practices of relatedness, personhood, and human life are articulated and negotiated. When related and live embryos are juxtaposed, an unexpected story emerges. Related embryos limit the possibility of embryo circulation within a particular family, whereas live embryos can circulate outside families. Embryos that are enmeshed in life debates can, as live embryos, be exchanged through adoption; or they can become researchable embryos, transformed into valuable and anonymous raw materials for the global biotechnology industry.

Cryopreservation is not automatic in Ecuador, as it appears to be in the United States and Europe. That difference prompts questions: Why is it that in certain Euro-American locales, the creation of frozen embryos is natural, and their "death" is contentious, whereas for some Ecuadorians, it is the creation, not the death, of embryos that makes cryopreservation so problematic? Part of the answer to this question can be found in the imperative of the life debates. But for many Catholic Ecuadorians unengaged in this debate, the frozen embryo is simply not as alive as it is in other contexts. Embryos are kin to be cared for. At least for now, it is their suspension, not their death, that makes them so hard to keep.

CONCLUSION · Care-Worthy

I began with a volcano. I'll end with a hurricane. In the days after Hurricane Katrina, a multistate consortium of police officers rescued a cryopreservation tank filled with 1,400 frozen embryos from a private hospital in New Orleans. One of those embryos was implanted, and sixteen months later Noah was born, named in remembrance of his watery journey (New York Times 2007). Noah's story was recounted by the conservative legal theorist Robert P. George and the philosopher Christopher Tollefson in the opening of their much-publicized 2008 manifesto *Embryo: A Defense of Human Life*. George and Tollefson argue that if the contents of the tank had not survived, "the toll of Katrina would have been fourteen hundred human beings higher than it already was, and Noah, sadly, would have perished before having the opportunity to meet his loving family" (George and Tollefsen 2008, 2). This argument is meant to bolster the pro-life side of the life debates, holding that human life begins at conception. But we could also consider Noah's story from another perspective. What made Noah and the other embryos worthy of the assistance and resources required for their rescue, while so many people were abandoned in Katrina's wake?

Life debates are loud, especially in the United States. Assisted reproduction has fueled these debates by making new entities, like embryos, to stand alongside the actors already involved: the fetus, the brain-dead, pro-life activists, and pro-choice activists. I hope that this book about practices of care and cultivation in relation to assisted reproduction in Ecuador will complicate North American life debates and related concerns about new reproductive technologies. In the United States, these technologies are often experienced as an artificial imposition upon natural reproduction. Synthetic hormones, incubators, third parties, and practitioners are seen as intervening in a process that should ideally involve only a woman and a man and whose outcome should be determined only by nature or God. In Ecuador, assisted reproduction has not provoked similarly intense debates about life or the problem of artificiality. Rather, in a place where assistance, not autonomy, is the very basis of existence, reproductive technologies have become one more form of assistance in a process that already involved the interventions of many people.

In this Ecuadorian reality, concerns about assisted reproduction center more on care than on debates about life. Existence is predicated on being worthy of care within a web of relations. This casts a different light on practices of assisted reproduction in the United States, which are so often framed within the context of the liberal individualism that informs the life debates. We might ask how and why so many resources are invested in the production of in vitro embryos in the United States. We can also ask how and why assisted reproduction carried out in private clinics in both nations is subsidized by state institutions and infrastructure. We can ask how different modes of care might contribute to racial formation. And we can ask why, in United States debates about assisted reproduction, God is called upon to arbitrate life but not to offer care.

With care relations as the frame, the post-Katrina embryo rescue highlights discrepancies of race and class that determined who was abandoned and who and what were saved in New Orleans. It also poses questions about the nature of existence. What conditions allow a person (who was once an embryo) to come into existence, and what kind of care will this person receive? The embryo rescue was carried out after a fertility doctor called a lawmaker, who called the governor. The mission involved National Guard trucks and flat-bottomed boats (Goldenberg 2007). The resources that went into first producing and then rescuing Noah were simply not available to the majority of the already-born residents of New Orleans, many of them poor and black. Their lives were deemed less worthy of care than the 1,400 embryos.[1]

The ways in which Ecuadorian IVF participants emphasize care toward related embryos, eggs, and IVF patients can prompt us to look at how different kinds of actors become care-worthy in specific contexts. According to the universal principle of life, often invoked in U.S. debates about preserving embryos, all human life is deemed worth saving. However, saving frozen embryos actually saves particular kinds of lives. If these embryos come into being as babies, they do so as the privileged and care-worthy children of parents who were able to spend substantial resources on producing a child. If they receive state assistance in the future, it is likely to be in the form of tax breaks for private home ownership rather than food stamps. The life debates tend to marshal resources on behalf of privileged individuals, unborn embryos, and privately funded embryo research, instead of expanding access to care, in the form of social welfare.

IVF patients, babies, and gametes are privately made in both nations, but state services and infrastructure affect and support their production. In an Ecuadorian crisis comparable to Hurricane Katrina, it is unlikely that the limited resources of the state's emergency services would be deployed to save embryos in Quito or Guayaquil. Nevertheless, the Ecuadorian state apparatus does shape assisted reproduction. IVF clinics have developed in the context of a poorly funded public health infrastructure, and they further national goals of creating a whiter populace. As in Ecuador, assisted reproduction in the United States remains unregulated.

There are vast material differences between state institutions and infrastructure in the two countries. In the United States, policing, security, schools, and public health care are more robust institutions. But discrepancies in access to publicly funded services are vast and racially marked. Such differences are evident in the kind of care that a private IVF clinic offered Noah's parents, as opposed to the kind of care the poor and black residents of New Orleans needed but didn't get. IVF practice is shaped by discrepancies in care provisioning, which in turn reinforce racial hierarchies.

IVF eggs, embryos, and patients are produced differently in the United States and Ecuador.[2] In the United States, sources of supplies and equipment are reliable, and routines and protocols well established. In this context, women's bodies and the gametes produced inside them and out are ministered to under stable regimens of care. In Ecuador, where it's much harder to coordinate people and things, the material world is seen as much less fixed or singular. It can be altered through resources and care.

The care that shapes the material world in Ecuador is notable and valued because it is hard to come by and coordinate. In this reality, bodies are more likely to be seen as particular rather than as exemplars of transcendent universal biological processes. Ecuadorian IVF patients become whiter as their bodies are attended to by private physicians: such care relations distinguish these women from those who use public medical services. These practices link care relations to the contingency of material reality, a link that provincializes Enlightenment assertions of the division between nature and culture, matter and spirit, individuals and groups.

In Ecuador the history of *mestizaje*, which presumes the plasticity of both blood and biological connection, is strikingly evident in the technosocial configurations that make up assisted reproduction. The divide between public and private medical care is one source of racial distinctions. Additionally, gamete donation and embryo cryopreservation in Ecuador uphold racial malleability: the ideal movements of these entities preserve or enhance a family's whiteness. It remains to be seen how private care and racial malleability might change through the shifts brought about with the commitment of Rafael Correa's administration to improving public health care.

Another difference between IVF in the United States and in Ecuador is the role of God. In the United States, pro-life supporters claim to have God on their side. Human life is considered sacred because God made it. Even so, he seems notably absent from IVF clinics, judging by ethnographic and media accounts of practitioner and patient experiences of assisted reproduction (see Becker 2000; Thompson 2005). In Ecuador, on the other hand, God's presence infuses the clinics. In a place with no social safety net, God's participation is crucial to harnessing the care and resources involved in assisted reproduction. For most doctors and lab biologists, and nearly all the IVF patients and families I encountered in Ecuador, relationships with God were hierarchical and paternalistic, rather like the patterns of mutual obligation established with kin, friends, children, doctors, and nurses. God was always present to be called on, never distant, impersonal, or bureaucratic.

Comparing IVF care relations in the United States and Ecuador requires attentiveness to variation within each nation. IVF, egg donation, and embryo cryopreservation practices in Quito differ from those in Guayaquil. The Duke study I described in the last chapter demonstrates a varied response to embryo cryopreservation in the United States as well (Lyerly et al. 2008). In Ecuador, these differences derive not from "culture" but from a history of divergent labor relations and economic systems that constitute kinship and personhood. In Guayaquil, with its relatively liberal history of "free" labor, care relations focus on the individual, whereas in Quito, paternalistic relations focus on larger family groupings that reflect the legacy of hacienda labor organization. In one context, the object of care is an individual whose life transcends his connections; in the other, he is a related member of a family that must maintain its own boundaries. What different material histories might produce divergent kinds of embryos in the United States?

Although I would like my observations of assisted reproduction in Ecuador to dislodge a sense of the IVF in the United States as standard practice and to complicate the idea of standard practice itself, I don't intend to romanticize assisted reproduction in Ecuador. The Ecuadorian emphasis on the malleability of nature, intertwining physiology, kinship and economy, and the involvement of God is hierarchal and racist, and for the most part it promulgates normative heterosexuality, femininity, and masculinity. Ecuadorian patients who seek embryo destruction, related egg donors, or expensive private medical services are no more critical of unequal resource distribution, exploitative labor practices, the sexual division of labor, or racial hierarchies than participants in United States life debates. In fact, the relational boundaries created by patients focused on care can be more exclusionary of collectivities like "the public" or "humankind" than the views of those on either side of the life debates who champion "the right to life" or "the right to choose" out of a more universalist sense of the reality of both "life" and "individuals."

Care relations in Ecuador, then, are cultivated within a racist and hierarchal order. IVF participants generally want their egg donors to be family members, often out of fear of racial degeneration or to keep material resources within the family. If they use anonymous gamete donors, they generally want them to be whiter. They want IVF and other reproductive treatments to make them into whiter women and to produce babies that are whiter and therefore more worthy of care. Neoliberal economic processes reinforce the value (and necessity) of private medical care, reflecting long histories of national corporeal identities (Roberts, forthcoming). Cultivating a being and body worthy of care by God, family, and medical patrons is part of the national whitening project at work in Ecuador since before independence in 1822. Carried out in private clinics and facilitated by private doctors through God's intervention, IVF has been taken up to assist in Ecuador's dream of a whitened nation.

And in Ecuador it's not only elites who come to have extra embryos. In the early 2000s, when I conducted this study, a substantial percentage of Ecuadorian IVF patients had very limited financial resources. Their use of assisted reproduction complicated earlier characterizations of assisted reproduction as stratified and exclusionary (Colen 1995; Ginsburg and Rapp 1995). The expansion of biotechnology around the world has made IVF accessible even to people of limited means. In Ecuador (as in much of Latin America), people of all classes use private medicine as much as they can in order to avoid public clinics and hospitals. In addition to serving the obvious goal of having a child, for these private patients, participation in assisted reproduction serves to cultivate care relations. The patients described at length in this book—Sandra, Consuelo, Teresa, Frida, and Vanessa—were not necessarily better off after they participated in assisted reproduction—many were in great financial debt—but they had become more care-worthy, even if only temporarily, during their IVF cycles. They had also become enmeshed in ongoing care relations with their families and with God, which involved a kind of desirable debt that they repaid in money, favors, deeds and children.

This constellation of relations helps to explain why despite the relatively recent arrival of IVF and the Catholic Church's condemnation of the procedure, it has been taken up with less anxiety in Ecuador than in the United States. Practices of assisted reproduction coincided with the ways in which children and relations were already made within a precarious material reality. Reproduction in private IVF clinics has become a site that activates paternalistic care relations that encompass extended families and God. In the face of scarce resources, economic instability, erupting volcanoes, and troubling hierarchies, doctors, biologists, and families mobilize to make patients' bodies fertile and whiter, all bundled together in God's laboratory.

NOTES

PREFACE

1. Ryan 2006. IVF success rates are notoriously difficult to evaluate. The most commonly used measure is the clinical pregnancy rate, which means a positive pregnancy test but not necessarily a "take-home" baby. In 2002–3, experts estimated that the overall clinical pregnancy rate in the United States was 20–30 percent. In 2003, La Red Latinoamericana de Reproducción Asistida (Latin American Assisted Reproduction Network), a multi-country accreditation board, reported a combined clinical pregnancy rate of 31.6 percent for its certified clinics across Latin America (RedLara 2003). At the Ecuadorian clinics where I worked, both La Red– and non-La Red–certified, clinicians reported to me clinical pregnancy rates of 25–40 percent. Without in-depth study it is difficult to account for these differences in pregnancy rates between clinics, but the point to keep in mind is that, although rates are improving, IVF fails most of the time.

2. See Becker 2000; Edwards 1999; Franklin 1997; Franklin and Ragoné 1998; Mamo 2007; Modell 1991; Ragoné 1994; Rapp 1999; Roberts 1998b; Strathern 1992a, 1992b, 2005; Thompson 2005.

3. See Bharadwaj 2002, 2005; Birenbaum-Carmeli and Inhorn 2009; Clarke 2009; Handwerker 1995; Inhorn 2003; Inhorn and Van Balen 2002; Kahn 2000; Pashigian 2009; Teman 2010; Tremayne 2009.

4. See Callon 1989; Haraway 1991, 1997; Latour 1988, 2005; Mol 2002.

5. See Cadena 2000; Leinaweaver 2008; Orlove 1998; R. Smith 1984; P. Wade 1993; Weismantel 2001.

INTRODUCTION

1. During my observations, no single women or partnered lesbians underwent IVF in the Ecuadorian clinics. One single woman underwent insemination with donor sperm. The clinicians were ambivalent about taking her as a patient.

2. By 2007 it was becoming more common for IVF practitioners to cultivate embryos in vitro to the blastocyst stage, so the transfer took place a few days later.

3. Sperm and eggs, which ideally combine into embryos in the incubator, are quintessential "entities in transition" (Turner 1969). They are liminal—an especially apt term given that liminality, described in the anthropology of ritual, frequently involves womblike spaces, darkness, and invisibility.

4. See Roberts 2009 for an extended discussion of Enlightenment autonomy in relation to medical technologies.

5. See Haraway 2008; Laet and Mol 2000; Latour 1987, 1988; Mol 2002; Rabinow 1996.

6. One of the primary justifications of the modern civilizing mission was the need to instill a division between matter and spirit in the lives of the colonized by establishing the validity of an "instrumentalist knowledge of nature" (Prakash 1999, 5) that promoted causal connections and scientific thought (Tambiah 1990). As part of that civilizing mission, anthropologists in the first half of the twentieth century documented the enchanted primitives, whose confused, animistic category mistakes allowed Europeans to feel like very special moderns indeed (Durkheim 1995; Latour 1993; Lévy-Bruhl 1935).

7. For example, one jar of human tubal fluid (HTF), which sold for as little as $50 in the United States, cost about $200 in Ecuador.

8. The term *zambo* (or *sambo*), meaning of mixed African and Amerindian heritage, may have come from the Kongo word *nzambu* (monkey).

9. On the theorization of care, see Mol 2008; Taylor 2008b.

10. Malleability has been considered a devalued state within the Enlightenment discourse of nature and subjecthood: it is associated with passivity and docility and with the abandonment of agency, especially for women. Saba Mahmood argues for a different view that takes into account the "malleability required of someone in order for her to be instructed in a particular skill or knowledge—a meaning that carries less a sense of passivity than one of struggle, effort, exertion, and achievement" (Mahmood 2005, 29).

11. By linking North America and Europe with biological determinism and fixity, I don't mean to make a totalizing claim about current understandings in the biological sciences or to imply that biological race means the same thing in all European and North American nations. However, even while biologists have become increasingly fascinated with the malleability and plasticity of biology in the last two decades (Keller

1995, 2000), biologists and geneticists have continued to make deterministic conflations of genes and race (Fullwiley 2008; Sunder Rajan 2006).

12. The ethnographic literature on assisted reproductive technologies and overlapping scholarship on kinship studies, queer family formation, and genomics is now enormous. But when I began this research, most of these studies focused on Europe and the United States. (For some important overviews, see Becker 2000; Birenbaum-Carmeli and Inhorn 2009; Edwards 1999; Franklin and Lock 2003; Franklin and Ragoné 1998; Inhorn and Balen 2002; Thompson 2002, 2005.) More recently, anthropologists and other scholars have come to recognize the ways in which science and technology (especially biomedical technologies) are central to the lives of people around the globe, even those on the economic margins. (See Anderson and Hecht 2002; Arnold 2000; Choudhuri 1985; Cueto 1988; Das and Dasgupta 2000; Lock 2002.) Part of this awareness has come from scholarship analyzing the very disparate ways in which assisted reproductive technologies function outside the global North (e.g., in India, China, Egypt, Lebanon, Israel, Iran, and Vietnam) in diverse religious and political contexts. (See Bharadwaj 2002; Handwerker 1995; Inhorn 2003; Kahn 2000; Pashigian 2002; Raspberry 2009; Teman 2010).

13. During the twentieth century, some Latin American nations, such as Mexico, Chile, and Costa Rica did develop relatively robust forms of state-funded health care and social security. These were subsequently dismantled under the banner of structural adjustment and neoliberal reforms (Gutmann 2007; Mesa-Lago 2008; Mooney 2009). In the majority of other Latin American nations, including Ecuador, socialwelfare programs barely got off the ground before first-world economic advisers began to campaign for their termination in order to alleviate national debt (Biehl 2005; Castro and Singer 2004; Ewig 2010; Zulawski 2007).

14. Consumer-based indicators showed an increase in poverty levels from 34 percent in 1995 to 46 percent in 1998, with about six million people living in poverty in a nation of twelve million. Income distribution in Ecuador is among the most severely imbalanced in the Andean region, with roughly 80 percent of the income share of GDP accruing to approximately 20 percent of the population (USAID 2000).

15. There is a widely acknowledged shortage of doctors in the public sector (CEPAR 2000), where they are paid as little as $450 a month, an extremely low professional salary in Ecuador. Sometimes doctors are not paid at all, leading to frequent local and national strikes simply demanding regular payment. Whereas in the 1990s about one-third of doctors worked in the private sector, by 2005 more than half did. Since the 1980s, a number of private medical schools have opened: these graduate more doctors every year who are even less inclined to work in the public health system (Alban 1998; Portes and Hoffman 2003; Vos et al. 2004).

16. Scholarly and press accounts indicate that funds are reaching their intended

destinations in social-welfare institutions and that there has been a measurable increase in the use of these institutions (Olson 2009).

17. In the early 2000s Ecuador had some of the highest indicators of poor health in Latin America (Crandall, Paz, and Roett 2005). The country spent only 2 percent of its annual budget on public health. In Latin America, only Haiti spent less (Vos et al. 2004). The social-security health service theoretically covered all workers in the country but in actuality covered only a small percentage. Police, military, and social-security health care services were all managed separately and received a much larger percentage of the health budget than public-sector health care. Thus, even though these institutions were funded by the state, they provided a much higher level of care for their disproportionately male recipients than the public health care system, with its disproportionately female recipients (Ewig 2010). At the time, the vast majority of health spending in Ecuador was private: 64 percent came from private sources, and 88.4 percent of that expenditure came directly from household incomes. This spending was not limited to the middle class or elites: 42.5 percent of the poor and 37 percent of the "poorest of the poor" (those whose incomes were 50 percent or less of the national poverty level) turned to the costly private sector rather than use free or low-cost public services (WHO 2005).

18. About 25 percent of the female patients I interviewed were exclusively housewives. Another 25 percent had their own small, informal businesses, often based at home, such as a sewing workshop or a store. Nurses and teachers, both low-paid and traditionally female professions, accounted for another 20 percent. Professionals—telecommunications specialists, accountants, executives, and doctors—made up another 20 percent. Five percent were students, and the final 5 percent were factory workers. I had much less information about the professions of male patients, but they varied as well. Some men were highly paid businessmen or entrepreneurs, two were wealthy owners of flower plantations, and several were government bureaucrats, who tended to have low salaries, around $300 a month. Several men were in the military or worked in the petroleum industry as engineers or mechanics. Some were carpenters or janitors. Several had their own small businesses, working as mechanics, mattress distributors, or microbus drivers.

19. My interview transcripts reflect the differences between these two regions. The transcripts with Quiteños are marked, for the most part, by a measured dialogue between my interlocutor and myself. My interviews with Guayaquileños, on the other hand, are filled with long passages of uninterrupted, rapid-fire monologues from my informants.

20. Despite the recent proliferation of evangelical churches in Latin America, only 5 percent of the IVF patients and none of IVF practitioners I worked with were evangelical. Nevertheless, as I describe in chapters 1 and 2, the influence of neoliberal evangelical Christianity on Ecuadorian reproductive, social-welfare, and economic policy has been profound.

21. The distinction I make between materialist and spiritual Catholics is inspired by the historian Pamela Voekel's distinction between "enlightened" Catholics—elite men engaged in Latin American modernist projects, influenced by the Protestant Reformation—and "baroque Catholics," who fashioned outward displays of their personal exchange relations with God (Voekel 2002).

22. Although Protestant mainline and evangelical churches have made significant inroads in Ecuador, the vast majority of Ecuadorians are still Catholic. In the IVF clinics I observed, only 5 percent of patients and none of the IVF clinicians defined themselves as Protestant or evangelical. The IVF patients and clinicians engaged in diverse forms of religious practice, but these were distinctions within Catholicism, not between different forms of Christianity.

23. See Benavides 2008 and Radcliffe and Westwood 1996 for a discussion of the place of *telenovelas* in Latin America.

CHAPTER 1. PRIVATE MEDICINE AND THE LAW OF LIFE

1. Ecuador has experienced as much political instability as neighboring nations but with less bloodshed. Since 1996, Ecuador has had eleven presidents: a number have been overthrown, some within days of assuming the presidency. Most observers have linked this ongoing political instability to the oil bust of the 1980s, which led to runaway inflation, increased corruption, banking scandals, and the austerity measures of the 1990s (Gerlach 2003; Sawyer 2004).

2. The TFR is defined as the average number of babies born to women during their reproductive years. A TFR of 2.1 is considered the population replacement rate (World Bank 2011).

3. Ecuadorians often asked me why North Americans have so few children when presumably they could afford more.

4. These responses match the findings of Lynn Morgan in the late 1980s among women in Northern Ecuador who held ambivalent attitudes about abortion. They were not comfortable with it but would never fully condemn it either, because the personhood of young children was contingent and negotiated (Morgan 1998).

5. Carizza was referring to two anomalies in pregnancy: the possibility of a sperm penetrating an "empty" egg, and tissue that should have been a fetus instead becoming abnormal tissue. In both of these rare cases a woman's body acts as if it were pregnant and produces the hormone HCG, indicating pregnancy, even though no fetus forms.

6. Women take birth-control pills while undergoing IVF to manage the timing of ovulation.

7. In Latin America, physicians have had a more integral role in government service, beyond serving in health posts and ministries, than in the United States (Voekel 2002).

8. See Leinaweaver 2008 for similar accounts of the difficulty of legal adoption in Peru.

9. *La "Viveza Criolla" en Argentina es la causa principal de una crisis moral, cultural, económica, social y política,* website, www.tabaquismo.freehosting.net/politica/argentinavivezacriolla.htm, accessed November 5, 2011.

CRAZY FOR BINGO

1. Most of the IVF aspirations I observed took seven to fifteen minutes. With prep and recovery time, the whole procedure usually lasted thirty to forty minutes.

2. North American names are very popular for babies in Ecuador.

CHAPTER 2. ASSISTED WHITENESS

1. The popular and medical literatures report a standard set of statistics on the causes of infertility among heterosexual couples worldwide: 40 percent female factor, 40 percent male factor, and 20 percent unknown. Occasionally the breakdown is 45 percent, 45 percent, and 10 percent (Vayena, Rowe, and Griffin 2002). In Ecuador and in Latin America more generally, however, the majority of infertility is diagnosed in women, with the most common diagnoses being blocked tubes and advanced maternal age. Ecuadorian IVF practitioners and other Latin American specialists at conferences have reported significantly lower rates of male-factor infertility diagnosis in Latin America. For instance in 2003, at the La Red conference in Punta del Este, Uruguay, the organizers presented statistics showing that only 12 percent of cases were designated as due to male infertility at La Red–certified clinics across Latin America. In the Ecuadorian clinics, I found that male-factor infertility was diagnosed 19 percent of the time (the rate was higher in clinics that performed ICSI, or introcytoplasmic sperm injection, which involves injecting individual sperm into an egg); and usually if a man was diagnosed with a problem, so was his female partner.

2. See Unnithan-Kumar 2004 for a discussion of the rise in cesarean-section rates worldwide.

3. Brazil and Venezuela are thought to have some of the highest C-section rates in the world, with numbers creeping toward 90 percent in private clinics (Althabe et al. 2004).

4. At the time, the most expensive private hospital in Quito, the Metropolitano, advertised its birth services by offering either "traditional births or cesareans." In Ecuador *tradition* is linked with indigeneity. In effect they were offering women the option of giving birth like either an Indian or a white woman.

5. This is not considered a risk for repeat C-sections in the United States.

6. See Gutmann 2007 for a discussion of masculinity and vasectomy in Mexico.

7. In the surgical realm, whiteness is linked to beauty. Plastic-surgery patients in Brazil and Venezuela want their surgery to be noticed, as a sign of their whiteness and their ability to overcome nature (Kulick and Meneley 2005; Ochoa 2008).

8. Marilyn noted that at thirty-nine, she was by far the oldest patient in Dr. Cabeza's clinic. After this experience, she went on to do an IVF cycle in the United States in the Los Angeles area, where her age was closer to the average for patients.

9. See Birenbaum-Carmeli 1998 for a comparison of IVF care in Israel and Canada with respect to paternalism and liberalism.

10. One woman told me that until she came to the clinic, she thought IVF meant the baby was grown in a big test tube, a fairly common perception. As we continued talking, it became clear that she still thought some doctors grew babies in test tubes. She was pleased that she was being allowed to choose to grow the baby in her own body.

11. See chapter 5 for a discussion of embryo disposal.

12. The clinicians who told female patients to cease work in order to pursue motherhood were most often "career" women themselves; however, they were often childless.

13. These practices are not limited to Ecuador. During her research on assisted reproduction in Mexico City, Lara Braff met a patient who was organizing a raffle to pay for her IVF cycle. The winner would get to send a musical group (one of the musicians was a friend of her husband) to serenade someone of his or her choice (Braff, personal communication; see also Braff 2010).

YO SOY TERESA LA FEA/UGLY TERESA

1. Foxes are associated with fertility, perhaps because they steal eggs from chicken coops. Many of the infertility remedies I heard about in Ecuador involved foxes.

2. Dr. Hidalgo wanted the donors to have proven fertility. He also believed that if they already had children, they would not regret donating their eggs.

3. Quiteñas of means regularly made a similar complaint, "You can't get good help these days," lamenting that the pool of *empleadas* (domestic servants) had left for Spain.

4. In Ecuador, the word *parentesco* is much more common than its English equivalent, *kinship*, which today only anthropologists use with any regularity.

CHAPTER 3. WHITE BEAUTY

1. Both physicians left the United States. Balmaceda returned to Chile, where he continues to practice IVF openly. In December 2010, Ricardo Asch was arrested in Mexico City under charges of fraud and tax evasion (Saillant 2010). U.S. authorities

hoped to have him extradited, but the Mexican government released him in March 2011. According to an unnamed government official in Mexico, Asch was released because his extradition would have placed him in double jeopardy, as he had been tried and cleared of the same charges in Argentina (Christensen 2011).

2. I use Mol's term *enactment*, with its emphasis on the constant need for renewal, rather than *construction*, which implies an end point and a completion (Mol 2002).

3. Nadia Abu El-Haj argues that individual race might become more malleable with the rise of personalized genomics. This approach to medicine incorporates the neoliberal valorization of individual efforts to manage one's susceptibility to race-based disease, offering a sense of racial plasticity that differs from biologically deterministic medicine (El-Haj 2007).

4. There is nothing subtle about the everyday racism directed toward Indians and Afro-Ecuadorians in Ecuador. Although recently more Afro-Ecuadorians have attempted to enter national political forums, they remain marginalized. The situation is somewhat different for indigenous people. Ecuador is home to one of the most visible and successful political indigenous groupings in the world. In the 1990s, indigenous movements fostered mass protests against five hundred years of occupation, the environmental devastation of Amazonian oil extraction, and globalization. These indigenous groups played a large part in the overthrow of President Jamil Mahuad in 2000. Since then the state has had to pay increased attention to the demands of indigenous activists and communities. Recent administrations have set up specific ministries to serve indigenous people. Despite these changes, racism directed at Indians and blacks is still commonplace throughout Ecuador.

5. According to the 2001 Ecuadorian national census, mestizos make up 77 percent of the populace, whites 10.46 percent, Indians 6.3 percent, and blacks 2.23 percent (INEC, National Institute of Statistics and Census of Ecuador 2002.)

6. The configuration of identity through religion has continued to the present day. A survey conducted in the early 1980s found that Ecuadorians, at least in the northern sierra, identified primarily as Cristianos (Catholics), rather than by race or class or nationality. Being Catholic was a sign of true personhood (Stutzman 1981).

7. Although the connection between race and religion is not unique to Ecuador or the Andes, their imbrication is more explicit there than in some other post-Enlightenment locales (Povinelli 2006, 147).

8. *Mestizaje* has been told through literature and art in different nations and different national periods (Stoler 1995). Latin American mid-nineteenth-century pedagogical novels of nation building were predominantly love stories in which heterosexual lovers of different *razas* (Indian and Spanish) overcame hardship and disapproval, producing hybrid children who formed new and modern nations (Sommers 2002). The virtues as well as the problems of mixture were also told through Mexican *casta* paint-

ings of the eighteenth century, which demonstrated how the mixture of different races could or could not achieve whiteness over several generations (Cadena 2000; Katzew 2004). These novels and paintings offered very different representations from earlier colonial narratives of mixture: in one of these, a native woman, Malinche, in what is now Mexico, betrayed her people and bore the first mixed (and degenerate) Mexican child (Melhuus 1996).

9. Ann Stoler details how race was formulated in Europe through the rise of liberalism, which undermined the social hierarchies determined by blood. In the face of an emergent bourgeois order that preached equality among individuals, biology, sexuality, and reproduction became the new means of naturalizing inequities (Stoler 1995).

10. Foucault characterized racism as a tactic, "a discourse of vacillations" (cited in Cadena 2000, 13) in the internal fissures of society, a means of creating internal biological enemies against whom society must defend itself (Foucault 2003). Whereas Foucault focuses on Jews, who became the internal enemies of emerging European nations, Ann Stoler considers the colonial encounter as the largest laboratory for making racial distinctions (Stoler 1995).

11. Eugenic thinking also varied throughout Latin America. Particular policies were contingent on the circumstances of these new nation-states. For instance, Peruvian elites in the 1920s and 1930s who championed *indigenismo*, the exploration and glorification of the nation's indigenous past, spurned even the soft eugenics of Brazil and Argentina, charging its proponents with the desire to "destroy the Indian" (Cadena, 2000, 85). Academics and scientists rejected outright the idea of deterministic biological races and instead argued that *mestizaje* was a spiritual essence (Cadena 2000).

12. Education mattered greatly to prospective patients in egg-donor selection. As in the United States, doctors recruited students and used the prestige of their universities as a marketing tool.

13. Wilson also explained to me that initially he had matched donors by blood type. This more "rational" method prevented children from learning of their origins on finding out that their blood type differed from that of the parents. I had never heard of this approach to matching before, but it certainly makes sense in a place where blood is associated with both religious identity and *raza*.

14. Wilson's Excel spreadsheet was a new bureaucratic technology (see Howell 1995), a small organizational innovation that participated in the ongoing process of enacting *raza*.

15. See Clark 1998 for a similar discussion of how, in the 1930s and 1940s, the Ecuadorian doctor and social reformer Pablo Arturo Suarez compiled a statistical study of peasants and the working class in Ecuador, attempting to show how living conditions, profession, income, hygiene, and consumption habits affected the biologi-

cal condition of the population. To North American eyes, his method of constructing statistical categories appears to be a conflation of class and race.

16. Browner or poorer-looking people were often intimidated at the entrances to malls. Hence, my mall interviews were conducted under very different circumstances from those of my home visits with patients of *bajos recursos* who lived in run-down parts of Quito. Even if the donors came from these neighborhoods, their lighter skin allowed access to the whiter venues of the malls. I would not have been sensitive to this policing if, early in my fieldwork, I hadn't entered a mall with an Afro-Ecuadorian man. The security guard began to stop him, but when he saw me, he let the two of us pass inside.

17. The title of this section is borrowed from the novel by Zadie Smith (Z. Smith 2005), which in turn borrows it from an essay by Elaine Scarry. Smith's novel is a meditation on aesthetic ideals, race politics, and academic life. The core conflict takes place between two American academics—one black, one white—who clash over the possibility of universal standards for beauty.

18. This representation of ugly blackness didn't make it into the American spinoff, *Ugly Betty*.

19. In the 1970s, the "Black is beautiful" campaign influenced ideas about beauty in the U.S. In 1993, *Time* put the beautiful face of the coming multicultural America on the cover. She was a computer composite of a blended future. This multiracial ideal has made it into American egg-donation clinics, where darker skin can be considered desirable to preserve a youthful appearance. One white professional woman explained to Charis Thompson that she selected her egg donor with an eye toward darker skin. She didn't want her child to have white skin like hers because it would wrinkle more easily (Thompson 2005).

20. With the recent outsourcing of surrogacy to India, it seems that some white couples from the United States are not worried about their baby's race being affected by that of a distant surrogate, who will presumably stay far away once the baby is born (Gentleman 2010). This practice, however, validates many early feminist concerns about the use of brown bodies for the reproduction of white bodies.

WHEN BLOOD CALLS

1. In most Hispanic regions, a child has two last names—one from the mother and one from the father. When a woman marries, she usually drops her mother's last name and adds her new husband's. Pamela had dropped her birth mother's last name and taken Frida's in addition to Arturo's.

2. *Varon* is another word for *hombre* (man), but with the more noble meaning of baron, signifying a strong man and bearer of burdens. Young boys are called *varones*.

CHAPTER 4. EGG ECONOMIES AND THE TRAFFIC BETWEEN WOMEN

1. CONAIE was able to change the wording of the law, but agrarian reform was still dismantled.

2. Perhaps it is fitting, given Lévi-Strauss's unexamined relationship to the biological, that some of the alternative models proposed for the origin of human sociality have been proposed by feminist sociobiologists and physical anthropologists. These accounts have focused on biological survival, such as the reframing project of "woman the gatherer" (Slocum 1975), the theory that human cooperative sociality arises from the adaptation to bipedialism that made birth more difficult and required aid from other females (Rosenberg 2001), and ethological research demonstrating that female primates are engines of political and economic life in their roles as providing mothers (Hrdy 1999). These theories all center on female activity in producing and brokering social life, something Lévi-Strauss left unexamined.

3. Anthropologists have noted that these distinctions elide another set of understandings of the world, whereby women, for instance, can be exchanged for cattle without either category being understood as inert objects (Hutchinson 1992; Valeri 1994). Rubin also described how women as exchanged entities are not inherently desubjectified, or made into objects, and she also contended that sex oppression did not begin with capitalism. But when men, as wage laborers, became the public transactors and women the private reproducers, power and rights came to rest even more solidly in the hands of those who were able to traffic in public (Rubin 1975).

4. Another important concern about egg donation involves the long-term effects of fertility hormones on the donors. Very few donors I spoke with in Ecuador knew anything about the potential health effects of these drugs.

5. See, for example, Lawson 2005; Howley 2005; BBC News 2004; Ahuja, Simons and Edwards 1999; Miles 2005.

6. There is very little anonymous organ donation in Ecuador.

7. In the United States, the fee for egg donation is $4,000–$5,000. Most donors are in college or college-educated, between the ages of twenty and thirty, and do not have children. Higher amounts are paid to women from groups that are considered scarce, particularly Jewish and Japanese donors.

8. One exception was Sonia Merlyn Sacoto, the lawyer working to regulate assisted reproduction in Ecuador (see chapter 1). She argued against paid remuneration for egg donors on the grounds that the body should remain outside the sphere of commerce. In her book, Sacoto writes that egg donation should be permitted only when it can be established that "the donor collaborates freely, motivated by sentiments of solidarity and altruism" (Sacoto 2006, 107).

9. In Dr. Leon's view, another problem with the closeness of known donation had

to do with bodily experience. "The *receptora* is uncomfortable about the pain that the donor is undergoing on her behalf—the blood, the injections. The *receptora* doesn't have to feel this when she uses an anonymous donor." Dr. Leon's advocacy of anonymous donation would concern opponents of body-parts sales who argue that the practice dehumanizes the donor. Dr. Leon was calling for just that effect.

10. See Roberts 2008 for a discussion of how biosociality—a term coined by Paul Rabinow—is not as relevant to a site like Ecuador, where the boundary between the biological and the social is less distinct.

11. Egg donation is nothing like donating a kidney in terms of the donor experience: the latter is far more invasive, requires a longer recovery time, and carries higher risks for the donor.

12. We can also wonder what might have happened if Lévi-Strauss had worked through structural accounts of other kinship exchanges, most obviously the exchange of children. The ethnographic record is rife with examples of exchanges of children and other goods between women and men and between women and women (Leinaweaver 2008; Modell 1995; Stack 1975) Indeed, one of anthropology's most heated scandals of the twentieth century concerned whether young women in Samoa had the right and ability to circulate themselves not just sexually but between households in order to find one that suited them (Freeman 1983; Mead 1953). See Scheper-Hughes 1984 for a discussion of the disparate social worlds that Margaret Mead's and Derek Freeman's informants inhabited. As a young anthropologist, Mead worked primarily with young women, whereas Freeman, an older man, worked with older men and chiefs, who seemed to have a vested interest in denying that adolescent girls had rights to circulate themselves.

CHAPTER 5. ON ICE

1. This organization, Snowflakes, connects couples with extra embryos to those who "need" them. The name *Snowflakes* emphasizes each embryo's uniqueness, while the organization's practice emphasizes the value of abstract life.

2. Note that this definition does not imply the absence of any conflict. Indeed, Roseberry (1993) has written of hegemony as providing a "language of contention," a framework within which conflicts are understood and pursued. The definition suggests that hegemony shapes conflicts in ways that stabilize inequality.

3. These differences should be considered in the context of population size in the respective countries. In the United States, with a population of roughly 300 million, there is approximately one frozen embryo for every 750 people. In the United Kingdom, with a population of 60 million, the ratio is 1:1,150, and in Spain, with a population of 40 million, the ratio is 1:1,000.

4. In Ireland, where Catholic doctrine is influential, IVF practitioners have come

up with another creative way to deal with the issue of extra embryos. "In an effort to minimize the risk of multiple pregnancies, [doctors] replaced surplus embryos in the woman's cervix, where they perished. This, as wryly pointed out by one critic, was equivalent in effect to putting them in her ear" (Egan 2005).

5. Some of the literature from La Red de Reproducción Asistida claims that embryos are never discarded in Latin American IVF clinics (Luna 2002).

6. See Clarke 2009 and Tremayne 2009 for a similar valuing of relations in the context of reproductive technologies in the Muslim world.

7. The study authors sympathized with this approach to compassionate destruction. They used the word *excess* seven times and *accumulation* five times to describe frozen embryos, and they positioned their study as a call "to limit increasing the number of stored embryos" (Lyerly et al. 2008, 507).

8. Thanks to Gay Becker for this term.

CONCLUSION

1. In a recent article, Anne Lovell describes the efforts to save New Orleans's public Charity Hospital, where so many of the city's black and poor babies were born in the twentieth century. The city shut down Charity Hospital after Hurricane Katrina to make way for a new research hospital and bioscience research corridor. The mainstream press linked the hospital to dependent welfare mothers and the unworthy indigent while valorizing the biotech development, where resources would be expended on things like frozen embryos. In response, the advocacy group Charity Hospital Babies demanded that the lives of those who had been born at Charity Hospital be taken into account in the reconstruction of the city, thus resisting "redesigning the city for white, middle-class residents and tourists" (Lovell 2011, 266).

2. Much of the controversy surrounding the woman dubbed Octomom (Nadya Denise Doud-Suleman), who had octuplets through IVF in Southern California in 2009, centered on the fact that she had received public assistance in the past. Media coverage suggested that assisted reproduction should benefit only those who don't need welfare.

REFERENCES

Ackerman, Sara. 2010. Plastic Paradise: Transforming Bodies and Selves in Costa Rica's Cosmetic Surgery Tourism Industry. *Medical Anthropology* 29(4): 403–23.

ACOG (American College of Obstetricians and Gynecologists), Committee on Ethics. 1994. Committee Opinion. *Preembryo Research: History, Scientific Background, and Ethical Considerations*. 136. April.

Adams, Vincanne, and Stacy Leigh Pigg. 2005. *Sex in Development: Science, Sexuality, and Morality in Global Perspective*. Durham, NC: Duke University Press.

Agamben, Giorgio. 1998. *Homo Sacer: Sovereign Power and Bare Life*. Stanford, CA: Stanford University Press.

———. 2000. *Remnants of Auschwitz: The Witness and the Archive*. Trans. D. Heller-Roazen. New York: Zone Books.

Aguilar-Monslave, Luis Antonio. 1984. The Separation of Church and State: The Ecuadorian Case. *Thought* 59 (233): 205–19.

Ahuja, K. K., E. G. Simons, and R. G. Edwards. 1999. Money, Morals and Medical Risks: Conflicting Notions Underlying the Recruitment of Egg Donors. *Human Reproduction* 14(2): 279–84.

Alban, Anthony Cavender Manuel. 1998. Compulsory Medical Service in Ecuador: The Physician's Perspective. *Social Science and Medicine* 47(12): 1937–46.

Allen, Catherine J. 1988. *The Hold Life Has: Coca and Cultural Identity in an Andean Community*. Washington, DC: Smithsonian Institution Press.

Althabe, Fernando, José M. Belizán, José Villar, Sophie Alexander, Eduardo Bergel, Silvina Ramos, Mariana Romero, et al. 2004. Mandatory Second Opinion to Reduce Rates of Unnecessary Caesarean Sections in Latin America: A Cluster Randomized Controlled Trial. *Lancet* 363(9425): 1934–40.

Anagnost, Ann. 1995. A Surfeit of Bodies: Population and the Rationality of the State in Post-Mao China. In *Conceiving the New World Order: The Global Politcs of Reproduction*, ed. Faye D. Ginsburg and Rayna Rapp. Berkeley: University of California Press.

Anderson, Warwick, and Gabrielle Hecht, eds. 2002. "Postcolonial Technoscience," special issue of *Social Studies of Science* 32(6): 791–825.

Andrade, Enrique Valle. 1994. "Cuando la sangre llama, la sangre mata" (When blood calls, blood kills). *Diario Hoy*. June 25. www.explored.com.ec/noticias-ecuador/cuando-la-sangre-llama-la-sangre-mata-30849–30849.html.

Arditti, Rita, Shelley Minden, and Renate Klein. 1984. *Test-Tube Women: What Future for Motherhood?* London: Pandora Press.

Ariès, Philippe. 1962. *Centuries of Childhood; A Social History of Family Life*. New York: Knopf.

Arnold, David. 2000. *Science, Technology, and Medicine in Colonial India*. New York: Cambridge University Press.

Asad, Talal. 1993. *Genealogies of Religion: Discipline and Reasons of Power in Christianity and Islam*. Baltimore: Johns Hopkins University Press.

———. 2003. *Formations of the Secular: Christianity, Islam, Modernity*. Stanford, CA: Stanford University Press.

Baker, Lee D., and Thomas C. Patterson. 1994. Race, Racism, and the History of U.S. Anthropology. *Transforming Anthropology* 5(1–2): 1–6.

Barth, Fredrik. 1954. Father's Brother's Daughter Marriage in Kurdistan. *Southwestern Journal of Anthropology* 10(164–71).

Barros, A. J. D., I. S. Santos, A. Matijasevich, M. Rodrigues Domingues, M. Silveira, Fernando C Barros, and C. Victora. 2011. Patterns of Deliveries in a Brazilian Birth Cohort: Almost Universal Cesarean Sections for the Better-Off. *Revista de Saúde Pública* 45 (4): 635–43. http://dx.doi.org/10.1590/S0034–89102011005000039. Bastien, Joseph William. 1979. Marriage and Exchange in the Andes. *Actes du LXIIe Congrès international des américanistes* 6:149–64.

BBC News. 2004. Egg and sperm donor cash proposal. November 11. http://news.bbc.co.uk/2/hi/health/4002829.stm, accessed October 11, 2011.

Becker, Gay. 2000. *The Elusive Embryo: How Women and Men Approach New Reproductive Technologies*. Berkeley: University of California Press.

Béhague, Dominique. 2002. Beyond the Simple Economics of Cesarean Section

Birthing: Women's Resistance to Social Inequality. *Culture, Medicine and Psychiatry* 26(4): 473–507.

Behar, Ruth, and Bruce Mannheim. 1995. The Couple in the Cage: A Guatinaui Odyssey. *Visual Anthropology Review* 11(1): 118–27.

Belizán, José M., Fernando Althabe, Fernando C. Barros, and Sophie Alexander. 1999. Rates and Implications of Caesarean Sections in Latin America: Ecological Study. *BMJ* 319 (7222): 1397–1402.

Belluck, Pam. 2005. It's Not so Easy to Adopt an Embryo. *New York Times*. June 12.

Benavides, O. Hugo. 2008. *Drugs, Thugs, and Divas: Telenovelas and Narcodramas in Latin America*. Austin: University of Texas Press.

Bharadwaj, Aditya. 2002. Conception Politics: Medical Egos, Media Spotlights, and the Contest over Test-Tube Firsts in India. In *Infertility Around the Globe*, ed. Marcia Claire Inhorn and Frank van Balen, 315–33. Berkeley: University of California Press.

———. 2005. Cultures of Embryonic Stem Cell Research in India. In *Crossing Borders: Religious and Political Differences Concerning Stem Cell Research*, ed. C.H. Wolfgang Bender and Alexandra Manzei, 325–41. Münster: Agenda Verlag.

Biehl, João Guilherme. 2005. *Vita: Life in a Zone of Social Abandonment*. Berkeley: University of California Press.

Biehl, João Guilherme, and Torben Eskerod. 2007. Will to Live: AIDS Therapies and the Politics of Survival. Princeton, NJ: Princeton University Press.

Birenbaum-Carmeli, Daphna. 1998. Reproductive Partners: Doctor–Woman Relations in Israeli and Canadian IVF Contexts. In *Small Wars: The Cultural Politics of Childhood*, ed. N. Scheper-Hughes and C. F. Sargent, 75–92. Berkeley: University of California Press.

———. 2009. Contested Surrogacy and the Gender Order: An Israeli Case Study. In *Assisting Reproduction, Testing Genes: Global Encounters with New Biotechnologies*, ed. Daphna Birenbaum-Carmeli and Marcia Claire Inhorn, 189–210. New York: Berghahn Books.

Birenbaum-Carmeli, Daphna, and Marcia Claire Inhorn. 2009. *Assisting Reproduction, Testing Genes: Global Encounters with New Biotechnologies*. New York: Berghahn Books.

Blakely, Mary Kay. 1983. Surrogate Mothers: For Whom Are They Working? *MS Magazine*, March, 18–20.

Bloch, Maurice, and Susan Guggenheim. 1981. Compadrazgo, Baptism and the Symbolism of a Second Birth. *Man* 16(3): 376–86.

Borneman, John. 2001. Caring and Being Cared For: Displacing Marriage, Kinship,

Gender and Sexuality. In *The Ethics of Kinship: Ethnographic inquiries,* ed. J.D. Faubion, 129–46. Lanham, MD: Rowman & Littlefield.

Borrero, Claudia. 2002. Gamete and Embryo Donation. In *Current Practices and Controversies in Assisted Reproduction,* ed. E. Vayena, P. Rowe, and P.D. Griffin, 166–76. Geneva: World Health Organization.

Bourdieu, Pierre. 1977. *Outline of a Theory of Practice.* Cambridge: Cambridge University Press.

Bowker, Geoffrey C., and Susan Leigh Star. 2000. *Sorting Things Out: Classification and Its Consequences.* Cambridge, MA: MIT Press.

Braff, Lara. 2010. Reconceiving Personhood: The Localization of Assisted Reproductive Technologies in Mexico City. PhD diss., University of Chicago.

Brown, Peter Robert Lamont. 1992. *Power and Persuasion in Late Antiquity: Towards a Christian Empire.* Madison: University of Wisconsin Press.

Browner, Carole. 1979. Abortion Decision Making: Some Findings from Colombia. *Studies in Family Planning* 10(3): 96–106.

Bryant, Sherwin K. 2008. Finding Freedom: Slavery in Colonial Ecuador. In *The Ecuador Reader: History, Culture, Politics,* ed. Carlos de la Torre and Steven Striffler, 52–67. Durham: Duke University Press.

Buechler, Hans C., and Judith-Maria Buechler. 1996. *The World of Sofía Velázquez: The Autobiography of a Bolivian Market Vendor.* New York: Columbia University Press.

Cadena, Marisol de la. 1995. "Women Are More Indian": Ethnicity and Gender in a Community near Cuzco. In *Ethnicity, Markets, and Migration in the Andes: At the Crossroads of History and Anthropology,* ed. B. Larson, O. Harris, and E. Tandeter, 329–48. Durham, NC: Duke University Press.

———. 2000. *Indigenous Mestizos: The Politics of Race and Culture in Cuzco, 1919–1991.* Durham, NC: Duke University Press.

Callon, Michel. 1989. Some Elements of a Sociology of Translation: Domestication of the Scallops and the Fishermen of St. Brieuc Bay. In *Power, Action and Belief,* ed. J. Law, 196–223. London: Routledge.

Canessa, Andrew. 2000. Fear and Loathing on the Kharisiri Trail: Alterity and Identity in the Andes. *Journal of the Royal Anthropological Institute* 6 (4): 705–20.

Canguilhem, Georges. 1991. *The Normal and the Pathological.* New York: Zone Books.

———. 1992. Machine and Organism. In *Incorporations,* ed. J. Crary and S. Kwinter, 45–69. New York: Zone.

Carsten, Janet, 2004, *After Kinship.* Cambridge: Cambridge University Press.

Castro, Arachu, and Merrill Singer. 2004. *Unhealthy Health Policy: A Critical Anthropological Examination.* Walnut Creek, CA: AltaMira Press.

Castro, Daniel. 2007. *Another Face of Empire: Bartolomé de las Casas, Indigenous Rights, and Ecclesiastical Imperialism*. Durham, NC: Duke University Press.

CEPAR (Centro de Estudios de Población y Desarrollo Social). 2000. *Endemain-III, Ecuador Informe General*. Quito: Centro de Estudios de Población y Desarrollo Social.

Chakrabarty, Dipesh. 2000. *Provincializing Europe: Postcolonial Thought and Historical Difference*. Princeton, NJ: Princeton University Press.

Charney, Paul. 1991. The Implications Of Godparental Ties between Indians and Spaniards in Colonial Lima. *The Americas* 47(3): 295–313.

Chen, Nancy N., and Helen Moglen. 2007. *Bodies in the Making: Transgressions and Transformations*. Santa Cruz, CA: New Pacific Press.

Christensen, Kim. 2011, Doctor with Ties to Fertility Scandal Won't Be Extradited by Mexico. *Los Angeles Times*. April 1. http://articles.latimes.com/2011/apr/01/local/la-me-0401-asch-20110401.

Choudhuri, Arnab Rai. 1985. Practising Western Science Outside the West: Personal Observations on the Indian Scene. *Social Studies of Science* 15:475–505.

Clark, A. Kim. 1998. Race, "Culture," and *Mestizaje:* The Statistical Construction of the Ecuadorian Nation, 1930–1950. *Journal of Historical Sociology* 11(2): 185–211.

———. 2002. The Language of Contention in Liberal Ecuador. In *Culture, Economy, Power: Anthropology as Critique, Anthropology as Praxis*, ed. W. Lem and B. Leach, 150–64. Albany: State University of New York Press.

Clark, A. Kim, and Marc Becker. 2007. *Highland Indians and the State in Modern Ecuador*. Pittsburgh, PA: University of Pittsburgh Press.

Clark, Gracia. 1994. *Onions Are My Husband: Survival and Accumulation by West African Market Women*. Chicago: University of Chicago Press.

Clarke, Morgan. 2009. *Islam and New Kinship: Reproductive Technology and the Shariah in Lebanon*. New York: Berghahn Books.

CNN. 2007. Tiniest Katrina Survivor Finally Born. January 16.

Cohen, Lawrence. 2004. Operability: Surgery at the Margin of the State. In *Anthropology in the Margins of the State*, ed. V. Das and D. Poole, 165–90. School of American Research Advanced Seminar Series. Santa Fe, NM: School of American Research Press.

———. 2005. Operability, Bioavailability and Exception. In *Global Assemblages: Technology, Politics, and Ethics as Anthropological Problems*, ed. A. Ong and S. J. Collier, 79–90. Malden, MA: Blackwell.

Cole, Joshua. 2000. *The Power of Large Numbers: Population, Politics, and Gender in Nineteenth-Century France*. Ithaca, NY: Cornell University Press.

Colen, Shellee. 1995. "Like a Mother to Them": Stratified Reproduction and West Indian Child Care Workers and Employers in New York. In *Conceiving the New World Order: The Global Politics of Reproduction*, ed. Faye D. Ginsburg and Rayna Rapp, 78–102. Berkeley: University of California Press.

Colloredo-Mansfeld, Rudi. 1998. "Dirty Indians": Radical Indigenas and the Political Economy of Social Difference in Modern Ecuador. *Bulletin of Latin American Research* 17(2): 185–205.

Comaroff, Jean, and John L. Comaroff. 2000. *Millennial Capitalism and the Culture of Neoliberalism*. Durham, NC: Duke University Press.

Comercio, El. 2004. Muchos Padres pagan para congelar y mantener sus embriones intactos. June 20.

Congreso Nacional, Función Ejecutiva, Ecuador. 2003. Código de la Niñez y Adolescencia 2002–100:1–55. Quito.

Cooper, Melinda. 2008. *Life as Surplus: Biotechnology and Capitalism in the Neoliberal Era*. Seattle: University of Washington Press.

Copeman, Jacob. 2009. Introduction: Blood Donation, Bio-economy, Culture. *Body and Society* 15(2): 1–28.

Corea, Gena. 1988. *The Mother Machine: Reproductive Technologies from Artificial Insemination to Artificial Wombs*. London: Women's Press.

Crandall, Russell, Guadalupe Paz, and Riordan Roett. 2005. *The Andes in Focus: Security, Democracy, and Economic Reform*. Boulder, CO: Lynne Rienner Publishers.

Crandon-Malamud, Libbet. 1991. *From the Fat of Our Souls: Social Change, Political Process, and Medical Pluralism in Bolivia*. Berkeley: University of California Press.

Cueto, Marcos. 1988. Excellence in the Periphery: Scientific Activities and Biomedical Sciences in Peru. New York: Columbia University Press.

Dalton, Rex. 1996. The Clinic of Lost Children. *Vogue*. March, 330–36.

Das, Veena, and Abhijit Dasgupta. 2000. Scientific and Polticial Representations : Cholera Vaccine in India. *Economic and Poltical Weekly* 35 (8–9): 633–44.

Daston, Lorraine 1992. Objectivity and the Escape From Perspective. In *The Science Studies Reader*, ed. M. Biagioli, 597–618. New York: Routledge.

Davila, Mario. 1971. Compadrazgo: Fictive Kinship in Latin America. In *Readings in Kinship and Social Structure*, ed. N. Graburn, 396–406. New York: Harper and Row.

Descartes, René. 1996. *Discourse on the Method; and Meditations on First Philosophy*. New Haven, CT: Yale University Press.

Descola, Philippe. 1994. *In the Society of Nature: A Native Ecology in Amazonia*. Cambridge: Cambridge University Press.

Doyle, Julie, and Katrina Roen. 2008. Surgery and Embodiment: Carving Out Subjects. *Body and Society* 14(1): 1–7.

Durkheim, Émile. 1995. *The Elementary Forms of Religious Life*. Trans. Karen Fields. New York: Free Press.

———. 1997. *The Division of Labor in Society*. Trans. W. D. Halls. New York: Free Press.

Edmonds, Alexander. 2010. *Pretty Modern: Beauty, Sex, and Plastic Surgery in Brazil*. Durham, NC: Duke University Press.

Edwards, Jeanette. 1999. *Technologies of Procreation: Kinship in the Age of Assisted Conception*. New York: Routledge.

Egan, Deirdre. 2005. Myths and Mothers: Women and IVF in Ireland. Paper presented at Reproductive Disruptions Conference, Ann Arbor, Michigan, May.

El-Haj, Nadia Abu. 2007. The Genetic Reinscription of Race. *Annual Review of Anthropology* 36:283–300.

Engels, Friedrich, and Ernest Untermann. 1902. *The Origin of the Family, Private Property and the State*. Chicago: C. H. Kerr.

Evans-Pritchard, E. E. 1937. *Witchcraft, Oracles and Magic among the Azande*. Oxford: Clarendon Press.

Ewig, Christina. 2010. *Second-Wave Neoliberalism: Gender, Race, and Health Sector Reform in Peru*. University Park: Pennsylvania State University Press.

Favret-Saada, Jeanne. 1980. *Deadly Words: Witchcraft in the Bocage*. Cambridge: Cambridge University Press.

Ferguson, James. 2006. The Anti-politics Machine. In *The Anthropology of the State: A Reader*, ed. A. Sharma and A. Gupta, 270–86. Blackwell Readers in Anthropology, 9. Malden, MA: Blackwell.

Foster, George M. 1953. Cofradia and Compadrazgo in Spain and Spanish America. *Southwestern Journal of Anthropology* 9(1): 1–28.

Foucault, Michel. 2003. *Society Must be Defended: Lectures at the College de France, 1975–76*. New York: Picador.

Franklin, Sarah. 1997. *Embodied Progress: A Cultural Account of Assisted Conception*. London: Routledge.

———. 2001. Biologization Revisited: Kinship Theory in the Context of the New Biologies. In *Relative Values: Reconfiguring Kinship Studies*, ed. Sarah Franklin and Susan McKinnon, 302–25. Durham, NC: Duke University Press.

———. 2006a. The Cyborg Embryo: Our Path to Transbiology. *Theory, Culture and Society* 23(7–8): 167–87.

———. 2006b. Embryonic Economies: The Double Reproductive Value of Stem Cells. *BioSocieties* 1(1): 71–90.

Franklin, Sarah, and Margaret M. Lock. 2003. *Remaking Life and Death: Toward an Anthropology of the Biosciences.* Santa Fe, NM: School of American Research Press.

Franklin, Sarah, and Helene Ragoné. 1998. *Reproducing Reproduction: Kinship, Power, and Technological Innovation.* Philadelphia: University of Pennsylvania Press.

Franklin, Sarah, and Celia Roberts. 2001. The Social Life of the Embryo. Paper presented at Ethnographies of the Centre, Lancaster, U.K., October.

———. 2006. *Born and Made: An Ethnography of Preimplantation Genetic Diagnosis.* Princeton, NJ: Princeton University Press.

Freeman, Derek. 1983. Margaret Mead and Samoa: The Making and Unmaking of An Anthropological Myth. Cambridge, MA: Harvard University Press.

Fullwiley, Duana. 2008. The Biologistical Construction of Race: "Admixture" Technology and the New Genetic Medicine. *Social Studies of Science* 38(5): 695–735.

———. 2011. *The Encultured Gene: Sickle Cell Health Politics and Biological Difference in West Africa.* Princeton, NJ: Princeton University Press.

Garcia, Mauricio, and Amalia Mauro. 1992. *El orden de adrentro y el orden de afuera.* Quito: Centro de Planificación y Estudios Sociales.

Gentleman, Amelia. 2010. India Nurtures Business of Surrogate Motherhood. *New York Times.* March 10. www.nytimes.com/2008/03/10/world/asia/10surrogate.html.

George, Robert P., and Christopher Tollefsen. 2008. *Embryo: A Defense of Human Life.* New York: Doubleday.

Gerlach, Allen. 2003. *Indians, Oil, and Politics: A Recent History of Ecuador.* Wilmington, DE: Scholarly Resources.

Giménez, Martha E. 1991. The Mode of Reproduction in Transition: A Marxist-Feminist Analysis of the Effects of Reproductive Technologies. *Gender and Society* 5(3): 334–50.

Ginsburg, Faye D., and Rayna Rapp. 1995. *Conceiving the New World Order: The Global Politics of Reproduction.* Berkeley: University of California Press.

Goldenberg, Suzanne. 2007. Rescued from Katrina: New Life for a Frozen Embryo. *Guardian* (U.K.). January 16.

Goody, Jack. 1959. The Mother's Brother and the Sister's Son in West Africa. *Journal of the Royal Anthropolgical Institute* 89(1): 61–88.

Gordon, Deborah. 1988. Tenacious Assumptions in Western Medicine. In *Biomedicine Examined: Culture, Illness, and Healing,* ed. M. M. Lock and D. R. Gordon, 19–56. Dordrecht: Kluwer Academic Publishers.

Guerrero, Andres. 1997. The Construction of the Ventriloquist's Image: Liberal Discourse and the "Miserable Indian Race" in Late 19th-Century Ecuador. *Journal of Latin American Studies* 29(3): 555–90.

———. 2003. The Administration of Dominated Populations under a Regime of Customary Citizenship: The Case of Postcolonial Ecuador. In *After Spanish Rule: Postcolonial Predicaments of the Americas,* ed. M. Thurner and A. Guerrero, 272–309. Durham, NC: Duke University Press.

Gutmann, Matthew C. 2003. *Changing Men and Masculinities in Latin America.* Durham, NC: Duke University Press.

———. 2007. *Fixing Men: Sex, Birth Control, and AIDS in Mexico.* Berkeley: University of California Press.

Handwerker, Lisa. 1995. The Hen That Can't Lay an Egg: Conceptions of Female Infertility in Modern China. In *Deviant Bodies: Critical Perspectives on Difference in Science and Popular Culture,* ed. J. Terry and J. Urla, 358–86. Bloomington: University of Indiana Press.

Haraway, Donna Jeanne. 1991. *Simians, Cyborgs and Women: The Reinvention of Nature.* London: Free Association.

———. 1997. *ModestWitness@SecondMillennium.FemaleManMeetsOncoMouse: Feminism and Technoscience.* New York: Routledge.

———. 1999. For the Love of a Good Dog: Webs of Action in the World of Dog Genetics. In *Genetic Nature/Culture: Anthropology and Science beyond the Two-Culture Divide,* ed. Alan Goodman, Deborah Heath, M. and Susan Lindee Berkeley: University of California Press, 111–31.

———. 2008. *When Species Meet.* Minneapolis: University of Minnesota Press.

Harris, Olivia. 2008. Alterities: Kinship and Gender. In *A Companion to Latin American Anthropology,* ed. D. Poole. 276–303 Oxford: Blackwell.

Harvey, David. 2005. *A Brief History of Neoliberalism.* Oxford: Oxford University Press.

Hermida, Jorge, Patricio Romero, Ximena Abarca, Luis Vaca, Maria Elena Robalino, and Luis Vieira. 2004. *Scaling-up and Institutionalizing Continuous Quality Improvement in the Ministry of Health of Ecuador, in the Context of the Law for the Provision of Free Maternity and Child Care.* Research Report no. 1, The Law for the Provision of Free Maternity and child care. www.lachsr.org/documents/thelawfortheprovision offreematernityandchildcarelfmc-EN.pdf. Accessed October 14, 2011.

Herold, Eve. 2006. *Stem Cell Wars: Inside Stories from the Frontlines.* New York: Palgrave Macmillan.

Horn, David. 1994. *Social Bodies: Science, Reproduction, and Italian Modernity*. Princeton, NJ: Princeton University Press.

Howell, Joel D. 1995. *Technology in the Hospital: Transforming Patient Care in the Early Twentieth Century*. Baltimore: Johns Hopkins University Press.

Howley, Kerry. 2005. Ma, Ma, Where's My Pa? Should Anonymous Sperm or Egg Donation Be a Crime? Reason.com. January 23. http://reason.com/archives/2005/01/23/ma-ma-wheres-my-pa, accessed June 18, 2011.

Hrdy, Sarah Blaffer. 1999. *Mother Nature: A History of Mothers, Infants, and Natural Selection*. New York: Pantheon Books.

Htun, Mala. 2003. *Sex and the State: Abortion, Divorce, and the Family under Latin American Dictatorships and Democracies*. Cambridge: Cambridge University Press.

Hubbell, Linda J. 1971. The Network of Compadrazgo among Middle-Class Mexican Women. Paper presented at the annual meeting of the American Anthropological Association, New York City. November.

Hume, David. 1964. *Hume on Religion*. Cleveland, OH: World.

Hutchinson, Sharon. 1992. Cattle of Money and the Cattle of Girls among the Nuer, 1930–83. *American Ethnologist* 19(2): 294–316.

Icaza, Jorge. 1968. *Huasipungo*. Buenos Aires: Losada.

Ignatiev, Noel. 1995. *How the Irish Became White*. New York: Routledge.

INEC (Instituto Nacional de Estadística y Censos). 2002. *Ecuador Censo 2001, 2002*. www.inec.gov.ec/home/Accessed October 12, 2011

Inhorn, Marcia. 1994. Interpreting Infertility: Medical Anthropological Perspectives. *Social Science and Medicine* 39(4): 459–61.

———. 2003. *Local Babies, Global Science: Gender, Religion, and In Vitro Fertilization in Egypt*. New York: Routledge.

Inhorn, Marcia Claire, and Frank van Balen. 2002. *Infertility around the Globe: New Thinking on Childlessness, Gender, and Reproductive Technologies*. Berkeley: University of California Press.

Irigaray, Luce. 1980. When the Goods Get Together. In *New French Feminisms*, ed. Elaine Marks and Isabelle de Courtivron, 107–10. Amherst: University of Massachusetts Press.

Ishiguro, Kazuo. 2005. *Never Let Me Go*. New York: Alfred A. Knopf.

Ivry, Tsipy. 2009. The Ultrasonic Picture Show and the Politics of Threatened Life. *Medical Anthropology Quarterly* 23(3): 189–211.

Kahn, Susan. 2000. *Reproducing Jews: A Cultural Account of Assisted Conception in Israel*. Durham, NC: Duke University Press.

Kasza, Gregory J. 1980. Regional Conflict in Ecuador: Quito and Guayaquil. *Inter-American Economic Affairs* 35(2): 3–42.

Katzew, Ilona. 2004. *Casta Painting: Images of Race in Eighteenth-Century Mexico.* New Haven, CT: Yale University Press.

Kaufman, Sharon. 2005. *And a Time to Die: How American Hospitals Shape the End of Life.* New York: Scribner.

Kaufman, Sharon, and Lynn Morgan. 2005. The Anthropology of the Beginnings and Ends of Life. *Annual Review of Anthropology* 34:317–41.

Keane, Webb. 2002. Sincerity, "Modernity," and the Protestants. *Cultural Anthropology* 17(1): 65–92.

———. 2006. Anxious Transcendence. In *The Anthropology of Christianity,* ed. F. Cannell, 308–24. Durham, NC: Duke University Press.

Keller, Evelyn Fox. 1995. *Reflections on Gender and Science.* New Haven, CT: Yale University Press.

———. 2000. *The Century of the Gene.* Cambridge, MA: Harvard University Press.

Kirsch, Thomas. 2004. Restaging the Will to Believe: Religious Pluralism, Anti-syncretism, and the Problem of Belief. *American Anthropologist* 106(4): 699–709.

Kohn, Eduardo. 2007. How Dogs Dream: Amazonian Natures and the Politics of Transspecies Engagement. *American Ethnologist* 34(1): 3–24.

Krupa, Christopher. 2010. State by Proxy: Privatized Government in the Andes. *Comparative Studies in Society and History* 52:319–50.

Kulick, Don, and Anne Meneley. 2005. *Fat: The Anthropology of an Obsession.* New York: Jeremy P. Tarcher.

Laet, Marianne de, and Annemarie Mol. 2000. The Zimbabwe Bush Pump: Mechanics of a Fluid Technology. *Social Studies of Science* 30(2): 225–63.

Lancaster, Roger N. 1992. *Life is Hard: Machismo, Danger, and the Intimacy of Power in Nicaragua.* Berkeley: University of California Press.

Landecker, Hannah. 2007. *Culturing Life: How Cells Became Technologies.* Cambridge, MA: Harvard University Press.

Lane, Kris. 2003. Haunting the Present: Five Colonial Legacies for the New Millennium. In *Millennial Ecuador: Critical Essays on Cultural Transformations and Social Dynamics,* ed. N.E. Whitten, 75–101. Iowa City: University of Iowa Press.

Larson, Brooke. 1999. Andean Highland Peasants and the Trials of Nation-Making during the Nineteenth Century. In *The Cambridge History of the Native Peoples of the Americas,* vol. 3, *South America,* ed. F. Salomon and S.B. Schwartz. Cambridge: Cambridge University Press.

———. 2004. *Trials of Nation Making: Liberalism, Race, and Ethnicity in the Andes, 1810–1910*. Cambridge: Cambridge University Press.

Lasch, Christopher, 1974. *Haven in a Heartless World: The Family Beseiged*. New York: Basic Books.

Latour, Bruno. 1987. *Science in Action: How to Follow Scientists and Engineers through Society*. Cambridge, MA: Harvard University Press.

———. 1988. *The Pasteurization of France*. Cambridge, MA: Harvard University Press.

———. 1993. *We Have Never Been Modern*. New York: Harvester Wheatsheaf.

———. 1999. *Pandora's Hope: Essays on the Reality of Science Studies*. Cambridge, MA: Harvard University Press.

———. 2005. *Reassembling the Social: an Introduction to Actor-Network Theory*. Oxford: Oxford University Press.

———. 2010. *On the Modern Cult of the Factish Gods*. Durham, NC: Duke University Press.

Lau, Estelle T. 1998. Can Money Whiten? Exploring Race Practice in Colonial Venezuela and its Implications for Contemporary Race Discourse. Michigan Journal of Race and Law 3:417–73.

Lawson, Amy. 2005. Chronic Shortage of Donors Puts IVF Clinics in Jeopardy, *Sydney Morning Herald*. September 18. www.smh.com.au/news/national/chronic -shortage-of-donors-puts-ivf-clinics-in-jeopardy/2005/09/17/1126750168474.html.

Layne, Linda L. 1999. *Transformative Motherhood: On Giving and Getting in a Consumer Culture*. New York: New York University Press.

LaBarre, Weston, and John Alden Mason. 1948. *The Aymara Indians of the Lake Titicaca Plateau, Bolivia*. Menasha, WI: American Anthropological Association.

Leach, Edmund. 1951. The Structural Implications of Matrilateral Cross-Cousin Marriage. *Journal of the Royal Anthropological Institute* 81:23–53.

Leenhardt, Maurice. 1979. *Do Kamo: Person and Myth in the Melanesian World*. Chicago: University of Chicago Press.

Leifsen, Esben. 2008. Child Trafficking and Formalisation: The Case of International Adoption from Ecuador. *Children and Society* 22(3): 212–22.

———. 2009. Adoption and the Governing of Child Welfare in 20th-Century Quito. *Journal of Latin American and Caribbean Anthropology* 14(1): 68–91.

———. 2010. Child Welfare, Biopower and Mestizo Relatedness in Quito Ecuador. In *Parenting after the Century of the Child: Traveling Ideals, Institutional Negotiations and Individual Responses*, ed. T. Thelen and H. Haukanes, 103–21. Farnham, U.K.: Ashgate.

Leinaweaver, Jessaca B. 2008. *The Circulation of Children: Kinship, Adoption, and Morality in Andean Peru*. Durham, NC: Duke University Press.

Leite, Iúri da Costa, Neeru Gupta, and Roberto do Nascimento Rodrigues. 2004. Female Sterilization in Latin America: Cross-National Perspectives. *Journal of Biosocial Science* 36(683–98).

Lévi-Strauss, Claude. 1969. *The Elementary Structures of Kinship*. London: Eyre & Spottiswoode.

Lévy-Bruhl, Lucien. 1935. *Primitive Mentality*. Boston: Beacon Press.

Literary Digest., 1917. Birth Control and Race Suicide. February 3.

Lock, Margaret M. 1993. *Encounters with Aging: Mythologies of Menopause in Japan and North America*. Berkeley: University of California Press.

———. 2002. *Twice Dead: Organ Transplants and the Reinvention of Death*. Berkeley: University of California Press.

Lock, Margaret, and Vinh-Kim Nguyen. 2010. *An Anthropology of Biomedicine*. Oxford: Wiley-Blackwell.

Lovell, Anne M. 2011. Debating Life after Disaster: Charity Hospital Babies and Bioscientific Futures in Post-Katrina New Orleans. *Medical Anthropology Quarterly* 25(2): 254–77.

Luna, Florencia. 2002. Assisted Reproductive Technology in Latin America: Some Ethical and Sociocultural Issues. In *Current Practices and Controversies in Assisted Reproduction*, ed. E. Vayena, P. Rowe, and P. D. Griffin, 31–40. Geneva: World Health Organization.

Lyerly, Anne Drapkin, Karen Steinhauser, Corrine Voils, Emily Namey, Carolyn Alexander, Brandon Bankowski, Robert Cook-Deegan, et al. 2008. Fertility Patients' Views about Frozen Embryo Disposition: Results of a Multi-institutional U.S. Survey. In *Fertility and Sterility* 93:499–509.

Lyons, Barry J. 2006. *Remembering the Hacienda: Religion, Authority, and Social Change in Highland Ecuador*. Austin: University of Texas Press.

Mahmood, Saba. 2005. *Politics of Piety: The Islamic Revival and the Feminist Subject*. Princeton, NJ: Princeton University Press.

Malinowski, Bronislaw. 1922. *Argonauts of the Western Pacific: An Account of Native Enterprise and Adventure in the Archipelagoes of Melanesian New Guinea*. New York: Dutton.

———. 1984. *Magic, Science, and Religion, and Other Essays*. Westport, CT: Greenwood Press.

Mallon, Florencia E. 1996. Constructing *Mestizaje* in Latin America: Authenticity,

Marginality, and Gender in the Claiming of Ethnic Identities. *Journal of Latin American Anthropology* 2(1): 170–81.

Mamo, Laura. 2007. *Queering Reproduction: Achieving Pregnancy in the Age of Techno-science.* Durham, NC: Duke University Press.

Mannheim, Bruce, and Krista van Vleet. 1998. The Dialogics of Southern Quechua Narrative. *American Anthropologist* 100(2): 326–46.

Marantz Henig, Robin. 2003. Pandora's Baby. *Scientific American.* May, 62–67.

Martin, Emily. 1992. *The Woman in the Body: A Cultural Analysis of Reproduction.* Boston: Beacon Press.

Marx, Karl. 1976. *Capital: A Critique of Political Economy.* Harmondsworth, U.K.: Penguin.

Mauss, Marcel. 1990. *The Gift: The Form and Reason for Exchange in Archaic Societies.* London: Routledge.

McKee, Lauris. 2003. Ethnomedicine and Enculturation in the Andes of Ecuador. In *Medical Pluralism in the Andes,* ed. J. Koss-Chioino, T. L. Leatherman, and C. Greenway, 131–47. London: Routledge.

McKinnon, Susan. 2001. The Economics in Kinship and the Paternity of Culture: Origin Stories in Kinship Theory. In *Relative Values: Reconfiguring Kinship Studies,* ed. Sarah Franklin and Susan McKinnon, 277–301. Durham, NC: Duke University Press.

Mead, Margaret. 1953. *Coming of Age in Samoa: A Psychological Study of Primitive Youth for Western Civilization.* New York: Modern Library.

Melhuus, Marit. 1996. Power Value and the Ambigious Meanings of Gender. In *Machos, Mistresses, Madonnas: Contesting the Power of Latin American Gender Imagery,* ed. M. Melhuus and K. A. Stolen, 230–59. London: Verso.

———. 2003. Exchange Matters: Issues of Law and the Flow of Human Substances. In *Globalisation: Studies in Anthropology,* ed. T. H. Eriksen, 170–97. London: Pluto Press.

Mesa-Lago, Carmelo. 2008. What the United States Can Learn from Social Security Reforms in Latin America. *LASA Forum* 34(2): 22–24.

Miles, Janelle, 2005. Human Egg Donors on Rise. *The Age* (Melbourne), September 7. www.theage.com.au/news/national/human-egg-donors-on-rise/2005/09/06/1125772522524.html.

Mintz, Sydney W., and Eric R. Wolf. 1950. An Analysis of Ritual Co-parenthood (Compadrazgo). *Southwestern Journal of Anthropology* 6(4): 341–68.

Modell, Judith. 1986. In Search: The Purported Biological Basis of Parenthood. *American Ethnologist* 13(4): 646–61.

———. 1991. Last-Chance Babies: Interpretations of Parenthood in an *In Vitro* Fertilization Program. *Medical Anthropology Quarterly* 5:124–38.

———. 1995. "Nowadays Everyone is Hanai": Child Exchange in the Construction of Hawaiian Urban Culture. *Journal de la Société des Océanistes* 100–101:201–19.

Mohr, James C. 1978. *Abortion in America: The Origins and Evolution of National Policy, 1800–1900*. New York: Oxford University Press.

Mol, Annemarie. 2002. *The Body Multiple: Ontology in Medical Practice*. Durham, NC: Duke University Press.

Mol, Annemarie, Ingunn Moser, and Jeannette Pols. 2010. *Care in Practice: On Tinkering in Clinics, Homes and Farms*. Bielefeld: Transcript Verlag.

Montoya, Rosario, Lessie Jo Frazier, and Janise Hurtig. 2002. *Gender's Place: Feminist Anthropologies of Latin America*. New York: Palgrave Macmillan.

Mooney, Jadwiga E. Pieper. 2009. T*he Politics of Motherhood: Maternity and Women's Rights in Twentieth-Century Chile*. Pittsburgh, PA: University of Pittsburgh Press.

Morgan, Lewis Henry. 1877. *Ancient Society; Or, Researches in the Lines of Human Progress from Savagery, through Barbarism to Civilization*. London: McMillan.

Morgan, Lynn. 1989. When Does Life Begin? A Cross-Cultural Perspective on the Personhood of Fetuses and Young Children. In *Abortion Rights and Fetal Personhood*, ed. E. Doerr and J. W. Prescott, 89–107. Long Beach, CA: Centerline Press.

———. 1998. Ambiguities Lost: Fashioning the Fetus into Child in Ecuador and the United States. In *Small Wars: The Cultural Politics of Childhood*, ed. N. Scheper-Hughes and C. F. Sargent, 58–74. Berkeley: University of California Press.

———. 2009. *Icons of Life: A Cultural History of Human Embryos*. Berkeley: University of California Press.

Morgan, Lynn, and Elizabeth F. S. Roberts. 2009. Rights and Reproduction in Latin America. *Anthropology News*, 12, 16.

———. Forthcoming. Reproductive Governance in Latin America. *Anthropology and Medicine*.

Nahman, Michal. 2008. Synecdochic Ricochets: Biosocialities in a Jerusalem IVF Clinic. In *Biosocialities, Genetics and the Social Sciences: Making Biologies and Identities*, ed. S. Gibbon and C. Novas, 117–35. London: Routledge.

Necochea López, Raúl. 2008. Priests and Pills: Catholic Family Planning in Peru, 1967–76. *Latin American Research Review* 43(2): 34–56.

Nelson, Diane M. 1999. *A Finger in the Wound: Body Politics in Quincentennial Guatemala*. Berkeley: University of California Press.

Nelson, Victoria. 2001. *The Secret Life of Puppets*. Cambridge, MA: Harvard University Press.

New York Times. 1995. Fertility Clinic Is Blamed in Theft of Eggs from Sedated Women. November 12.

Nouzeilles, Gabriela. 2003. Hysteria in Turn-of-the-Century Buenos Aires. In *Disease in the History of Modern Latin America: From Malaria to AIDS*, ed. D. Armus, 51–75. Durham, NC: Duke University Press.

O'Connell, Marvin. 1986. The Roman Catholic Tradition since 1545. In *Caring and Curing: Health and Medicine in the Western Religious Traditions*, ed. R. L. Numbers and D. W. Amundsen, 108–45. New York: Macmillan.

O'Connor, Erin. 2007. *Gender, Indian, Nation: The Contradictions of Making Ecuador, 1830–1925*. Tucson: University of Arizona Press.

Ochoa, Marcia. 2008. Perverse Citizenship: Divas, Marginality, and Participation in "Loca-lization." *Women's Studies Quarterly* 36(3–4): 146–69.

Olson, David. 2009. Still in Its Infancy, Ecuador's Free Health Care Has Growing Pains. *Press-Enterprise* (Riverside, CA). September 19.

Ong, Aihwa. 2006. *Neoliberalism as Exception: Mutations in Citizenship and Sovereignty*. Durham, NC: Duke University Press.

Ong, Aihwa, and Stephen J. Collier. 2005. *Global Assemblages: Technology, Politics, and Ethics as Anthropological Problems*. Malden, MA: Blackwell.

Orlove, Benjamin. 1998. Down to Earth: Race and Substance in the Andes. *Bulletin of Latin American Research* 17(2): 207–22.

Ortiz, Ana. 1997. "Bare-Handed" Medicine and Its Elusive Patients: The Unstable Construction of Pregnant Women and Fetuses in Dominican Obstetrics Discourse. *Feminist Studies* 23(2): 263–88.

Oudshoorn, Nelly. 1994. *Beyond the Natural Body: An Archaeology of Sex Hormones*. New York: London: Routledge.

Palmié, Stephan. 2002. *Wizards and Scientists: Explorations in Afro-Cuban Modernity and Tradition*. Durham, NC: Duke University Press.

Pashigian, Melissa. 2002. Conceiving the Happy Family: Infertility and Martial Practices in Northern Vietnam. In *Infertility around the Globe: New Thinking on Childlessness, Gender, and Reproductive Technologies*, ed. Marcia Claire Inhorn and Frank van Balen, 134–51. Berkeley: University of California Press.

———. 2009. Inappropriate Relations: The Ban on Surrogacy with In Vitro Fertilization and the Limits of State Renovation in Contemporary Vietnam. In *Assisting Reproduction, Testing Genes: Global Encounters with New Biotechnologies*, ed. Daphna Birenbaum-Carmeli and Marcia Claire Inhorn, 164–88. New York: Berghahn Books.

Paul, Annie Murphy. 2010. *Origins: How the Nine Months Before Birth Shape the Rest of Our Lives*. New York: Simon and Schuster.

Pinto, Sarah. 2004. A Logic of Needles: Excess and the Illegitimate Economy of Labor-Inducing Drugs in Rural North India. Paper Presented at the Society for the Social Studies of Science, Paris, August 2004.

———. 2008. *Where There Is No Midwife,* New York: Berghahan Books.

Pitt-Rivers, Julian. 1973. Race in Latin America: The Concept of Raza. *Archives euro-péennes de sociologie* 14(1): 3–31.

Poblete, Juan. 2002. Governmentality and the Social Question: National Formation and Discipline. In *Foucault and Latin America: Appropriations and Deployments of Discursive Analysis,* ed. B. Trigo, 137–51. New York: Routledge.

Poole, Deborah. 1991. Review of *Compadrazgo: Ritual Kinship Relations in an Andean Peruvian Community. American Anthropologist* 93(3): 755–56.

———. 1997. *Vision, Race, and Modernity: a Visual Economy of the Andean Image World.* Princeton, NJ: Princeton University Press.

———. 2004. *Between Threat and Guarantee: Justice and Community in the Margins of the Peruvian State.* In *Anthropology in the Margins of the State,* ed. Veena Das and Deborah Poole, 35–65. Santa Fe, NM: School of American Research Press.

Portes, Alejandro, and Kelly Hoffman. 2003. Latin American Class Structures: Their Composition and Change during the Neoliberal Era. *Latin American Research Review* 38(1): 41–82.

Povinelli, Elizabeth A. 2006. *The Empire of Love: Toward a Theory of Intimacy, Genealogy, and Carnality.* Durham, NC: Duke University Press.

Prakash, Gyan. 1999. *Another Reason: Science and the Imagination of Modern India.* Princeton, NJ: Princeton University Press.

Pribilsky, Jason. 2007. *La Chulla Vida: Gender, Migration, and the Family in Andean Ecuador and New York City.* Syracuse, NY: Syracuse University Press.

Rabinow, Paul. 1996. Artificiality and Enlightenment: From Sociobiology to Biosociality. In *Essays on the Anthropology of Reason,* ed. P. Rabinow, 91–111. Princeton, NJ: Princeton University Press.

———. 1999. *French DNA: Trouble in Purgatory.* Chicago: University of Chicago Press.

Radcliffe, Sarah, and Sallie Westwood. 1996. *Remaking the Nation: Place, Identity and Politics in Latin America.* London: Routledge.

Raffles, Hugh. 2002. *In Amazonia: A Natural History.* Princeton, NJ: Princeton University Press.

Ragoné, Helena. 1994. *Surrogate Motherhood: Conception in the Heart.* Boulder, CO: Westview Press.

Ramberg, Lucinda. 2009. Magical Hair as Dirt: Ecstatic Bodies and Postcolonial Reform in South India. *Culture, Medicine, and Psychiatry* 33:501–22.

Rapp, Rayna. 1999. *Testing Women, Testing the Fetus: The Social Impact of Amniocentesis in America*. New York: Routledge.

Raspberry, Kelly. 2009. The Genesis of Embryos and Ethics In Vitro: Practicing Preimplantation Genetic Diagnosis in Argentina. In *Assisting Reproduction, Testing Genes: Global Encounters with New Biotechnologies*, ed. Daphna Birenbaum-Carmeli and Marcia Claire Inhorn, 213–38. New York: Berghahn Books.

Ratcliffe, Peter. 2001. *The Politics of Social Science Research: Race, Ethnicity, and Social Change*. Basingstoke, U.K.: Palgrave.

Rattner, Daphne. 1996. On the Hypothesis of the Cesarean Birth Rates Stabilization in Southeastern Brazil. Revista de Saúde Pública 30 (1): 19–33.Ratzinger, Cardinal Joseph. 1987. *Instruction on Respect for Human Life in its Origin and on the Dignity of Procreation*. *Congregation for the Doctrine of the Faith*. Rome. February 22.

RedLara, 2003. *Resultados Para Latinoamérica: Año 2003*. www.redlara.com/images/arq/resulo3.pdf, accessed October 14, 2011.

Rivero, Yeidy M. 2003. The Performance and Reception of Televisual "Ugliness" in *Yo Soy Betty la Fea*. *Feminist Media Studies* 3(1): 65–81.

Roberts, Elizabeth. 1998a. Examining Surrogacy Discourses: Between Feminine Power and Exploitation. In *Small Wars: The Cultural Politics of Childhood*, ed. N. Scheper-Hughes and C. Sargent.93–110 Berkeley: University of California Press.

———. 1998b. "Native" Narratives of Connectedness: Surrogate Motherhood and Technology. In *Cyborg Babies: From Techno-sex to Techno-tots*, ed. J. Dumit and R. Davis-Floyd, 193–211. New York: Routledge.

———. 2006. God's Laboratory: Religious Rationalities and Modernity in Ecuadorian In-Vitro Fertilization. *Culture, Medicine, and Psychiatry* 30(4): 507–36.

———. 2007. Extra Embryos: Ethics, Cryopreservation, and IVF in Ecuador and Elsewhere. *American Ethnologist* 34(1): 188–99.

———. 2008. Biology, Sociality and Reproductive Modernity in Ecuadorian In-Vitro Fertilization: The Particulars of Place. In *Biosocialities, Genetics and the Social Sciences: Making Biologies and Identities*, ed. S. Gibbon and C. Novas, 79–97. London: Routledge.

———. 2009. American Death. *Focaal: European Journal of Anthropology* 54:114–19.

———. 2010. Ritual Humility in Modern Laboratories: Or, Why Ecuadorian IVF Practitioners Pray. In *The Problem of Ritual Efficacy*, ed. W. S. Sax, J. Quack, and J. Weinhold, 131–49. Oxford Ritual Studies. Oxford: Oxford University Press.

———. 2011. Abandonment and Accumulation: Embryonic Futures in the United States and Ecuador. *Medical Anthropology Quarterly* 25(2): 232–53.

———. Forthcoming. Scars of Nation: Surgical Penetration and the Ecuadorian State. *Journal of Latin American and Caribbean Anthropology.*

Roberts, Elizabeth F. S., and Nancy Scheper-Hughes. 2011. Medical Migrations. *Body and Society* 17(2–3): 1–30.

Robertson, J. A. 2006. Compensation and Egg Donation for Research. *Fertility and Sterility* 86(6): 1573–75.

Rodriguez, Clara E. 2000. *Changing Race: Latinos, the Census, and the History of Ethnicity in the United States.* New York: New York University Press.

Rofel, Lisa. 1999. *Other Modernities: Gendered Yearnings in China after Socialism.* Berkeley: University of California Press.

Rose, Nikolas S. 1999. *Powers of Freedom: Reframing Political Thought.* Cambridge: Cambridge University Press.

Roseberry, William. 1993. Hegemony and the Language of Contention. In *Everyday Forms of State Formation*, ed. G. M. Joseph and Daniel Nugent, 355–66: Duke University Press.

Rosenberg, Charles E. 1979. The Therapeutic Revolution: Medicine, Meaning, and Social Change in Nineteenth-Century America. In *The Therapeutic Revolution: Essays in the Social History of American Medicine*, ed. M. J. Vogel and C. E. Rosenberg, 3–25. Philadelphia: University of Pennsylvania Press.

Rosenberg, K. and W. Trevathan. 2001. The Evolution of Human Birth. *Scientific American.* May, 72–77

Rubin, Gayle. 1975. The Traffic in Women: Notes on the "Political Economy" of Sex. In *Toward an Anthropology of Women*, ed. R. R. Reiter, 157–210. New York: Monthly Review Press.

Ruilova, Hugo Corral. 1974. Ecuador. *Studies in Family Planning* 6(8): 272–73.

Ryan, Caroline. 2006. More than 3m Babies Born from IVF. BBC News. June 21. Prague. http://news.bbc.co.uk/2/hi/health/5101684.stm.

Sacks, Karen. 1975. Engels Revisited: Women, the Organization of Production, and Private Property. In *Towards an Anthropology of Women*, ed. R. R. Reiter, 311–24. New York: Monthly Review Press.

Sacoto, Sonia Merlyn. 2006. *Derecho y reproducción asistida.* Quito: Cevallos.

Sahlins, Marshall. 2011. What Kinship Is. *Journal of the Royal Anthropological Institute* 17(1): 2–19.

Saillant, Catherine. 2010. Fugitive in UC Irvine Fertility Scandal Arrested in Mexico City; U.S. Hopes to Extradite Him. *Los Angeles Times.* December 27.

Sawicki, Jana. 1991. *Disciplining Foucault: Feminism, Power, and the Body*. New York: Routledge.

Sawyer, Suzana. 2004. *Crude Chronicles: Indigenous Politics, Multinational Oil, and Neoliberalism in Ecuador*. Durham NC: Duke University Press.

Scheper-Hughes, Nancy. 1984. The Margaret Mead Controversy: Culture, Biology, and Anthropological Inquiry. *Human Organization* 43(1): 85–93.

———. 1992. *Death without Weeping: The Violence of Everyday Life in Brazil*. Berkeley: University of California Press.

———. 2005. The Last Commodity: Post-human Ethics and the Global Traffic in "Fresh" Organs. In *Global Assemblages: Technology, Politics, and Ethics as Anthropological Problems*, ed. A. Ong and S. J. Collier, 145–67. Malden, MA: Blackwell.

Schneider, David. 1980. *American Kinship: A Cultural Account*. Chicago: University of Chicago Press.

Scrimshaw, Susan C. M. 1985. Bringing the Period Down: Induced Abortion in Ecuador. In *Micro and Macro Levels of Analysis in Anthropology: Issues in Theory and Research*, ed. B. R. DeWalt and P. J. Pelto, 121–46. Boulder, CO: Westview Press.

Sharma, Aradhana, and Akhil Gupta, eds. 2006. *The Anthropology of the State: A Reader*. Malden, MA: Blackwell.

Sharp, Lesley Alexandra. 2006. *Strange Harvest: Organ Transplants, Denatured Bodies, and the Transformed Self*. Berkeley: University of California Press.

Silverblatt, Irene Marsha. 2004. *Modern Inquisitions: Peru and the Colonial Origins of the Civilized World*. Durham, NC: Duke University Press.

Simmel, Georg. 1990. *The Philosophy of Money*. New York: Routledge.

Siok, Wai Ting, Charles A. Perfetti, Zhen Jin, and Li Hai Tan. 2004. Biological Abnormality of Impaired Reading Is Constrained by Culture. *Nature* (431): 71–76.

Slocum, Sally. 1975. Woman the Gatherer: Male Bias in Anthropology. In *Toward an Anthropology of Women*, ed. R. R. Reiter, 36–50. New York: Monthly Review Press.

Smith, Carol A. 1996. Myths, Intellectuals, and Race/Class/Gender Distinctions in the Formation of Latin American Nations. *Journal of Latin American Anthropology* 2(1): 148–69.

Smith, Raymond Thomas. 1984. *Kinship Ideology and Practice in Latin America*. Chapel Hill: University of North Carolina Press.

Smith, Zadie. 2005. *On Beauty*. New York: Penguin.

Sommers, Doris. 2002. Love and Country: An Allegorical Speculation from Foundational Fictions; The National Romances of Latin America. In *Foucault and Latin America: Appropriations and Deployments of Discursive Analysis*, ed. B. Trigo, 103–24. New York: Routledge.

Stack, Carol B. 1975. *All Our Kin: Strategies for Survival in a Black Community*. New York: Harper & Row.

Steinbrook, Roberts. 2006. Egg Donation and Human Embryonic Stem Cell Research. *New England Journal of Medicine* 354(4): 324–26.

Stepan, Nancy. 1991. *The Hour of Eugenics: Race, Gender, and Nation in Latin America*. Ithaca, NY: Cornell University Press.

Stern, Alexandra Minna. 2006. Yellow Fever Crusades: US Colonialism, Tropical Medicine, and the International Politics of Mosquito Control. In *Medicine at the Border: Disease, Globalization and Security, 1850 to the Present*, ed. A. Bashford, 41–59. Basingstoke, U.K.: Palgrave Macmillan.

Stevenson, Lisa. 2009. The Suicidal Wound and Fieldwork among Canadian Inuit. In *Being There: The Fieldwork Encounter and the Making of Truth*, ed. J. Borneman and A. Hammoudi, 55–76. Berkeley: University of California Press.

Stiffler, Steven. 2008. The United Fruit Company's Legacy in Ecuador. In *The Ecuador Reader: History, Culture, Politics*, ed. Carlos de la Torre and Steven Striffler, 239–49. Durham, NC: Duke University Press.

Stolberg, Sheryl Gay. 2005. House Approves a Stem Cell Research Bill Opposed by Bush. *New York Times*. May 25.

Stoler, Ann Laura. 1995. *Race and the Education of Desire: Foucault's History of Sexuality and the Colonial Order of Things*. Durham, NC: Duke University Press.

Strathern, Marilyn. 1985. Kinship and Economy: Constitutive Orders of a Provisional Kind. *American Ethnologist* 12(2): 191–209.

———. 1992a. *After Nature: English Kinship in the Late Twentieth Century*. Cambridge: Cambridge University Press.

———. 1992b. *Reproducing the Future: Essays on Anthropology, Kinship, and the New Reproductive Technologies*. New York: Routledge.

———. 2005. *Kinship, Law and the Unexpected: Relatives Are Always a Surprise*. New York: Cambridge University Press.

Stutzman, Ronald. 1981. El Mestizaje: An All-Inclusive Ideology. In *Cultural Transformations and Ethnicity in Modern Ecuador*, ed. N. Whitten, 45–94. Urbana: University of Illinois Press.

Sunder Rajan, Kaushik. 2006. *Biocapital: The Constitution of Postgenomic Life*. Durham, NC: Duke University Press.

Swanson, Kate. 2007. Revanchist Urbanism Heads South: The Regulation of Indigenous Beggars and Street Vendors in Ecuador. *Antipode: A Journal of Radical Geography* 34(4): 708–28.

————. 2010. *Begging as a Path to Progress: Indigenous Women and Children and the Struggle for Ecuador's Urban Spaces*. Athens: University of Georgia Press.

Tambiah, Stanley Jeyaraja. 1990. *Magic, Science, Religion, and the Scope of Rationality*. Cambridge: Cambridge University Press.

Taussig, Michael. 1980. *The Devil and Commodity Fetishism in South America*. Chapel Hill: University of North Carolina Press.

————. 1986. *Shamanism, Colonialism, and the Wild Man: A Study in Terror and Healing*. Chicago: University of Chicago Press.

Taylor, Christopher C. 1992. *Milk, Honey, and Money: Changing Concepts in Rwandan Healing*. Smithsonian Series in Ethnographic Inquiry. Washington, DC: Smithsonian Institution Press.

Taylor, Jannelle. 2000. An All-Consuming Experience: Obstetrical Ultrasound and the Commodification of Pregnancy. In *Biotechnology and Culture: Bodies, Anxieties, Ethics*, ed. Paul Brodwin, 147–70. Bloomington: Indiana University Press.

————. 2008a. *The Public Life of the Fetal Ultrasound: Technology, Consumption and the Politics of Reproduction*. New Brunswick, NJ: Rutgers University Press.

————. 2008b. On Recognition, Caring and Dementia. *Medical Anthropology Quarterly* 22 (4): 313–35.

Teman, Elly. 2010. *Birthing a Mother: The Surrogate Body and the Pregnant Self*. Berkeley: University of California Press.

Temkin, Owsei. 1977. *The Double Face of Janus and Other Essays in the History of Medicine*. Baltimore: Johns Hopkins University Press.

Thompson, Charis. 2001. Strategic Naturalizing: Kinship in an Infertility Clinic. In *Relative Values: Reconfiguring Kinship Studies*, ed. Sarah Franklin and Susan McKinnon, 175–202. Durham, NC: Duke University.

————. 2002. Fertile Ground: Feminists Theorize Infertility. In *Infertility Around the Globe*, ed. Marcia Claire Inhorn and Frank van Balen, 52–78. Berkeley: University of California Press.

————. 2005. *Making Parents: The Ontological Choreography of Reproductive Technologies*. Cambridge, MA: MIT Press.

Ticktin, Miriam. 2011. How Biology Travels: A Humanitarian Trip. *Body and Society* 17(2–3): 139–58.

Titmuss, Richard Morris. 1971. *The Gift Relationship: From Human Blood to Social Policy*. New York: Pantheon.

Torre, Carlos de la. 2006. Ethnic Movements and Citizenship in Ecuador. *Latin American Research Review* 41(2): 247–59.

————. 2008. Civilization and Barbarism. In *The Ecuador Reader: History, Culture,*

Politics, ed. Carlos de la Torre and Steven Striffler, 267–70. Durham, NC: Duke University Press.

Tremayne, Soraya. 2009. Law Ethics, and Donor Technologies in Shia Iran. In *Assisting Reproduction, Testing Genes: Global Encounters with New Biotechnologies,* ed. Daphna Birenbaum-Carmeli and Marcia Claire Inhorn, 144–63. New York: Berghahn Books.

Turner, Victor Witter. 1969. *The Ritual Process: Structure and Anti-structure.* Chicago: Aldine.

Unnithan-Kumar, Maya. 2004. *Reproductive Agency, Medicine and the State: Cultural Transformations in Childbearing.* New York: Berghahn Books.

USAID (U.S. Agency for International Development). 2000. *Ecuador.* www.usaid .gov/pubs/bj2001/lac/ec/.

Valeri, V. 1994. Buying Women but Not Selling Them: Gift and Commodity Exchange in Huaulu Alliance. *Man* 29(1): 1–26.

Vayena, Effy, Patrick Rowe, and David Griffin, eds. 2002. *Current Practices and Controversies in Assisted Reproduction.* Geneva: World Health Organization.

Verdesoto, Luis, Gloria Ardaya, Roque Espinosa, and Fernando Garcia. 1995. *Rostros de la famila ecuatoriana.* Quito: UNICEF.

Voekel, Pamela. 2002. *Alone before God: The Religious Origins of Modernity in Mexico.* Durham, NC: Duke University Press.

Vos, Rob, Jose Cuesta, Mauricio Leon, Ruth Lucio, and Jose Rosero. 2004. *Ecuador: Public Expenditure Review 2004, Health,* 1–80. Quito: Secretaria Técnica del Frente Social.

Wade, Nicholas. 2003. Clinics Hold More Embryos Than Had Been Thought. *New York Times.* May 9.

Wade, Peter. 1993. Race, Nature and Culture. *Man* 28(1): 17–34.

Waldby, Catherine. 2002. Stem Cell, Tissue Cultures and the Production of Biovalue. *Health* 6(3): 305–23.

Waldby, Catherine, and Robert Mitchell. 2006. *Tissue Economies: Blood, Organs, and Cell Lines in Late Capitalism.* Durham, NC: Duke University Press.

Wall, J. T., J. Xu, and X. Wang. 2002. Human Brain Plasticity: An Emerging View of the Multiple Substrates and Mechanisms That Cause Cortical Changes and Related Sensory Dysfunctions after Injuries of Sensory Inputs from the Body. *Brain Research Reviews* 39(2–3): 181–215.

Weismantel, Mary. 1995. Making Kin: Kinship Theory and Zumbagua Adoptions. *American Ethnologist* 22(4): 685–704.

————. 1997. White Cannibals: Fantasies of Racial Violence in the Andes. *Identities: Global Studies in Culture and Power* 4(1): 9–43.

————. 2001. *Cholas and Pishtacos: Stories of Race and Sex in the Andes*. Chicago: University of Chicago Press.

Wexler, Alice. 1995. *Mapping Fate: A Memoir of Family, Risk, and Genetic Research*. Berkeley: University of California Press.

WHO (World Health Organization). 2005. *Statistics by Country or Region; Ecuador*. www.who.int/countries/ecu/en/.

Williams, Derek. 2001. Assembling the 'Empire of Morality': State Building Strategies in Catholic Ecuador, 1861–1875. *Journal of Historical Sociology* 14(2): 149–74.

Wilson, Ara. 2004. *The Intimate Economies of Bangkok: Tomboys, Tycoons, and Avon Ladies in the Global City*. Berkeley: University of California Press.

World Bank. 2011. *Fertility Rate, Total (Births per Woman)*. http://data.worldbank.org/indicator/sp.dyn.tfrt.in, accessed Oct 14, 2011.

Zelizer, Viviana A. Rotman. 1994a. *Pricing the Priceless Child: The Changing Social Value of Children*. Princeton, NJ: Princeton University Press.

————. 1994b. *The Social Meaning of Money*. New York: Basic Books.

Zenit. 2003a. Church in Spain Proposes Unfreezing of "Spare" Embryos. July 29. www.zenit.org/article-7890?l=english.

————. 2003b. Why Adoption of Frozen Human Embryos Could be Acceptable. www.zenit.org/article-17406?l=english.

————. 2005. Lives In Limbo: Debate over the Future of Frozen Embryos. www.zenit.org/article-17663?l=english.

Zulawski, Ann. 2007. *Unequal Cures: Public Health and Political Change in Bolivia, 1900–1950*. Durham, NC: Duke University Press.

INDEX

abandonment, 184, 198–200, 202, 207

abortion: botched abortions, 40, 67, 82; Child and Adolescent Civil Code on, 42; Church opposition to, 36; clandestine abortion, 40; embryo disposal as, 196, 202; forced abortion, 103; IVF treatment after, 34; as judgment of God, 34, 66; legality of, 32, 39–40, 41, 48, 49; rates in Latin America, 22, 40; representation of embryos as babies, 190; rights-based discussions of, 66–67; women's experiences of, 32–35, 49, 66, 196

Abu El-Haj, Nadia, 224n3

Ackerman, Sara, 89

adoption: anonymity of birth mother, 167–68; attitudes towards, among Indians, 121–22; on basis of child's beauty, 134; cultivation of physical similarity, 166; egg donation compared with, 133–34, 163–64; extra-legal adoption, 64, 65; of frozen embryos, 186, 192; genetic risks of, 167; regional differences, 163

advertisements for IVF procedures, 46, 51, 126, 127f4, 159

Afro-Ecuadorians, 26, 201, 224n4

Agamben, Giorgio, 187

Alfaro, José Eloy, 60

altruism, 162, 170–72

American Society for Assisted Reproductive Technology, 188

Ana (egg donor), 133, 179

Anabela (Frida's niece), 138–39, 140, 142, 143, 144–47, 149, 157, 179

Andean market women, 156–57

Andrade, Enrique Valle, 148, 149

Andrade, Marco (pseud.), 42–43, 51

Andrés (Teresa and Manuel's son), 106, 107, 108–11, 123, 124, 125, 135–36

animal imagery, 81, 85, 86

anonymous egg donations: as abandonment, 198; adoption instead of, 163–64; confidentiality in, 159, 227–28n9; donor recruitment, 102, 104, 116, 126, 127f4, 225n12; as economic transactions, 150, 158, 176; and issues of relatedness, 113, 143, 165–66, 189,

Ferguson, James, 58

Fernando (patient), 203

fertility control, 22, 38–39, 41, 78, 82

fertilized eggs as pre-embryos, 47, 190, 196

financing of IVF treatments: bingo games, 74, 98, 99, 101, 155; debt accrual, 25, 58, 71–72, 74, 80, 104, 107, 138–39, 154–55, 157–58, 172–73; fundraising for, 74, 98, 99–100

Flor (patient), 202

Foucault, Michel, 225n10

fox imagery, 103, 223n1

fragility of female elites, 79–80, 81, 83, 86

Franklin, Sarah, 2–3, 190, 206

Frazier, Lessie Jo, 97

Freeman, Derek, 228n12

Frida (patient): economic assistance for Anabela, 179; need for valuables and input, 179; rejection of blood imperative, 143, 149; on relatedness, 149, 157; relations with husband, 139, 140–41, 142; as single mother, 141–42; tensions with family members, 138–39, 140, 142–46; twin birth, 139, 140–41, 142

frozen embryos: biovalue of, 208–9; donation of, 184, 186; external circulation of, 202, 206, 207; for medical and scientific purposes, 188; rescue value of, 211; temporality of, 195, 201–2, 204, 208–9. *See also* cryopreservation

games of chance, 74, 98, 99–100, 101, 155, 223n13

García Moreno, Gabriel, 59–60

gender: ability to exchange, 152; in constituting *raza*, 128; exchanging women into structural men, 152; infertility, 79, 177, 222n1; roles in the marketplace, 151–52, 156–57

genetics: adoption, 167; blood, 166, 171;

as determining physiology, 136–37; epigenetics, 21; genes in constituting race, 122; genetic connection, 113; genetic engineering, 42, 43; genetic transmission through egg donation, 133, 150, 166; malleability of genes, 164–65; preimplantation genetic diagnosis (PGD), 143–44; relatedness, 50, 163, 165, 166, 168

George, Robert P., 211

gestation, 72, 171, 190

gift economies, 153, 156–57, 172, 176

God: on abortions, 34, 40, 66; assistance required from, xxii, 15–16; cited on cryopreservation, 202; doctors as God-like, xxiii, 55, 88, 194; on embryo abandonment, 184; enlisted in gambling, 99–100; extra embryos, 204; fertilization, 7–9, 10; gendering of, 87; human capabilities compared with God's work, 54–56; infertility as punish-ment from, 33, 35; invoked by IVF practitioners, xxii, 7–8, 10–11, 28, 33, 54–55, 100, 139; of materi-alist Catholics, 26–27; in national whitening project, 215; in nature, 13–14, 15, 56, 212; paternalistic rela-tions with, 6–7, 9, 24, 38, 214, 216; patient relations with, 6–7, 15–16, 34, 38, 40, 54, 72, 99–100, 139, 182, 184; pregnancy as the will of, 11, 34, 55, 89, 139, 173, 181–82; in pro-life debates in the United States, 211, 212, 214; promises made to, 15, 34, 173; regional differences in relationships with, 26; technology and, 12–16

godparenthood *(compadrazago)*, 73, 156, 174–75

Great Britain, 162, 190–91, 206, 208, 210

Grünenthal Group, 52

Guayaquil, 27map 1, 158, 208

Guayaquileños: on adoption, 163, 164; on anonymous egg donation, 158, 163,

Guayaquileños *(continued)*
165, 202, 203; Catholic Church influence on, 208; characteristics of, 26, 187, 220n19; circulation of embryos among families, 208; on cryopreservation, 194–95, 202, 208, 214; on donation of live embryos, 189, 197; genetics in understanding of relatedness, 168, 208; on personhood, 166, 187; Quiteños compared with, 26, 28; relationship with God, 26, 28

Gupta, Akhil, 62

Gutiérrez, Lucio (President of Ecuador), 36, 42, 63

haciendas: autonomy of haciendados, 59–62; labor, 28, 58, 60, 61, 75, 214; national whitening project on, 19, 61, 75, 89; paternalism of, 57, 75, 89, 214

Haraway, Donna, 3

Harris, Olivia, 149

hegemony, 91, 228n2

heterosexuality, xxii, xxiii, xxiv, 6–7, 12, 30, 150, 215, 222n1, 224n8

Dr. Hidalgo: on child's whiteness, 106, 111, 123–24; clinical policies toward embryo storage and disposal, 199, 200; concerns about state intervention, 47, 51; egg donation, 104, 158, 223n2. *See also* Irene (egg donor); Teresa (patient)

homosexuality, 53

hormones and hormone treatments: cross-cultural perceptions of, 4, 89, 90–91, 94–95; dosages, 18, 93, 192, 194; effects on egg donors, 227n4; emotional distress as result of, 4, 90–94; impact on women's physiology, 90–92, 95; ovarian hyperstimulation, 17–18

Htun, Mala, 40

huasipungeros (debt peons), 58, 59

human sociality, 150, 151–52, 227n2

Hume, David, 13–14

Hurricane Katrina, 211–13, 229n1

Hurtig, Janise, 97

incest, 151, 175, 176

Indians: attitudes toward adopted children, 121–22; behavior identifying, 128, 133–34; child birth, 78, 82, 83, 85–86; exploitation of, 59, 117; in hacienda labor force, 28, 58, 59, 60, 61, 75, 118, 214; as IVF patients, 126–27; kinship practices, 118, 122; miscegenation, 61, 75, 113, 116, 118–19, 124; nation building, 118, 122; *pishtaco*, 80, 86; racial optimism, 19, 119; stereotypes of, 26, 78, 85–86, 121, 123, 124, 134, 148–49, 224n4; subjugation of Indian women, 61, 75, 113, 116, 119, 124; as taxpayers, 59; transformation of Indians into mestizos, 20, 110, 119, 225n11; tribalism of, 19; *trigueño oscuro*, 128. *See also* mestizaje/mestizos

indigenous peoples: behavior identifying, 128, 133–34; in eugenic thinking, 225n11; in hacienda system, 58–60; *indigenismo*, 225n11; political activism of, 224n4

individual: abortion and the rights of the individual woman, 48–49, 66; capability of changing race, 114, 115; in the family sphere, 207, 208, 209; genetics, 168, 224n3; liberal discourse of individual rights, 48; as the object of care, 214, 215; whitening of, 115

individual autonomy: desirability of, 16; nature, xxiv; of women, 66

individualism: citizenship, 19; individual rights and neoliberal governance, 22; in life debates, 187, 205, 212, 215

individuality: neoliberalism, 22; tribalism, 19

infertility: alternative treatments for, 34, 35, 181; as complaint of elite women,

79; as corporeal punishment, 33, 35; emotional distress, 91–94; as God's punishment, 33, 35; life circumstances as causing, 91–95; male-factor infertility, 79, 177, 222n1; poverty, 100; relaxation as cure for, 91–93

Ingrid (egg donor), 170, 171, 196, 201

Inhorn, Marcia, 205

intimate economies (Wilson), 153

Irene (egg donor), 102, 104–5

Irigaray, Luce, 152

IVF children: death of, 98, 184–85; egg donors' relations with, 148, 171, 175; embryos identified/conceptualized as babies, 180, 190, 191, 195; fathers of, 123, 124, 125, 142; genetically inherited traits, 163, 165, 166; health complications from multiple births, 183–84, 185, 191; kinship ties, 124–25, 130–31, 132, 143, 145; knowledge of their IVF origins, 73, 81, 143, 154–56, 165, 168; multiple births, 72, 182–84, 195; privileging of, 135–36, 211–13, 229n1; resemblance to parents as desirable, 73, 104, 106, 107–9; sperm donors on, 130–31, 132; valorization of, 154–56, 172, 176; whiteness of, 74, 104, 106, 107–9

IVF procedures, xf1; advertisements for, 46, 51, 126, 127f4, 159; after abortion, 34; as artificial, xxiii, 12, 14, 55, 56, 212; care relations after, 95–96; Catholic Church on, xxii, 33, 37, 45–47, 54–56, 159, 208; clinic infrastructure maintenance, xxii, 17–18, 21, 199, 218n7; criticism of, 86–87, 191; C-sections, 22, 72, 73, 81–84, 106, 183; embryo transfer, 32, 50–51, 70–72, 89–97, 180, 191–92, 204–5, 209–10; emotion distress as result of, 4, 90–94, 144; impact of physiological differences on, 17–18; multiple births, 72, 182–84, 191, 195, 229n2; *nuestra*

realidad, 3, 4, 17–18, 20, 21, 51, 199; ontological choreography in, 6, 169–70; quality of life after, 30, 108–9; success rates, xxii, 30, 217n1; United States government involvement in, 188–89, 209–10; vaginal penetration, 174. *See also* cryopreservation; donation headings; economic aspects of IVF treatments; embryo headings; financing of IVF treatments; God; hormones and hormone treatments

Dr. Jaramillo, 68, 69–72, 81, 86, 158, 197

Javier (Anabela's husband), 139, 143, 145–46, 172

José (Rosa's husband), 163

Juan Carlos (Vanessa's husband), 180

Junta de Beneficencia, 98–99

Kant, Immanuel, 154, 187

Kaufman, Sharon, 188

kinship: adopted children, 121–22; anonymous embryo donations, 113, 189, 197, 198, 202, 203; babies resembling egg donors, 145; biographies of, 209; blended families, 140; blood relations, 143, 147–49, 166, 168–69, 170–72, 175–76; boundaries of, 188; children of reproductive technology, 130–31, 132; cryopreservation, 193, 201, 202; economy of, 154, 157–58; egg donation as debt payment, 138–39, 157–58, 172–73, 177; English kinship, 207; exchange relations, 156, 165, 177–78, 228n12; family member as egg donor, 138–39, 140, 142–45; genetics, 113, 208; identifying maternity, 143, 147; marriage arrangements, 152–53; materiality of care, 149; practical kinship, 152, 153; race kinked to kinship practices, 121–22; skin color, 107, 123, 126; tensions with family members, 138–39, 140, 142–46; through care and

210; donor recruitment, 102, 104, 116, 126, 127f4, 225n12; malls, 128–29, 226n16; reciprocal female exchange, 5, 153, 155–57; separation of home and, 153–54, 156; shortage of donor eggs, 158, 162; women in, 78, 138–39, 142–43, 152, 156–57, 159, 177

marriage, 78, 140, 152, 153–54

materialist Catholics, 26–27, 28

matter/spirit, 149, 151, 213, 218n6

Mauss, Marcel, 153, 207, 208

McKinnnon, Susan, 151

Mead, Margaret, 228n12

media coverage: advertisements for IVF procedures, 46, 51, 126, 127f4; assisted reproductive technologies, 41, 45–46, 47, 112–13; extra embryos, 205–6; Latin American doctors helping Latin American women in their quest for lighter, 112; portrayals of infertility as complaint of elite women, 79; *telenovelas*, 29, 30, 139

men: absence of male partners during procedures, 170–73, 177; abuse of intrafamilial egg donation, 178; on anonymous donations, 176; children from other relationships, 140, 142, 145, 182–83; coercion of Indian women by whiter man, 19, 61, 75, 113, 116, 119, 124, 125; on cryopreservation, 195; on familial donations, 176; gendering of reproductive surgery, 79, 84–85, 220n18; in kinship systems, 151; male-factor infertility, 79, 177, 222n1; in national whitening project, 19, 61, 75, 89, 113, 116, 119; sons desired by, 140, 141, 145–46; on stepdaughter as donor, 176; support for egg donation, 70–71, 141, 146, 160–61, 171, 172–73

mental health professionals, 64–65, 87, 163

mestizaje/mestizos: in art and litera-

ture, 224–25n8; in assisted reproduction, 214; caste hierarchies, 117; Creole elites and, 118; crillos, 18–19, 118, 119, 126; as distinguished from Indians, 59, 80, 110; Ecuadorian law as, 49–50; history of, 110, 115–18, 224–25n8; Indians transformed into, 20, 110, 119, 225n11; informal adoption among, 64; middle class identified with, 25; *pishtaco*, 80, 86; racial optimism, 19–20, 119, 121; racial pessimism, 119; *raza*, 18–19, 20, 116–18, 120–21, 124, 126, 128, 224–25n8; 225n14; tax protests of, 59; transformation of Indians into mestizos through education, 20. *See also* race and racism; whiteness and whitening

middle-class women, 25, 79–80, 83–84, 102

Milena (doctor), 126, 128

miracles, 13–14, 99, 100

miscarriages, 80, 89, 95, 96, 144, 173, 195

miscegenation, 61, 75, 113, 116, 118–19, 120, 124

modernity: autonomy, xxiv, 6, 13–14, 16, 42, 62, 212; Enlightenment, 12–15, 56–57, 60, 117, 149, 151, 162, 213, 218n10; family size, 39, 94; fertility problems caused by modern behaviors, 77, 96; genetic discourses in, 207–8; individual rights, 48; kinship practice, 121–22; the modern civilizing mission, 13, 218n6; nation-building policies, 21, 60; population control, 22, 23, 37, 38–39, 41, 78, 82; spiritual assistance, 11, 14–15; surveillance of elite women, 9, 118–19. *See also* malleability

Mol, Annemarie, 3, 16

Dr. Molina: anonymous egg donations, 158; clinical innovations, 95–96, 126, 127; cryopreservation, 182; Diego (Dr. Molina's son), 18, 46, 198–99; disposal of embryos, 198–99, 203;

Dr. Molina *(continued)*
  donor matching, 126, 127; God's
    assistance invoked by, xxii, 33, 139;
    impact of Catholic doctrine on, 52,
    62, 67; Wilson (Dr. Molina's son), 17,
    95, 126, 128, 159, 199, 225n13
money economies, 153, 154
Montoya, Rosario, 97
Morgan, Lewis Henry, 178
Morgan, Lynn, 38, 221n4
multiple births, 72, 98, 182–84, 191, 195,
    229n2
Muslim countries, 205

Natalie (Frida's twin daughter), 140
national whitening project, 19–20, 61,
    75, 89, 115–16, 119, 122, 124–29, 132–
    33, 135
nature: and the construction of race, 114–
    15; culture and, xxii, 2, 21, 95, 114,
    213; God's intervention in, 13–14, 15,
    56, 212; individual autonomy, xxiv;
    laboratory-produced embryos, 2,
    56; malleability of, xxiv, 215, 218n10;
    national differences in understanding,
    xxiv; and the realty of deities in, 11,
    13–14, 15, 56, 212; and relatedness,
    135; women as natural patients, 79.
    See also biology; genetics
neoliberalism, 22, 23, 24, 212–13, 219n13,
    224n3
nerves, 91, 92, 170
New Guinea, 207
New Orleans, Louisiana, 211, 213, 229n1
niece-to-aunt donations, 138–39, 140,
    142, 143, 144–47, 149, 157, 173–75,
    179
North America: adoption in, 166–67;
    circulation of embryos outside fam-
    ily groupings, 205; egg donations in,
    176; middle-class life in, 157; multi-
    cultural celebration of mixed beauty,
    135; relatedness, 135, 176; valuing of

transcendent life, 205. *See also* United
    States
nuestra realidad, 3, 4, 17–18, 20, 21, 51,
    169, 199

Octomom, 229n2
Ong, Aihwa, 150
ontological choreography (Thompson),
    6, 169–70
Opus Dei, 45, 49, 53, 54
organ donation, 159, 177
Ortiz, Ana, 21

Dr. Padilla, 10, 11, 96, 155, 158, 170,
    172–73
paid egg donations, 154, 158, 160–63,
    227n7, 227n8
Parredes, Mariana de Jesús, 97
parto normal (vaginal birth), 81, 83, 84,
    85–86
paternalism: attitudes towards women
    patients, 20, 57, 61, 68–72, 75, 86–89,
    115–16, 159, 216; of doctors, 20, 34–
    35, 57, 61–62, 68–72, 75, 86–89, 115–
    16, 159, 165, 216; gamete and embryo
    selection by doctors, 19–20, 102,
    115–16, 122–23, 125–26, 194, 200,
    202, 206; on the haciendas, 57, 75,
    214; national whitening project, 19–
    20, 61, 75, 89, 115–16, 122, 124–29,
    132–33, 135; patients' lack of medical
    knowledge, 84, 87, 88, 90, 91, 99,
    103, 196, 223n10; in private IVF clin-
    ics, 20, 34–35, 57, 61, 62, 68–72, 75,
    86–89, 115–16, 159, 216; in relations
    with God, 6–7, 9, 24, 38, 214, 216;
    reproductive governance, 22, 38, 39,
    41, 78, 82
patients: on abortion, 40, 221n4; adop-
    tion considered by, 64, 65, 167, 181;
    age of, 96, 102, 223n8; on anonymous
    egg donation, 170–71; bed rest, 72,
    93, 95–97, 196; care relations, 13, 15–

relatedness: adoption, 167; blood relations, 143, 147–49, 166, 168, 170–72,
175–76; embryos, 165–66, 203, 204,
205–6, 209–10; English kinship, 207;
genetics, 50, 133, 150, 163, 165, 166,
168, 171; kinswomen as egg donors,
138–39, 140–47, 149, 153, 157, 170–75,
177, 179, 196, 201; marriageability,
168–69; nature and, 135; privileged
over life, 205; regional differences
on, 163; strategic naturalizing, 135;
through care and cultivation, 121,
130–31, 135–36, 166–67; in U.S.-
based assisted reproduction, 135
relaxation, 72, 91–94, 95–97, 196
reproductive governance, 22, 38, 39, 41,
78, 82
reproductive rights: access to abortion,
32–35, 37, 39–40, 49, 66, 67; access
to health care, 33, 40, 63–64, 65–66,
213, 214, 229n1; birth control, 36, 53,
69; of egg donors, 70–71, 160–61,
161–62; family size, 39, 94; right to
life of the unborn, 41–42, 48, 51. *See
also* life debates
res mancipi, 207
res nec mancipi, 208
resources *(recursos):* for abortion, 37, 67;
bajos recursos, 62, 81, 154, 226n16; debt
relations in private IVF clinics, 34, 61,
62, 64, 66, 71–72, 81; for IVF treatments, 25, 74, 98, 99–100, 101, 155,
223n13
right-to-life organizations, 41–42, 190
Roberts, Celia, 190
Rosa (IVF patient), 163
Roseberry, William, 228n2
Rubin, Gayle, 151, 152, 161, 178–79,
227n3

Sacoto, Sonia Merlyn, 47–50, 66, 209,
227n8
Sahlins, Marshall, 207

sambo, 73, 117, 218n8
Samoan women, 228n12
Samuel (Eliana's husband), 195
Sandra (patient), 32–35, 37, 66, 67
la sangra llama (blood calls), 143, 147
Santa Catalina convent, 52, 57
Sawyer, Suzanne, 148
scarring, 76, 80–82, 86
Schneider, David, 157
SEMER (Sociedad Ecuatoriana de
Medicina Reproductiva), 44–46
semi-pensionada (half-service) births,
73, 83
sex: abstinence from sexual relations
prior to donation, 139, 161; asexuality of IVF, 56; *casta,* 18–19, 117–18,
224–25n8; coercion of Indian women
by whiter man, 19, 61, 75, 113, 116,
119, 124, 125; egg donors as sexually active, 131, 133; heterosexuality,
xxii, xxiii, xxiv, 6–7, 12, 30, 150, 215,
222n1, 224n8; homosexuality, 53;
incest, 151, 175, 176; kinship, 151–52,
227n3, 228n12; market women, 156–
57, 159; mestizaje, 119, 224n8; miscegenation, 61, 75, 113, 116, 118–19, 124;
normalization of women patients, 79;
perfection of the race, 77, 115, 225n11;
selection of sex partners, 19, 124;
select the sex of a child, 143–44;
sexual oppression, 151–52, 177–78,
227n3; sperm donation and sexual
pleasure, 129; surveillance of elite
women, 9, 118–19; traffic in women,
151–52, 227n3; virginity, 10, 11, 12,
129, 133, 161, 174; whitening project,
119; women's sexual activity, 33, 37,
66, 70; women's sexual domination
by white men, 19, 61, 75, 108, 113, 116
sex and sex roles, 152
sexed medicalized treatments. *See* hormones and hormone treatments;
surgery

212–13; oversight of private clinics, 21, 38, 43–47, 51–52, 57–58, 61–62, 67; population control, 22, 37, 38–39, 41, 78, 82; presidency, 36, 38, 41, 42, 63, 214; public education, 19, 20, 76; reproductive governance, 22, 39, 41, 78, 82; rights to health care, 41; social welfare, 23, 98–99, 155, 162; whitening as national project, 19–20, 61, 75, 89, 115–16, 119, 122, 124–29, 132–33, 135; women and state-building, 63, 77, 115, 225n11. *See also* haciendas; public health care and hospitals

stem-cell research, 42, 186, 206, 209, 210

Stepan, Nancy, 77, 119, 120

Stoler, Ann, 225n9, 225n10

Strathern, Marilyn, 6, 151, 154, 162, 207

stress, 4, 77, 86, 90–94, 96, 97, 144

Suarez, Pablo Arturo, 225–26n15

surgery: cesarean births (C-sections), 22, 72, 73, 81–84, 106, 183; dilation and curettage (D&C), 80; gendering of reproductive surgery, 79, 84–85, 220n18; *pishtaco,* 80, 86; plastic surgery, 80–81, 135, 223n7; reinforcement of whiteness, 85; scarring, 76, 80–82, 86; as unnecessary, 79, 84–85, 99, 220n18; uterine cyst removal, 32, 33, 68, 69

surrogacy, xxiii, 136, 154, 162, 176, 226n20

Tatiana (patient), 88, 92–94, 95, 202

Taussing, Michael, 53

telenovelas, 29, 30, 139

Temkin, Owsei, 91

Teresa (patient): anonymous gamete donation, 113; cultivation of son's beauty, 135, 136; family life of, 103; Indian identity of, 102, 115, 134; on son's skin color, 109, 111, 122–23, 136;

successful pregnancy, 105; whitening project, 116, 122

Thompson, Charis, 135, 169–70, 176

Titmuss, Richard, 162

Tollefson, Christopher, 211

traffic in women, 151–52, 227n3

Trascendiendo Fronteras en Medicina (Transcending Frontiers in Medicine), 50

trigueño, 126, 128, 131

trigueño oscuro, 128

twin birth, 139, 140–41, 142, 155

UC Irvine fertility clinic scandal, 112, 113, 116, 137, 223–24n1

ugliness, 109, 110, 133, 141

United Nations Fund for Population Activities, 39

United States: access to assisted reproduction services, 213, 229n2; clinical pregnancy rates, 217n1; compensation for egg providers, 162, 227n7; cryopreservation regulation in, 188–89; embryo donation in, 206; free market circulation of extra embryos, 209–10; God in pro-life debates, 211, 212, 214; government involvement in IVF research, 209–10; hormone treatments in, 90–91; Hurricane Katrina, 211–13, 229n1; profile of egg donors, 227n7; racial malleability in, 114; right-to-life groups in, 190

universality: beauty standards, 109–10, 113–14, 116, 124, 134–36; embryos and the universal quality of life, 187, 212; the human body as non-universal, 6, 17–18, 91, 114, 213; local biologies, 2, 3, 4, 115; national differences in assisted reproduction, xxii–xxiii, 12, 90–91, 135, 154, 157–58, 162, 188–91, 198, 205–6, 208, 209–14, 217n1, 219n12, 227n7, 229n2; *nuestra realidad,* 3, 4,

Text: 10.25/14 Fournier
Display: Fournier
Compositor: BookMatters, Berkeley
Printer & Binder: IBT Global